Melancholy Dialectics

A volume in the series

Critical Perspectives on Modern Culture

Edited by David Gross and William M. Johnston

Melancholy Dialectics

Walter Benjamin and the Play of Mourning

Max Pensky

The University of Massachusetts Press   Amherst

Copyright © 1993 by

The University of Massachusetts Press

All rights reserved

Printed in the United States of America

LC 92-42229

ISBN 0-87023-853-1

Designed by Mary Mendell

Set in Bodoni Book

Printed and bound by Thomson-Shore, Inc.

Library of Congress Cataloging-in-Publication Data

Pensky, Max, 1961–

Melancholy dialectics : Walter Benjamin and the play of mourning /
Max Pensky.

p.   cm. — (Critical perspectives on modern culture)

Includes bibliographical references and index.

ISBN 0–87023–853–1 (alk. paper)

1. Benjamin, Walter, 1892–1940—Philosophy.   2. Melancholy in
literature.   3. Grief in literature.   I. Title.

PT2603.E455Z796   1993

838'.91209—dc20   92–42229 CIP

British Library Cataloguing in Publication data are available.

For my mother and my father

Contents

Acknowledgments

My thanks to those who have helped me through the long life of this project: to the Fulbright Foundation for supporting a research year at the Johann Wolfgang-Goethe Universität and to the many friends and colleagues for their ideas, suggestions, and criticisms, especially David Bathrick, Paul Breines, Susan Buck-Morss, Josef Früchtl, Jürgen Habermas, Axel Honneth, Michael Mahon, Thomas McCarthy, Dennis J. Schmidt, and Gary Smith. My thanks to Clark Dougan of the University of Massachusetts Press for his unflagging patience and support. And above all else, thanks to Katherine Lucas Anderson.

Melancholy Dialectics

Introduction

Is this the landscape image of that one-way street
That you want to walk down?
I almost doubt it. But know
Where you should go.
There are so many streets with paths of return
One doesn't see.
And when direction leads to an impasse:
It's not true that nothing can happen.
There is no negotiating at a collision;
It is the lightning strike.
And finding yourself transformed utterly:
It's no illusion.
In ancient days all paths led
Somehow to God and His Name.
We are not pious. We stay in the Profane
And where God once stood, stands: Melancholy.
—Gershom Scholem

At the close of her work on melancholy and literature, *Black Sun*, Julia Kristeva reveals the conception of melancholia that had implicitly guided her analysis: while the psychological-literary syndrome of melancholy is triggered, articulated, transformed, half-remembered, or suppressed by the textual dance of a cultural history, melancholy itself remains, behind its masks, "essential and transhistorical." The depressive, deathly fixation of melancholia, "the most archaic expression of the unsymbolizable, unnameable narcissistic wound,"[1] self-lacerating longing for the prelinguistic Thing, obsessive-repetitive, necessary, and impossible search for the metalinguistic in language, for the unpossessible in desire, for meaning beyond any significa-tion—this symptomatology, Kristeva reveals, articulates itself within texts, guides the productive imagination of authors, sinks out of sight to emerge again.

Melancholy possesses an inward history. It attaches itself to the characteristic forms of literary expression of an epoch. It invades the very capillaries of the text. Its mode of erotic representation and ma-nipulation, its grammar, its essential problematic of illness and in-sight, all combine into a constellation of cognitive, libidinal, and se-mantic regularities that, in its unhurried historical creep, "produces," creates, forms. In this way Kristeva observes an inner connection between melancholia and writing. Modernist literature is melancholy; conversely, melancholy writing bears within it something disturbingly, undeniably modern.

But, for Kristeva, "this writing is today confronted with the postmod-ern challenge. . . . The point now is to see in the 'malady of grief' only one moment of the *narrative synthesis* capable of sweeping along in its complex whirlwind philosophical meditations as well as erotic protec-tions or entertaining pleasures." The constellation of melancholia sinks, revealing its exact, somehow chiral reflection. "The postmodern is closer to the human comedy than to the abyssal discontent"; the world of hell, of the theology of evil as deprivation of meaning, has transformed itself from a literature of emergency, a *difficult* literature, into something more familiar, more accessible, and more comfortable. The crisis of meaning that drove modern literature into the secrets of its own inner illness now appears as the occasion for a good time; the converse of meaning is no longer "abyssal" meaninglessness but the pleasures of indeterminacy; the comic dance of representations within the exhilarating space that dead meaning has left behind. Postmodern sentiments toward a relaxation of a peculiarly modern narcissistic tension—sentiments that urge us not to worry about subjectivity, about indeterminacy, about nothingness—insist on "truth without tragedy, melancholia without purgatory."[2]

For Kristeva, this transposition of a language of melancholia into its buffoonish alter ego allows us to see that, in the history of melancholia, this *comédie humaine* is just as essential—just as "transhistorical"—as the abyssal discontent.

> A new amatory world comes to the surface within the eternal return of historical and intellectual cycles. Following the winter of discontent comes the artifice of seeming; following the whiteness of boredom, the heartening distraction of parody. And vice versa. Truth, in short, makes its way amid the shimmering of artificial amenities as well as asserting itself in painful mirror games. Does not the wonderment of psychic life after all stem from those alternations of protections and downfalls, smiles and tears, sunshine and melancholia?[3]

If this strange image can provide us with little comfort—if it is more a secret than a public insight into the "truth" of postmodern thought—it can at least suggest a very Nietzschean challenge. What once was melancholy now seems foolish. If Kierkegaard could still understand the truth that "melancholia is the ailment of our age," resounding "even in its frivolous laughter," that it has "deprived us of courage to command, of courage to obey, of power to act, of the confidence necessary to hope,"[4] for the present, pagan laughter has the final word.[5] The problems that once drove us to grub and grasp inconsolably in the earth for dark inspiration now provoke at best a good-natured smirk, no hard feelings, at the spectacle of a mind so productively bent on acquiring what does not exist, what one would in any case not want.

What seems funny now will not always be so. Enough concentration on those problems that, to this "amatory world," seem to constitute a world well lost will, in the repetitive cycle, bring back with a vengeance what a simple laugh can still dispel. Feelings will become very hard; smirks will freeze into grimaces. The whole weeping, laughing, mournful celebratory spectacle of psychic life will perform another of its infinite self-reversals, and we will not understand how those crises of meaning that torture us could conceivably have appeared to the older generation as parodic, light, charged with the eroticism of ambiguity, as if they did not have the power to crush our lives. Such is the "wonderment" of it all, for Kristeva, for one who has captured this mystical historiography and who can observe the infinite cycling of metaphysical worlds where *we* see only the ahistorical fixity of our own.

For such a privileged perspective, melancholia is indeed here forever, since it corresponds to the very ground of our emergence as speaking and acting persons. But a melancholy world is only a world awaiting its own parody.

Thus Kristeva proclaims herself as a *cultural critic* who, by pulling herself out of the endless historical and intellectual cycle of melancholy/comedy, wins an insight into the power and the ephemerality of both. The trick, from this Olympian perspective, is to observe and contemplate the physiognomy of the dance of representations, for only in such a form can the critic glimpse truth, flitting from tree to tree in a forest of symbols. The calm heroism of the self-expelled becomes the aesthetic posture of the cultural analyst. Writing is the murmur that such a heroic critic emits at the sight of truth.

The vision of an essential, even dualistic history of melancholia that Kristeva summons forth determines the implicit understanding of the role of cultural criticism as well. Such a Nietzschean *amor fati* is of course compatible neither with a commitment to revolutionary political change nor to any gradualist reform that would justify itself according to a vision of rational emancipatory progress. Criteria for political action, insofar as they exist, remain fundamentally aesthetic ones. Critique, as collective therapy, can diagnose and thus ease individuals' symptoms. But melancholy will assert its ancient rights over any writing that presumes to undo it. Following a time-honored practice, Kristeva prescribes sublimation. The political quietism implicit in Kristeva's vision of a melancholy history is, in distinct contrast to Kristeva's own detached voice, itself melancholy.

Melancholy remains primary. This Kristeva admits in the first lines of *Black Sun:* "For those who are racked with melancholia, writing about it would have meaning only if writing sprang out of that very melancholia."[6] The juxtaposition of the world-metaphysical conclusion of Kristeva's writing about melancholia with its confessional-epistemological opening reveals the "trick" of Kristeva's work. The irreducible paradox of self-reference inherent in writing "about" melancholia appears precisely at the point where the writing attempts to situate itself at the edge of the melancholy vision of the world, where writing about melancholia would constitute some essential break from the narcissistic depths of subjective contemplation so characteristic of the melancholy view of things, and could thereby constitute the *meaning* of the abyssal meaninglessness that the melancholic experiences: the truth about melancholy, the "truth content" of melancholy literature.

Yet, insofar as writing about the incommunicable, about melancholy, could only "mean" its intention insofar as it springs from its object, *"melancolie redet sich selber"*: melancholy always speaks and writes itself. The horizon beyond the interiority of melancholy is withdrawn as insistently as writing approaches it. The Thing, the unnameably, irretrievably withheld, whether the messianic day or the mother, absolute truth or eternal peace, establishes the impossibility and necessity of melancholy writing by its absolute absence. In this sense, the cultural critic who writes through/about melancholic culture is, for all her perspectival achievements, perhaps even more savagely thrown back into the radical immanence of depression. In the curiously hermetically sealed paradox of melancholy writing, no aesthetic pleasure of the "wonderment of psychic life" could compensate for the incalculable pain that would have to be exacted to reach it. There is, of course, always a practical dimension to the subjection to writing. Like Burton, who "write[s] of melancholy, by being busy to avoid melancholy,"[7] Kristeva's melancholy writing has at least an anaesthetic effect—it fills the "whiteness of boredom," the blank page, with writing and thus avoids what for thousands of years has been regarded as the fatal chink in the psychic shield through which melancholy enters: idleness, *acedia*. (Baudelaire, more than anyone else, recognized that the transformation of *spleen* into writing required the frenzied battle against boredom.)

But if this is all, if melancholy writing, under the sign of its own impossibility to achieve what it needs, as writing *about* melancholia, to achieve, merely provides either more or less pain—in what sense can we speak of a cultural critic? If the (postmodern) break in the phenomenology of melancholia appears not as its negation but only as its parody, what purpose would a cultural critique of melancholia possibly serve? Would "critical" mean anything in this context, apart perhaps from a certain sharpened awareness of the stakes involved in melancholy writing, an increased interest in the analgesic effect of writing itself? What, in other words, would it mean to write critically "about" melancholia? It is with this question that I would like to justify beginning a book about Walter Benjamin with these comments on Julia Kristeva.

No one was more sensitive to the question of the theological and political effects of writing than Walter Benjamin. Indeed, the transformations and inner developments of his conception of the purpose and effect of writing could be taken as a key or legend to the "phases" of his conception of criticism. From his early conviction concerning the redemptive dimension in the act of critical writing through the attempt, following the study of the German *Trauerspiel*, to develop critical writing as a mode of engaged political *praxis* among the milieu of Left intellectuals of the Weimar Republic, to the much more complex and ambiguous attempt, in the context of the *Passagenwerk*, to find a mode of critical construction capturing the energy of the montage, the conception of writing constitutes a category of central importance for Benjamin's work. Thus a question about melancholy writing, writing about melancholy, provides a point of entry into the exceedingly strange role of the idea of melancholy in Benjamin's work.

One gets a sense of the sheer extent of this role by a juxtaposition of two short, roughly simultaneous texts by Benjamin, "Linke Melancholie" and "Agesilaus Santander."

In 1931, the leftist Weimar journal *Die Gesellschaft* published a short review by Benjamin entitled "Leftist Melancholia."[8] The review itself, quite apart from its subject matter, can be taken as an ecapsulation of the frustrations and delays that plagued Benjamin's productive career: the piece had actually been submitted several months earlier to the *Frankfurter Zeitung*, which, with the smaller and more politically radical journal *Die literarische Welt*, had published the majority of the numerous works that Benjamin's career as literary critic had produced. Itself far removed from the radical political demands that Benjamin's essays and reviews had acquired over the second half of the 1920s, the *Frankfurter Zeitung* had published so many of Benjamin's reviews in large measure due to the personal intervention of its editor, Siegfried Kracauer.[9] In the case of "Linke Melancholie," however, there was no intervention: the review was rejected by the editor of the newspaper's feuilleton.

From his very first review of Fritz von Unruh, Benjamin's self-understanding of his role as a professional critic in the Weimar cultural sphere articulated itself in the form of increasingly devastating attacks on his "leftist" colleagues. As Benjamin would claim in "The Author as Producer," by expressing their opposition in texts destined to become the objects of aesthetic enjoyment, left-wing intellectuals transform their allegiance to the working class into a weapon of reaction far more powerful than any reactionary ideology. Thus, for example, *Neue Sachlickeit* revealed "a political tendency, however revolutionary it may seem," that "has a counterrevolutionary function as the writer feels his solidarity with the proletariat only in his attitudes, not as a producer."[10]

Critique, directed not at a general reading public but at (or against) the much smaller circle of writing, Left-oriented intellectuals, therefore aimed at the mobilization of intellectuals in the interests of revolutionary political change. It worked for the revelation of the hidden class interests that tied Left intellectuals to the ruling bourgeoisie, the ruthless exposure of the hypocrisy by which the ruling class exerted its power through "leftist" literature. By directing explosive critical charges into the mass of his own peers, Benjamin intended his reviews to blast apart the secret complicity between cultural expression and political domination, forcing his contemporaries to come to a clear self-understanding of their own activity, and thus consciously and unambiguously to choose their class loyalties—in this sense, literary critique claims the status of radical political praxis.[11] As a moment in the process of decision that an intellectual of the Left must undertake, critique is one mode of strategy in political struggle; it is a method for the promotion of political decisiveness on the part of intellectuals who are otherwise emphatically disinclined toward unambiguous political convictions. In this sense, the category of decisiveness—a key concept in Benjamin's thought as for Weimar political theories in general—wins a prominent role in Benjamin's politically motivated literary reviews. This is most clearly visible in "Linke Melancholie."

The strategy of politically decisive critique—critique as a rough shove at the backs of dithering, angst-ridden Left intellectuals—finds in Erich Kästner's poetry a target apparently supremely worthy of shoving. And it is the harshness of the shove that moved the editors of the *Frankfurter Zeitung*, in any case not overly pleased with Benjamin's increasingly polemical work, to reject the review.

As for Kästner himself, one could say that his own star had risen very quickly in the constellation of Weimar Left intellectuals. The son of working-class parents (his father was a factory worker in Dresden), he had begun training as a schoolteacher, and the stark discipline and mindlessness of the pedagogy he encountered in the Prussian *Lehrerseminar* had a similar effect that it had for the young Benjamin, forming a conviction of the importance of childhood, of the awakening and mobilizing of the moral-critical powers of discernment of the child, and of a Left literary pedagogy. Indeed, Kästner was most successful as a writer for children. Despite the wide popular success of many of his adult writings (especially before the war), he insisted that children's books were his most significant achievements. [12]

After service in the war, Kästner had become an active journalist and reviewer, and a member of the circle of critics and writers associated not only with *Neue Sachlickeit*, but also in particular with the journal *Weltbühne* and its leading contributors, Hiller, Tucholsky, von Ossietzky, and Zweig. In 1928, still in his twenties, Kästner published a collection of poems, *Herz auf Taille*, and the immediately and immensely popular children's book, *Emil und die Detektive*. More poetry, *Lärm im Spiegel*, followed in 1929, and *Ein Mann gibt Auskunft* in 1930. The novel *Fabian* appeared the following year.

Kästner's work in this period, both in the novel and in the poems, was a self-consciously politicized form of writing. According to Kästner's own convictions, literature could play a political-didactic function only once it was stripped of its own effete pretensions and, in a clear and simple voice, could reveal and condemn the moral turpitude and hypocrisy of contemporary society. Thus his poems, cool and precise observations of concrete images of social injustice, deliberately refuse the turgid emotions, the *Weltschmertz* and the interiority of expressionism. Their broad purpose is social critique, accomplished by a mixture of satire, sarcasm, and moral outrage. The images that they frequently depict—of apathetic politicians, bloated and mindless bureaucrats, monstrous generals, human relationships hollowed out by greed or devastated by poverty and neglect—paint a panorama of the moral vacuum of Weimar culture. One might say that they attempt to present poetically the graphic images of Grosz's drawings.

Benjamin was certainly not alone in condemning Kästner's work, or in accusing Kästner of promoting a form of political resignation and quietism under the banner of leftist moral indignation. Indeed, "Linke

Melancholie" should surely be seen as a part of a broader debate concerning the political role of the Weimar Left intellectual, as well as a debate specifically concerning the political dimension of Kästner's *Gebrauchlyrik,* a debate that came to a head over the publication of the novel *Fabian,* whose bleak portrait of contemporary Berlin was criticized both for being too blatantly political and for presenting a pessimism so extreme that it effectively argued against the possibility of concrete political change.[3]

Benjamin's position in this debate is unmistakable, as can also be readily seen in his critique of Kästner's colleague Mehring the year before.[4] (In fact, one might say that the venomous "Linke Melancholie" is the result of a year-long slow burn.) While the violence of Benjamin's critique of Kästner proved too much for the staid *Frankfurter Zeitung,* it was certainly in keeping with polemical charges flying back and forth in *Die Weltbühne, Die literarische Welt, Die Gesellschaft,* or *Die Front* precisely over the political effect of *Neue Sachlickeit.*[5] Benjamin insists that the *use* of the *Gebrauchslyrik,* contrary to Kästner's intentions, is the support of the same morally desolate culture that Kästner presumes to attack. But while Benjamin's critical view is clear enough, the mode of this critique is fascinating. "Linke Melancholie" deals only cursorily with Kästner's poems. It proceeds almost directly to the mobilization of a concrete political charge against not only Kästner, but also the entire milieu of Left intellectuals of *Neue Sachlichkeit:* Benjamin accuses them all of melancholia.

"The predilection for Kästner's poetry," writes Benjamin, "is immediately related to the rise of a social class which took naked possession of its own position of economic power, and prided itself as no other on the nakedness, the unmasked character of its economic physiognomy." Thus Kästner's poems arise from—and ultimately reflect back—the experience of the *Linksbürgertum* (although Kästner himself was, unlike Benjamin, of working-class origins). "Their subject matter and effect remain restricted to this stratum, and Kästner's rebellious accents are just as ineffectual for the dispossessed as his irony is at striking the industrialists." Rather than insisting on the political mobilization of the writer, the poems merely describe the desperation and sadness of a bourgeoisie that, while "upset" by social injustice, has no interest in acting against it. In this way, "all appearances notwithstanding," the poems reflect and defend "the interests of this middle stratum of agents, journalists, department heads," serving to support an unjust regime by transforming revolutionary opposition into objects of aesthetic appreciation.

This secret reactionary function is common to the entire *Neue Sachlickeit* movement:

> Left-radical publicists like Kästner, Mehring or Tucholsky are the decayed bourgeoisie's proletarian mimicry. Politically, their function is to bring forward not parties but cliques; literarily, not schools but styles; economically, not producers but agents. . . . Their political meaning exhausts itself in the reversal of all revolutionary reflexes insofar as they ever could have touched the bourgeoisie, into objects of distraction, of amusement, made available for consumption. And, in fact, this left intelligentsia has been, for the last fifteen years, the continual agent of all the spiritual booms and busts [*Konjunkturen*] from Activism through Expressionism up until *Neue Sachlickeit*. But the left intelligentsia's political meaning is exhausted by the transposition of revolutionary reflexes—insofar as they ever came up among the bourgeoisie—into objects of distraction, of amusement, presented for consumption.[16]

Neue Sachlickeit, merely the latest in the ebb and tide of politically correct literary fashions, having long since squandered its small capital of political relevance, now fatuously follows the tired, ritualized formula of literary protest, hollow irony, self-congratulation. No *praxis* could conceivably be produced by this weary introspection; but then, "from the beginning, it had nothing else in mind than to enjoy itself a bit in its negativistic calm. The metamorphosis of the political struggle from a demand for decision [*Zwang zur Entscheidung*] to an object of enjoyment, from a means of production to an article of consumption—that is this literature's latest hit."[17]

Such a transformation, however, appears here for Benjamin suddenly in a different, indeed far more ancient light. The slothful retreat from political engagement—the transformation of decisiveness into febrile contemplation—awakens a deeper charge: "Tortured stupidity: this is the latest of two millennia of metamorphoses of melancholy."[18] The mournfulness that is the deepest source of Kästner's poetic voice has now been named. But the melancholy mind, the depressive-productive syndrome that produced the baroque *Trauerspiel,* or Baude-laire's allegory, assumes its contemporary form as mere fatuousness and sloth: *acedia* without the corresponding moment of occult insight; *taedium vitae* without allegorical destruction.

Several points can be raised here. First, it is important to note that Benjamin's claim does not imply that Kästner and his colleagues have somehow inaugurated a voice of passivity and resignation that apes or imitates, is "like" the historical voice of melancholia, a voice that so gripped Benjamin's imagination in his theoretical writings. On the contrary, "tortured stupidity" *is* melancholia, is the latest—the newest and also the last, *"die letzte"*—mode of melancholy's historical ap-pearance. In this sense, the contemporary diagnosis of Benjamin's Left intellectual colleagues includes a historical dimension not readily apparent in the context of one particular debate concerning the politi-cal worthiness of left-wing writers. Benjamin is also concerned with the present, twentieth-century stage in a history of melancholia. This stage is characterized by the appropriation of what had always been a senti-ment or syndrome associated with a spiritual and economic elite—of thinkers, writers, contemplators—by a middle class that was success-ful in fashioning even a sentiment of hopelessness into a force of political reaction, precisely by fostering the rise of writers whose hope-lessness was dedicated to, and therefore identified with, the critique of that same class.

Benjamin sees the convoluted paradox of melancholy writing in its particularly political dimension. Melancholy infects any political cause that it seeks to support, for the melancholic's support (of any-thing) is always tinged with the atmosphere of meaninglessness. Politi-cally, meaninglessness translates into resignation, the precise nega-tion of decisiveness. A melancholy politics thus glides into a secret, half-willing collaboration with the forces it seeks to oppose. This is the invariable result when melancholy, like all other syndromes and affec-tations of "high" literature, is de-auraticized, removed from its esoteric aloofness, and thrust onto the political and economic stage.

Benjamin thus argues that *contemporary* melancholy writing must necessarily lose the appearance of political detachment. Like other forms of high art, it becomes political by the elimination of the cultural milieu in which the act of writing can maintain its remoteness from its status as a productive force. The question is the manner in which melancholia's political dimension will be articulated. For Benjamin, the case of Kästner reveals that the ancient links between melancholia and *acedia*, passivity, and indecision assume a contemporary form in which the political effect of writing neatly, indeed dialectically negates the author's intention. Moreover—and this is the essential point—this supremely dangerous dialectical reversal appears due not only to the power of ideological refunctioning so characteristic of capitalism, but also to a dialectical predilection inherent in the "history of melancholia" itself.

It is this strange combination of a history of melancholia, articulating itself in current political conditions that activate its transhistorical tendency toward passivity in a particularly pernicious way, that so disturbs Benjamin. The reactivation of the ur-old in the form of the new was an image of the mythic whose significance for criticism Benjamin himself recognized all too clearly. As Rolf Tiedemann observes, the close of "Linke Melancholie," in which Benjamin compares Kästner's writing to flatulence, observing that "constipation and melancholy have always gone together,"[19] clearly signals Benjamin's new appreciation of Brecht, whose "political lyric" provides one of the few contemporary political alternatives to the *Gebrauchslyrik*.[20] But the same observation also demonstrates a very different genealogy, tracing back, I suspect, to Benjamin's reading of Erwin Panofsky and Fritz Saxl's essay on Dürer's print *Melancolia I*[21] (itself deriving its guiding interest from Aby Warburg's earlier essay on Luther, Melanchthon, and the astral occult[22]) and in particular its analysis of the medical symptomatology of melancholy by Rufus of Ephesius, a contemporary of Galen.

A critique of melancholy writing, then, taking full account of then present circumstances, appears as the urgent project of *smashing* or arresting the hold of melancholia over Benjamin's own colleagues. If Kristeva can now see writing about melancholia as a source of appreciation of the wonderment of sociopsychic life, Benjamin, in the last years of the Weimar Republic, understood a critique of melancholia as a demand for decisiveness and thus a victory over, rather than a redemption of, the object of critique. Critique is a strategic act in a politics of intervention, directed toward the heart of the present, against a politics of melancholia.

Whether Kästner himself would have understood the charge of

modern melancholia Benjamin made against him is not clear. It is evident, however, that Benjamin's own attitude toward melancholia is far more complex than his critique of Kästner alone would imply.

Benjamin wrote the fragment "Agesilaus Santander" on Ibiza in 1933. Gershom Scholem has devoted a lengthy analysis to this two-page text. He has revealed the intricate, sad constellation of failed loves that forms its web of references, the complex dance of reversals and substitutions with which Benjamin describes his relation with his personal, satanic angel, anagramatically hidden within the title, and the half-ironic, half-mystical preoccupations with fate and subjection to astral forces that make the text so haunting. Above all, however, what emerges from Scholem's hermeneutic adventure is the bottomless sadness and isolation that are encoded in every syllable of the text. Under Scholem's gaze, "Agesilaus Santander" is transformed from a murky fragment of esoterica into a moving and utterly personal document of an event of self-recognition. The demonic angel encrypted within the fabric of "everyday" linguistic experience, the mysterious causality of names and stars, the hopeless enmeshment of erotic and creative life—all these point to the thrall of the occult that persisted for Benjamin despite his most vigorous efforts to adopt an exoteric mode of expression. It was a fascination that clearly touched Benjamin's own most personal experiences; one that was activated above all during times of deep personal crisis, such as Benjamin's stay on Ibiza. There, during a period apparently as painful as it was productive, Benjamin could reflect that the satanic angel whose power he had captured, however briefly, in his erotic and creative existence, paid Benjamin back for his presumption by "taking advantage of the circumstance that I came into the world under the sign of Saturn—that star of the slowest revolution, the planet of detours and delays."[23]

Scholem explains that Benjamin was trying to express the conjunction of circumstances that had resulted in the destruction of his marriage, the revolutionary transformation of his creative life, and his passion for Jula Cohn, a friend of his youth. Even Scholem, for all his personal insight and hermeneutical delicacy, confesses that this passage, relating the image of Klee's watercolor *Angelus Novus* to the circumstances of Benjamin's birth, and these in turn to the "masculine" or "feminine" form of the ambiguously satanic angel itself, remains hermetic. It is perhaps just as well.[24] But Benjamin's admission that he was born "under the sign of Saturn," that is, that he was born a melancholic, makes this passage unique. It is the only place, as Scholem observes, where Benjamin reveals his own melancholy character.[25] The Hebraic images of malevolent and beneficent angels, secret names, and divine vengeance here combine magically with a different occult vocabulary: the ancient history of saturnine melancholy, the syndrome brought about by subjection to the effects of the baleful planet. The author of the *Ursprung des deutschen Trauerspiels*, the expert on the history and phenomenology of the occult history of saturnine melancholia, and the savage critic of the "tortured stupidity" of the "newest" phase of melancholia's "two-thousand year history" are one and the same.

It has often been remarked that Benjamin's work displays a curious entwinement of two otherwise thoroughly heterogenous features. On the one hand his thought, particularly his early thought, frequently articulates itself in elements of a never fully developed metaphysical doctrine or code, which appears as isolated fragments, apparently waiting to be reintegrated into a permanently deferred system. On the other hand, these esoteric breezes from other planets are often combined with fragments of completely personal experience, whose significance in their context could be grasped only by those intimately familiar with Benjamin and his life. Indeed, Bernd Witte has argued that this trait, essentially identical to the incessant "quoting out of context" that Benjamin found to be the essence of the allegorical vision, places severe restrictions on the comprehensibility of Benjamin's work and seriously compromises the scholarly integrity of his historical studies.[26] Adorno, who with Scholem was best able to observe this trait both in Benjamin's speech and in his writing, argues forcefully that this juxtaposition of extremely personal experience with gestures toward the ineffable absolute constitutes a dialectical tension that provides Benjamin's thought with its remarkable clarity and power.

Benjamin was able to fashion images in which the sheer concreteness of the historical object or the lived moment could remain intact. "What Benjamin said and wrote sounded as if it were conjured up out of a secret depth. Its power, however, came from its evidentness. It was free of any affectation of occult doctrine, the preserve of initiates."[27] Far from establishing a preserve of private meaning, Benjamin's characteristic voice aimed at the destruction of the limits placed on subjective experience, limits that imposed themselves as the false-idealist, ultimately mythic distinction between the absolutely concrete and the transcendent universal. Thus, one might say that the characteristic infusion of fragments of concrete experience into the articulation of metaphysical conception was itself an essential methodological component of a consistent line of attack in Benjamin's critical thinking. The tension produced by such juxtapositions could explore the real with a messianic interest, without betraying its commitment to the things themselves, and produce images whose transcendent force would be contained within their absolute historical concreteness and graphicness.

Such a conception of the energy of thinking and writing underlies the production of the energized image, energized by the messianic cessation of happening, the explosive concentration of meaning into the liberated, profaned fragment, the forgotten text, the skull, the arcade, the useless commodity. It is true that this tension is dangerous. It underlies the occasionally unmediated theology and esoteric aloofness of Benjamin's early theory, as well as the very ambiguous relationship between allegorical and dialectical image in Benjamin's later thought. But without this tension—between the personal and the absolute, the concrete and the transcendent, the messianic and the mythic— Benjamin's own writing would itself collapse into unmediated collections of the concrete or unmediated wishes for the end of history.

The maintained tension between historical object and messianic futurity, between subjective concentration and objective revelation, is in essence a tension arising from the possibility of meaning; better, it is a productive tension maintained at the moment of dialectical suspension in which the necessity and impossibility of meaning are held frozen for the contemplating subject. In this sense we may begin to pose a question concerning the role of melancholia in Benjamin's thought. For Benjamin, the idea of melancholia clearly implied vastly more than "mere" sadness, not a simple, that is undialectical, personal mood, temperament, or constitution. Nor, by the term *melancholia*, could we mean some essentiality, some real being, that could be referred to as directing or inspiring Benjamin's thinking "from the outside."

As a *way of seeing*, melancholia is more than a subjective mode of apprehension and conceptualization, more than an unproductive schematism, but at the same time something we could only talk about "under the sign of the subject"; in terms of the contemplative adventures of the isolated thinker. If the melancholy subject "produces" melancholy objects, then those objects themselves also constitute a world, a realm of objects of contemplation that in turn constitute the melancholy way of seeing. Between melancholy subject and melancholy objects, this way of seeing subsists in the dialectical interval between these two constituted moments. The form of vision that draws the speculative subject ever deeper into the interrogation of the creaturely also establishes the realm of the objective as a complex puzzle awaiting its decipherment. Melancholy occupies the space that separates Benjamin's "messianic" and "materialistic" gaze—it is a space that is carved between the subject and the object by a question concerning the possibility of meaning; a space Benjamin sought his life long to fill with the storehouse of images yielded up to him and constructed in his shocking, healing writing.

This fundamental dialectical feature of melancholia, which I am here introducing in a purely provisional way, of course must be elaborated at much greater length. I would like to argue that such an elaboration will show that *melancholia* is a term that will lead us to an appraisal of the heart of Benjamin's critical vision—and to a confrontation with that vision's unresolved paradoxes as well. For the present, it is enough to remark, as a very preliminary justification for this path of argument, that the creative tensions in Benjamin's thought that I have been describing seem to have led both Adorno and Scholem to the idea of melancholia, on independent but intimately related paths.

Reflecting on the dialectic of the personal and the metaphysical in Benjamin, Scholem observes that "behind many of Benjamin's writings stand personal, indeed most personal experiences which by projection into the objects of his works disappeared or were put into code, so that the outsider could not recognize them or at least could do no more than suspect their presence. Such is the case, for example, in *The Origin of German Trauerspiel* with the theory of melancholy, by which he described his own constitution." This example is a central one for Scholem; indeed, the "angel of history," Benjamin's lifelong companion from his first musings on Klee's *Angelus Novus* to his last theses is

for Scholem "basically a melancholy figure, wrecked by the immanence of history, because the latter can only be overcome by a leap that
does not save the past of history in an 'eternal image,' but rather in a
leap leading out of the historical continuum into the 'time of now,'
whether the latter is revolutionary or messianic."[28]

Adorno, for his part, extends a similar claim: "The peculiar imagistic quality of Benjamin's speculation, what might be called his myth-
icizing trait, has its origin in his melancholy gaze, under which the
historical is transformed into nature by the strength of its own fragility
and everything natural is transformed into a fragment of the history of
creation."[29] Intimately familiar with Benjamin's earliest work, and
convinced of the untrammeled and abiding purity of Benjamin's mystic
vision, Scholem reads Benjamin's melancholy as the quintessentially
Jewish persistence of a loyalty to the order of creation, arising not
despite but precisely out of the universality and endlessness of historical catastrophe. Adorno, who watched the enormous difficulties that
presented themselves to Benjamin as this mystical understanding of
history searched for a materialist mode of expression, understands better than Scholem the productive contradiction that lies at the heart of
Benjamin's melancholy. Adorno saw how attuned Benjamin's thought
was to the unstable rhythms of contradiction and understood the heavy
price that Benjamin had to pay for this.

Imagistic thinking gravitates naturally toward extremes, trans-
gresses the limits that it places upon itself. For Benjamin's frozen
dialectic, no less than for Hegel's dialectic of absolute motion, contradiction fuels speculation but inflicts pain. Melancholy insights into the
images of reconciliation threaten that mythologizing moment in which
the source of pain is transmuted from concrete historical conditions to
"existence" as such. Happiness, the moment of missing contradiction,
is both as intimate and as utterly alien to the melancholy mind as the
permanently withheld antithesis.[30] Misery, the absence of meaning, of
a stable identity, of the image of harmony and completion, is the force
that drives the contemplative mind onward, but also is the price paid
by the human being. Though Benjamin rightly rejected the violence to
the concrete that Hegel's dialectic demanded, his "highway of despair"
and Hegel's are, at least in this regard, the same. Benjamin's liquidation of the idealist brutality of the Hegelian dialectic was, by the same
token, only possible through a Kierkegaardian exploration to the very

bottom of the well of subjective inwardness. If, like Kierkegaard, Benjamin was able to make this black hole produce a little light of its own, it was a task that consumed "life" in the process.

Benjamin was, by all accounts, a sad man. This sadness was more than an arbitrary and hence accidental feature of personality—it entered into a creative, essential, complex relation with Benjamin's work, and thus demands an analysis that attempts to understand this relation, the link between a subjective character itself possessing objective, historically illuminating referents, and a body of theoretical work demonstrating the strong, indeed constitutive influence of a personal constitution. "Sadness—which is different from the simple fact of being sad—was his nature," writes Adorno, "as Jewish awareness of the permanence of danger and catastrophe as well as the antiquarian tendency to see the present transformed into the ancient past, as if by enchantment."[31]

But if sadness was Benjamin's nature, and if, moreover, we wish to extend a claim that this sadness lies at the base of a talent for contradictory thinking essential for Benjamin's critical vision, the attempt to explore this melancholia must also confront a series of contradictions raised by the idea of melancholy writing. Benjamin, born under Saturn, attacks Kästner and his cohorts for melancholy writing. He demands a moment of recognition, in which contemporary melancholia would be forced to reveal its duplicity with the agents of oppression, and he proclaims a critique that, stripped of all its esoteric, contemplative ornament, would publicly demand a decisive commitment to political action. This critical demand is not merely opposed to melancholia—it is precisely antithetical to it. If melancholia had always borne connotations of the intensity of subjective contemplation, Benjamin demands a postsubjective, socially engaged form of thinking and writing. Connected at least since the Renaissance with occult and esoteric doctrines of metaphysical correspondences, astral influences, and secret truths, melancholia is attacked by Benjamin with an explicitly and self-consciously exoteric, materialist, "crude" political critique. Benjamin's critique will be decisive; melancholia has for two thousand years been closely associated with an inability to act decisively. "Linke Melancholie" does not merely direct critical writing against melancholia. In its very being it aligns itself directly against it, negating it, attempting to overcome it. But this implies that Benjamin, at least in the period of his most overtly political critical writing, is struggling to annihilate the very "nature" that, at least for Adorno, constituted a central source of his critique itself.

It would not have been the first time that a melancholic exploited his own melancholia in order to overcome it, to transform it into its opposite. Indeed, one might even say that this is the most characteristic feature of melancholy writing, its most stubborn paradox. Melancholy, according to this old supposition, is a source of critical reflection that, in its ancient dialectic, empowers the subject with a mode of insight into the structure of the real at the same time as it consigns the subject to mournfulness, misery, and despair. The very image of meaninglessness, whose objects populate the melancholy landscape, are themselves produced from a more hidden conviction, of an originary dimension of lost, destroyed, or withheld meaning. Such a dimension is thus cryptically encoded into the very objects of melancholy despair; as objects of contemplation, they become both the keys to a secret body of insight and the reminders of the impossibility of recovering what was lost. This duality in the status of melancholy objects—which for both Benjamin and Kristeva extends to the reality of written language—both spurs the course of melancholy reflection onward (or downward) and locks it into its essential paradox. Produced from melancholy, a melancholy writing could only *transcend* itself through the exercise of its own characteristic forms of cognition. But by doing so, would such a writing transcend melancholy, or reflect itself infinitely back upon itself? Would such a writing not lose the dimension of critical writing? In Benjamin's case, would it not lose the explosive, unambiguous, practical relation to political action that he so badly wants it to have?

"For those who are racked with melancholia, writing about it would have meaning only if writing sprang from that same melancholia." Reading this observation in the context of Benjamin's writing may help us understand a bit better the contradictions raised by the juxtaposition of "Linke Melancholie" and "Agesilaus Santander." We could put the matter in this way: read together, the two texts represent a crystalline moment of pure opposition—the struggle against melancholy and melancholy writing, and the moment of insight into the melancholy of Benjamin's own nature. Understood in the context of a development of Benjamin's critical and theoretical writings, however, the juxtaposed texts capture a moment of contradiction within a longer story, a struggle with and against melancholia that occupied Benjamin for most of his productive life. It is a struggle whose stakes were very clear to Benjamin. For us to appreciate the terms of this struggle, however, a brief excursus into the history of the idea of melancholia is indispensable.

Recent historical analyses of the idea of melancholia often tend to begin with the claim that—notwithstanding the presence of the idea in virtually every historical epoch in Western culture from ancient Greece onward—the epoch in question, the one chosen by the historian of melancholy, is *particularly* worthy of interest. The classical conception of melancholy as a particular disease of humoral imbalance, in the broader context of the doctrine of humoral pathology, can be understood as the medical-ethical core of the "melancholy disposition."[32] The theories of melancholic (saturnine) planetary influences, which the Renaissance inherited from Arabian and medieval Western astrology, underlie the persistent strand of speculation in which melancholy is associated with occult doctrines, as well as the conviction that melancholia expressed the entwinement of personal genius with cosmological structure.[33] The lamentation and moralizing over decay, transience, and human *vanitas* characteristic of baroque melancholy expresses best the melancholic theme of intense mourning or hopelessness in the face of the universality of death and the reality of sin.[34] As poetic device from eighteenth-century classicism[35] through the nineteenth-century elegy[36] to romanticism and symbolism, melancholy appears as a particularly consistent trope, indicating the intense "sweet sadness" and isolation of the poet who must struggle for the distillation of beauty from the material of worldly experience.[37] Each epoch, each discourse, apparently, can extend a claim to represent the core of melancholia.

Such is the ubiquity of the idea of melancholia in medical, theological, and aesthetic discourses in the West that all these claims are plausible. Read together these claims point not just to the admirable protean quality of the idea of melancholia, but also to its continued fascination, its grip on the human imagination, which survives through its endless permutations.

In a very preliminary way, one might say that this fascination owes its tenacity to a dialectical vigor residing in the very heart of the idea of melancholy: the representation of the simultaneity of otherwise rigorously heterogenous properties of the human experience of the world, characterized above all by the combination of properly transcendental insights into a realm of ultimate reality with the most immanent and "creaturely" preoccupations with the physical or the private. Thus, for example, a historical hallmark of descriptions of the melancholy state, sadness, normally represented as an entirely subjective and hence interior or private emotion, appears in melancholy in an intimate, indeed dialectical relationship with cognition of the "objective" world of things. The melancholic's sadness is at once private and also derived from the objective status of the cognized world; conversely, the cognized world is at once objectively present and also synthesized under the sign of infinite sadness. Likewise, insofar as physical and mental illness has normally been understood as a concrete weakening or distortion of the subjective faculties, it wins its dialectical moment in the idea of melancholia insofar as it is consistently related to a heightening or intensification of a certain power of spiritual perception or insight into the nature of the world. Melancholia appears under the dialectic of illness and empowerment.

This dialectical synthesis of illness and (spiritual) empowerment thus repeats the more fundamental dialectic of (sad) subjectivity and objective nature and leads to a hierarchical series of dialectical oppositions explored in discourses about melancholia—oppositions between immanent and transcendent spiritual attitudes, for example, the simultaneous yearning for the disclosure of absolute truth and the intensive concentration on the sheer materiality of the physical world; or between the medieval doctrine of *acedia* as the sin of sloth and inactivity and the notion of melancholia as a sort of autonomous spiritual vocation in which the disdain for action could be interpreted as a sign of true insight, an ennobling withdrawal from an inconsequential world.

A dialectic of genius and illness, of spiritual empowerment and paralytic sadness, of subjective intensification and an absorption into the realm of objects, Saturn as giver of vision and thief of sanity . . . a preliminary sketch of the dialectic of melancholia would not be complete without a further observation: if melancholia is the schema of a set of extraordinary juxtapositions of immanent and transcendent moments in human experience, it is also the schema of a certain *produc-

tive impetus that arises from these juxtapositions. Melancholia, as Benjamin would observe in the *Ursprung des deutschen Trauerspiels*, is as much as anything a discourse about knowledge, about the urge toward the acquisition and articulation of a privileged insight into the world—hence a metasubjective form of disclosure—in such a way that this knowledge could be rendered accessible *for* the contemplative subject. Thus the productive-cognitive dimension of melancholia, the search for absolute knowledge on the part of the subject immersed in the radically contingent, is a theme quite familiar to the history of philosophy; in fact one could say that it is the question of idealism itself. It extends beyond this history, however, and addresses both the cognitive contradictions arising from such a search and the emotional or private consequences that are produced by its necessary failure. Melancholia is a discourse about the necessity and impossibility of the discovery and possession of "objective" meaning by the subjective investigator.

Understood as a pathological affliction, or as a temperament that threatens to become pathological, melancholia (literally, "black fluid" or black humor) has its origins in the (originally Pythagorean) doctrine of humoral pathology. The doctrine is based on a vision of bodily and spiritual health as a balance or harmony of the four bodily humors, black and yellow bile, phlegm and blood; deficiency or preponderance of any of these could arise from a variety of environmental or internal causes. Health thus consisted of a coordination of the internal balance of the humors and their corresponding organs with the harmonious relationship of the entire organism to its external environment. Melancholia in this doctrine is, accordingly, conceived as the syndrome caused by the preponderance of black bile, and thus takes its place in a table of diseases occasioned by preponderance of the corresponding humor. Melancholy symptoms could thus be charted with precision as could phlegmatic, choleric, or sanguine ones.

Under such a scheme, a disease was to be distinguished from a characteristic temperament or mode of behavior only quantitatively, according to the amount of the preponderant humor. Thus melancholic, choleric, phlegmatic, or sanguine conditions could emerge as explanatory accounts for specific personality traits, which themselves were not necessarily to be regarded as pathological or even as undesirable.[38]

The direct connection between physical pathology and abnormal temperament—between physical and spiritual conditions—and a disharmony or imbalance of the constitution made the doctrine of humoral pathology a powerful descriptive paradigm, one that fit extremely well with the Pythagorean fascination with mathematical, natural, and cosmological proportion. Even after the doctrine of humoral pathology became less directly associated with Pythagorean cosmology, it continued to accumulate natural and cosmological references extending far beyond the realm of physical pathology. The four humors came to be regarded as corresponding not just to particular temperaments, but also to the four seasons, the four elements, and the four stages of life, which in turn were in some instances meant to represent the corresponding temperament or disease symbolically or, in other cases, could be introduced as factors or even causes of the disease. By the time that "melancholia" first appeared in Hippocratic medical literature as an identifiable and treatable disease, the original Pythagorean humoral theory had thus grown and been refined into a fairly precise and comprehensive schematism of the interrelation between human physical and mental life and the broad physiognomy of observable nature.[39]

Under this theory, then, melancholia appears as the preponderance of black bile, the cold and dry bodily humor, associated with the earthly and the low, late adulthood, and the spleen. Symptoms of such a preponderance include, according to Hippocrates, lethargy, coldness, slowness, "aversion to food, despondency, sleeplessness, irritability," or "fear and depression which are prolonged." In general, Hippocratic physicians tended to attribute the onset of melancholia to seasonal changes, improper diet, old age—such "mild" melancholies were not serious and could be treated with changed diet or distracting entertainment, especially music.[40] In severer cases, however, melancholia threatened madness and delirium, suicidal tendencies, or even death.[41] The melancholic becomes slow and heavy, feels the energy of the living organism ebb, is tormented by delusions, is incapable of enjoying simple pleasures, is morbidly obsessed with death. Unable to enjoy human company, the pathological melancholic launches on a self-imposed exile, on a solitary path toward insanity. In such cases, treatment became extraordinarily difficult.[42]

By Galen's time, the doctrine of humoral pathology had thus provided the basis for a remarkably detailed description of the symptomatology of melancholia. Moreover, whereas the other humoral disequilibria had remained by and large descriptive categories for the organic source of certain specific dispositions or feelings, melancholia emerges clearly as temperament and profound disease, a sort of global syndrome that clearly fascinated and challenged the best of classical physicians. The developed symptomatology and therapies remained remarkably unchanged in a medical discourse that would continue virtually without interruption until the demise of the paradigm of humoral pathology in the seventeenth century. This image of the sad, brooding, lonely, bored, hopeless, irritable, and possibly mad melancholic thus consistently elicited a special respect from physicians who must have been especially moved by an affliction that, as they repeatedly observe, seemed to be such a total disease, taking away the enjoyment of even the most trivial compensatory pleasures that make life tolerable. Furthermore, the medical consensus remained that the melancholic disease was at least etiologically related to factors that extended beyond the sufferer's body. The melancholic's subjective feelings of despair and sadness may have been immediately caused by the preponderance of black bile, but this preponderance in turn was related to a broader disharmony with the natural world, perhaps even to certain facts—the onset of old age, for example—that were simply universal features of the human experience and that could thus be regarded as "pathologies" or disharmonies only by the extension of the discourse of melancholia beyond its narrower medical parameters and into philosophical, aesthetic, or theological discourses.

Even after the decay of the paradigm of humoral pathology, this characteristically global gesture in the explanation of melancholy symptoms continues. The seventeenth-century debates on the causes of melancholy from a mechanistic conception of the body therefore concerned how melancholia was to be understood as a *mental disease*, recapitulating in different terms the older insight that melancholy disease was intimately related with a melancholy temperament or disposition, itself not subject to medical treatment. In *Madness and Civilization*, Foucault argues that the very shift from an essentialist to a mechanist paradigm of the organic body led to the development of the conception of mental illness in the seventeenth century, a development in which melancholia was one of the key terms. The "disordered movement of the brain," rather than a symptom, became the (mechanical) cause of the "essential break with truth" of the melancholy mind;[43] a break that thus reverberates throughout the entire organism. This global departure from normalcy, insofar as its causality violates the limits of reason itself, thus could no longer be regarded as a physical disease. Melancholics, who until that time were regarded as patients, became, in the Age of Reason, liable to confinement by the state.

Profound melancholia continued to be regarded as a particularly convoluted mental illness, a "clean break" with standards of rational normalcy, until the present century. The peculiar characteristic of "clinical" melancholia, its legacy from the discourse of humoral pathology according to which the depressive symptoms of the melancholic were referred to features extending beyond the melancholic and into the objectively structured world in which the disease occurred, was also obliquely preserved.

Thus Freud's "Mourning and Melancholia" (1915) could argue that the distinction between these two kinds of object loss consisted not just in the melancholic intensification of feelings of despair and joylessness, but further in the melancholic's "extraordinary diminution of his self-regard, an impoverishment of his ego on a grand scale." Thus, while both mourning and melancholia result from psychic strategies in the response to the deprivation of a libidinal object, in which the resentment or anger at such a withdrawal is projected onto compensatory objects, melancholics turn such feelings on themselves. This pernicious circularity implies that while mourning is a perfectly acceptable and temporary response to the dissolution of a valued libidinal bond, melancholy is puzzlingly permanent and virtually untreatable. Typically, the original libidinal bond whose loss results in melancholia is not readily visible. The resulting "dissatisfaction of the ego on moral grounds" consists in uninterrupted self-reproach, whose strength seems to increase as the original libidinal object, the true target of all the melancholic's reproaches, recedes. Melancholy thus appears to Freud as a peculiar mode of self-deception, which in turn launches into its own vicious circle: the reproaches that the ego heaps upon itself only fuel the awareness of the absence of the erotic attachment, and this awareness, however dim, is the fuel for increased self-torment. Still, Freud often seems less than completely convinced by his own arguments, as if he himself had a presentiment that there was more to say about melancholia than this somewhat desultory classification as a peculiarly persistent form of self-abuse. There is a sense, Freud writes, in which the melancholic is not "wrong" but indeed perfectly justified in the reproaches that he heaps upon himself, for "it is only that he has a keener eye for the truth than other people who are not melancholic. When in his heightened self-criticism he describes himself as petty, egoistic, dishonest, lacking in independence, one whose sole aim has been to hide the weaknesses of his own nature, it may be, so far as we know, that he has come pretty near to understanding himself; we only wonder why a man has to be ill before he can be accessible to a truth of this kind."[44]

Despite his almost exclusive concern with the self-abusive dimension of melancholia—excluding its cognitive content—Freud does not speculate on the originary libidinal bond in question here, which is a pity, insofar as such speculation might have led him to explore the strange implications of his conception of melancholia for his understanding of the relation of the ego to its libidinal objects. Rather than merely one example of an object relation, in which the reproaches for the dissolution of the relation turn for whatever reason back upon the ego, melancholia could well mark the limit of the very notion of "object-relation"—not the deprivation of the object, but the impossibility of an object relation, the region in which all erotic attachments fail, could be in question.

This, at any rate, is the position that Kristeva develops from her own Lacanian reading of Freud. If love, as a striving for attainment of union with an erotic object, is always "meaningful" in the sense that it is an act of symbolization, then melancholia is the disorder that arises precisely when the ability to establish and maintain such acts breaks down. For Kristeva, then, melancholia becomes closely associated with meaninglessness and is thus characterized most exactly by "asymbolia" and inhibition, the breakdown of the "depressed narcissist's" entire set of signifying bonds, which secures the possibility of object relations themselves. The signifier itself fails to perform its compensatory function. The total withdrawal of the depressive from the realm of meaningful action, of possibility, thus traces back to the originary libidinal wound: the loss not of the object, but of the thing, the mother (death), "the real that does not lend itself to signification, the center of attraction and repulsion, seat of the sexuality from which the object of desire will become separated":

> Ever since that archaic attachment [to the Thing] the depressed person has the impression of having been deprived of an unnameable, supreme good, of something unrepresentable, that perhaps only devouring might represent, or an *invocation* might point out, but no word could signify. . . . Knowingly disinherited of the Thing, the depressed person wanders in pursuit of continuously disappointing adventures and loves; or else retreats, disconsolate and aphasic, alone with the unnamed Thing.

"What is melancholia?" Kristeva concludes: "Merely an abyssal suffering that does not succeed in signifying itself and, having lost meaning, loses life."[45]

The sense of a desolating loss of originary meaning, which resonates through Kristeva's analysis, touches upon one of the deepest sources of melancholy writing. The category of loss—of life force, of joy, of the originary, presymbolic Thing, of "meaning"—is so central to the idea of melancholy because loss itself is so thoroughly a dialectical concept. In it is compacted the dim claim that such originary meaning was once, if not "possessed" by the ego, then once in a state of immediacy predating the painful separation of subjectivity from its objects. Loss subtly presupposes that such a state of affairs is, however feebly and unsatisfactorily, accessible through memory, through intentional or unintentional discoveries of correspondences or traces, through the repetitive allegorization of the objects of experience. Memory and forgetting settle as constituent, mournful properties of the realm of objects of intuition and knowledge.

Melancholia as loss of originary meaning thus implies, if not a theology, then something close to it. The "recovery" of meaning is the most pressing possibility that is given to the melancholy subject, but only under the sign of the impossibility of such a recovery *for* the symbolizing, law-imposing subject itself. "Meaning" is the ultimate loss; not the meaning that the strength of the subject can impose, arbitrarily, upon experience, but rather the meaning that would come bursting forth from behind the surface of experience only by the impossible recovery of a receptivity that would predate the subject *qua* subject. The objects that proliferate in the economy of the symbol thus themselves "stand for" the loss of meaning in their very signifying function. It is this very proliferation of signs that draws the melancholic's attention, both as the exact schematic representation of the sites of the melancholic's loss and as the only possible medium in which the Thing could be glimpsed. The chaotic mass of symbolic signification—of names—"means" the loss of meaning. It therefore signifies in a double motion. For the melancholic who is able to recover from the paralytic, illogic thrall of loss—who can sublimate it—meaning translates into the continually frustrated fascination with the rifts and discontinuities that remain in the proliferation of signs. In this way Kristeva understands the "melancholy jouissance" of the allegorical.[46]

For the sublimating melancholic, "imagination" operates "like a tense link between Thing and Meaning, the unnameable and the proliferation of signs." In the dance of failed or jumbled meanings allegory represents the tension of melancholy itself. It contains within its motion the incessant, stroboscopic alternation between the exaltation of meaning and the abjection of meaninglessness contained in the act of signification. The "resurrectional jubilation" of assigned significance occurs only within the imaginative space of the object as already dead. For Kristeva, this structural ambiguity or alteration between meaning and meaninglessness, life and death, exaltation and despair, lying at the heart of allegoresis, is nothing other than an insight into the very structure of imagination itself.[47]

If it is true that melancholia articulates itself most vividly as a dialectic of loss and recovery, of signification and meaningless (or of I and Thing), then this might serve to underscore the impressive emotive-cognitive richness that has been associated with it. The melancholic's torment is the price paid for a special insight into the real nature of "the" world, the presymbolic conditions that predetermine the symbolizing subject itself. Beauty as sublimation, or the "continually disappointing adventures" into language, are the frustrating significative enterprises that the melancholic dedicates to the loss of originary meaning. But the very pain of this realization also constitutes a kind of insight into the truth of the subject that could not have been accomplished in any other way.

In the peripatetic *Problemata Physica*, the author wonders "why it is that all those who have become eminent in philosophy or politics or poetry or the arts are clearly melancholics, and some of them to such an extent as to be affected by diseases caused by the black bile?"[48] Tossing off an impressive list of heroes, artists, and philosophers, all "melancholics by constitution," the author introduces an explanatory analogy. He compares the black bile with wine, observing that, beyond the physical similarities of the two fluids, the effect of wine on the mind and body of the drinker is like the effects of degrees of preponderance of the black bile. A certain small amount produces beneficial effects; indeed, it can result in a change in the constitution that, although not yet "intoxicating," with its connotation of the presence of an alien toxin, appears as a heightening of the powers of insight or discernment, of an empowerment of the mind and the emotions. If, however, the preponderance of this *pharmakos* is increased, the poisonous effects emerge, and what was empowerment of the senses and intellect is transformed into a progressive degradation of the faculties. Among those who naturally possess a preponderance of black bile—those who "constitutionally possess the temperament"—rather than having got it through some environmental cause, "there is straightaway the greatest variety of characters, each according to his mixture." These characters range from those who are indistinguishable from those of a "harmonious" mixture to those whose degree of preponderance is great enough to effect a transition from melancholy character to melancholy disease. It follows that within this range of melancholics, "those . . . in whom the black bile's excessiveness is relaxed toward a mean, are melancholy, but they are more rational and less eccentric and in many respects even superior to others either in culture or in the arts or in statesmanship."[49]

Thus a *sophrosyne* of excess—a moderate amount of preponderance of the humor—is the mixture that produces the melancholy character, the presence of the healing toxin that intoxicates the mind and grants it "superior" powers. Such a character, the author observes, certainly does not thereby lose the depression, brooding, or "state of grieving" that is produced by the condition. Moreover, to the extent that it is dependent on the body's mastery of what is otherwise toxic, the character is inherently unstable. Insofar as the body "successfully" masters the preponderance of bile, the character drifts toward mediocrity; insofar as it fails, it approaches madness.[50] Such a precarious state of being— which a psychoanalytic discourse would want to describe in terms of more or less successful sublimation—marks the melancholic as literally "outstanding"; capable of superior achievements in intellect and perception, but by the same token constitutionally excluded from the normalcy of a social continuum in which and on which the melancholic's powers must be exercised. The sorrow arising from the character itself is thus met halfway by the sorrow arising from the isolation and loneliness that are the effects of the melancholic's unhappy mean.

This peripatetic notion of melancholy as the simultaneity of morbidity and genius, and the implication of a *good* melancholy that one could effect by consciously achieving a sort of mean between normalcy and madness, was a short-lived and fairly isolated event in the classical texts on melancholia and would remain more or less dormant until the creative reappropriation of classical literature in the Florentine Renaissance, especially in Ficino and the ideal of *heroic* melancholy. Far more characteristic of the role of melancholia in Western culture was its tendency to migrate from medical into theological and ethical discourses. The original medical texts of late antiquity, migrating to Arabia in the tenth and eleventh centuries, become associated with astrological bodies and properties. Melancholia becomes connected with Saturn, the cold, dark, and slow planet, and thence the correspondence, Saturn-melancholia, with Chronos, the classical god of time, who is now transfigured into the god of sadness and morbidity, of delay.[51]

This connection, apparently made on the basis of the natural similarities between the observed qualities of the planet and the dark and cold melancholy temperament, posited the planet as the cause of the condition. Later on, the accounts of planetary properties and influences grew increasingly complex in Arabic medical and cosmological speculations and brought about a gradual fusion of the two sciences.

As this form of medical-cosmological science made its way back to Europe in the eleventh century, the idea of Saturn as an underlying cause of melancholia became more prominent. Moreover, it was connected with an older mythical heritage of the actions and properties of the Olympic pantheon; thus the association of melancholy with Saturn, and Saturn with the god Chronos, Chronos with time and universal death as well as harvest and the change of the seasons, laid the foundation for an astonishing allegorical complexity attached to the original medical accounts of the melancholy disposition.

The complex and selective process with which medieval and Renais-

sance artists and philosophers reinterpreted classical motifs and figures in their reappropriation of the classical idea of melancholia
resulted in the transformation of a dialectic of illness and insight into
one of individual genius and cosmological forces. Medieval conceptions of the melancholy disposition tended to associate it with the
antique affliction of the *taedium vitae;* translated into the terminology
of Christian doctrine, the loss of interest in life became expressed as
acedia, the cardinal sin of sloth. A lapse of personal ethical discipline
could expose the soul to the baleful influences of Saturn; indeed *acedia*
was conceived as the special danger of monastic discipline, insofar as a
link was perceived among the retirement from active life into contemplation, a heightened and intensified awareness of the passage of
time (i.e., boredom), and the onset of saturnine melancholia. The
black bile thus becomes associated not only with enforced inactivity,
but also with contemplation, and in this way an older peripatetic link
between deep contemplation, solitude, and the hostile and debilitating
effects of the black bile is renewed, this time in ethical terms. Furthermore, such a relationship is, for example according to Hildegard of
Bingen, consciously related to the theological state of fallen humanity
itself. As a cardinal sin, melancholia proceeds as a direct consequence of the Fall. [52]

The medieval conviction that deep sadness was an appropriate
spiritual attitude did occasionally lead to speculations concerning the
possible status of melancholia as a signal of spiritual transcendence or
as an anamnestic trace of divine nostalgia. [53] But the dialectics of
affliction and empowerment merge most clearly with that between loss
and recovery, or meaning and meaninglessness, in the Renaissance
image of heroic melancholia. The Renaissance recovery of the Aristotelian ideal of genius as a delicate balance between mediocrity and
madness was read through the astrological and religious reformulations
of melancholia as a sinful affliction arising from the influence of
Saturn. The complex synergy of emotive, medical, metaphysical, and
cognitive factors at work in this sort of appropriation constitutes the
image of the heroic melancholic. The *vita speculativa* promises occult
insight into the structure of the cosmos, but places the contemplator at
risk of falling so far under the influence of Saturn that speculation will
give way to mournful paralysis. Heroic melancholy, for example in
Ficino or Melanchthon, thus consisted not only in striking the delicate

balance between too much and not enough black bile, but also in mastering and harnessing the very power of Saturn that threatened the investigator with madness, in order to recover the sources of individual genius from the same planet. Ficino's system of astral coordinates and powers served as a spiritual-celestial blueprint for this strategy.

What is striking about Ficino's *Vita Triplici* as well as the ideal of Renaissance heroic melancholy as a whole is its self-consciously dialectical nature. The process whereby the individual sets out to master Saturn is the same process of individual self-formation. Cosmological structure and personal temperament and strength of will coincide in the production of a new kind of subjectivity, one that has self-consciously forged itself at the intersection of dialectical oppositions. Grief and sorrow do not disappear; the "sorrowful investigator" has, rather, discovered their true nature and use.

The theme of the ideal of heroic melancholy in the Renaissance, especially in Ficino, will return again and in detail through an examination of Benjamin's theory of Renaissance and baroque melancholia in the *Ursprung des deutschen Trauerspiels*. For the moment, it is mentioned only to indicate that the discourse of melancholia finds in it the truest and most powerful historical image of its dialectical structure. This image is that of the individual who struggles to forge subjective inwardness with metaphysical truth, developing each to its extreme in order to bring out and control the truth content of the other. It points to the theme of melancholy not just as a dialectic of lost meaning, or of illness and insight, or of self and its half-forgotten origin, but also to melancholy as a remarkable, difficult form of subjective temperament in which these traits are unified, however fragilely or transiently, into an expressive whole.

In the *Ursprung des deutschen Trauerspiels*, Benjamin noticed the odd state of affairs that arises from a reconstruction of the history of melancholia, particularly its Renaissance incarnation. "However obvious the distinction between the astrological and the medical systems in the theory of the melancholic temperament," he wrote, ". . . however obvious it must seem that the harmonious speculations, which were concocted out of both, had only a coincidental relationship to empirical reality, all the more astonishing, all the more difficult to explain, is the wealth of anthropological insight to which the theory gives rise."[59]

Anthropological insight of the kind Benjamin himself observes in the history of melancholia can at least be pointed to by a few observations concerning the sociological aspects of the melancholy type. The puzzled question of the *Problemata Physica*—why it is that so many creative people are melancholic—can, as Lawrence Babb has suggested, be answered by the simple fact that melancholia is, as much as a genuine cognitive state, an affectation meant to indicate deepness and tortured creativity. It is just this "tortured stupidity" that Benjamin observes in his own contemporary incarnation of the melancholy type.[55] But this itself would not answer why the image of the melancholy type exerts such an attraction.

Two descriptive regularities of the melancholy type can be introduced to suggest a sociology of melancholia: solitude and the inability to act. Categories such as these provide means for analyzing the cultural and intellectual condition of Benjamin's early theory of *Trauer*. Since its pre-Socratic origin melancholia has been closely associated with solitude. The temperament that makes the melancholic sad and that grants the melancholic a heightened insight into the structure of the real also renders the melancholic unfit for human society (Heraclitus is perhaps the most vivid early portrait of this phenomenon). Greek physicians often prescribed forced companionship as a treatment against black bile.[56] In the *Problemata Physica*, the connection between melancholy and genius implies that genius itself is incompatible with integration into the *polis*.

Enforced solitude is the image of the flight into interiority of the melancholy, romantic artist,[57] and introduces a particularly sharp connection between the hyperintellectual melancholic and social criticism as well. Melancholy isolates; conversely, the enforced isolation from social institutions and practices produces both melancholy sadness and the alienation necessary to gain a critical insight into the structure of society itself. Even in Gryphius's "Einsamkeitssonnette," melancholia grants the sufferer the insight that human society and industry is, at all levels, "vanity, only vanity"; the bile is a corrosive substance that strips off the veil of human pretension and allows the sufferer to see the world as it truly is.[58] The melancholic is, like it or not, in a state of continual and total rebellion against the real.[59]

In *Melancholie und Gesellschaft*, the sociologist Wolf Lepenies finds in this image of the lonely, excluded melancholic rebel a specific category of social rebellion. Following Robert Merton, Lepenies identifies melancholia as a simultaneous rejection of both the means and the ends of sanctioned social behavior.[60] For Merton, melancholia constitutes a specific form of rebellion: the despair and hopelessness of the melancholic arise from the concrete or imagined condition of utter helplessness in the face of a social order experienced as oppressive or stifling. From this perspective, melancholia is a retreat from and a total rejection of society, due not only to the repressive function of social norms but also to the total effect of society, which the melancholic experiences as suffocating. The melancholic's rebellion is therefore a passive one. Under the conviction, whether justified or not, that all avenues toward effective action have been closed off, the melancholic rebel recedes into a resigned interiority, brooding over the very conditions of the impossibility of action themselves. Lepenies thus refers to the *Zurückgezogenheit* or retreat into interiority characteristic of melancholics, accompanied by "a homesickness for the past and apathy for the present."[61]

In this way the loneliness and isolation of the melancholic enters into a complex relation with another aspect, hopelessness concerning the prospect of significant action. The melancholic's indifference and paralysis—*acedia*—is often observed as the effect of the melancholy disorder. From a descriptive sociological perspective, Lepenies reverses this relationship and argues that the "melancholy disease" appears textually with objective historical conditions in which the subject is closed off from meaningful avenues for active self-expression.

Lepenies does not argue for a strictly causal relationship between enforced inaction and melancholia. Rather, he introduces the idea of *Handlungshemmung*—the disinclination or inability to act—as a way of indicating the ambiguity attending the phenomenon. The absence of real alternatives for action could be the immediate, concrete result of social conditions, for example of complete marginalization, slavery, or imprisonment. It could just as easily attach itself to the self-understanding of a socioeconomically privileged social stratum whose traditional role is undergoing rapid and disorienting change, for example, aristocratic elites during the rise of the bourgeoisie.[62] Perceived or real disempowerment can in many instances come mutually to influence each other, for example in the case of a social class that, as a response to concrete disempowerment, rejects the entire possibility of change through organized action.

As a reaction to situations of real or perceived disempowerment, melancholia projects itself from the sphere of instrumental social action onto progressively more global spheres of reference. The personal or group experience of *Handlungshemmung* thus becomes the occasion for melancholy speculations on the futility of action and the meaninglessness of life as such. An ideology of pessimism, of the futility of action, is closely related to indecisiveness. Indecisiveness is nothing other than the mode of action of the brooding melancholic who, convinced by contemplation of the meaninglessness of practical means and ends, nevertheless is obliged to pretend otherwise.[63] For Lepenies, then, the spectrum of affective and cognitive states of melancholia appears as a range of subliminatory or compensatory responses to the experience of *Handlungshemmung*.

Lepenies, who is interested not in what melancholia is, but in what people seem to mean when they describe themselves as melancholic,[64] refrains from speculating on the philosophical significance of self-descriptions of melancholia. But the argument connecting melancholic descriptions with concrete sociohistorical conditions in which the ability to act has been compromised or abrogated suggests pushing the analysis, and asking whether the dialectical structure of melancholy thought itself does not bear an interesting relation to the conditions in which it is articulated. *Handlungshemmung*, we might claim, has a *complex* relation to sadness and reflection. The particular strategies whereby a historically situated thinker confronts the tasks of thought arise from a complex, mediated relationship between concrete historical factors and elements that belong to the nature of thinking itself. Melancholia articulates itself as the set of variable historical appearances, under the condition of *Handlungshemmung*, of a set of dialectical oppositions that themselves transcend particular historical circumstances. This postulate becomes particularly relevant when we consider the synergy of historical and cognitive factors involved in the formation of Benjamin's earliest theories of critical writing.

1   Trauer and Criticism

Dear sir, I have always had a desire to see things as they appeared before they showed themselves to me.—Franz Kafka, "Gespräch mit dem Beter"

Our truly essential experiences are encapsulated and invisible in our lives, as seeds. That which is fruitful in the fullest sense lies enclosed within the hard shell of the incommunicable, of immediacy. Nothing distinguishes genuine productivity from its failed or inauthentic forms more clearly than the question: has the man experienced at the right time—between fifteen and twenty-five— what seals his mouth, what silences him, makes him knowing and reflective, what gives him an experience to which he will always testify, never betray, never rashly reveal?—Walter Benjamin, "Theologische Kritik. Zu Willy Hass"

In May of 1916, Martin Buber wrote to the then twenty-three-year-old Walter Benjamin to solicit from him a contribution for the inaugural issue of Buber's journal, *Der Jude*. Benjamin refused Buber's request. The characteristics of this refusal are revealing not just for the extraordinary "political" sensibilities that Benjamin had developed, in large measure as a result of his withdrawal from the German Youth Movement and his rejection of both Buber's existential Judaism and the Zionist alternative, but for critical-political sensibilities that would remain fundamental for years to come. Benjamin understood Buber's invitation and his own refusal to collaborate as highly moral-political acts not just because of his and Buber's antagonistic positions concerning the war, but also because of Benjamin's fundamental opposition to a conventional understanding of the political in general.

Scholem recalls that Benjamin had at first considered presenting his refusal to contribute to *Der Jude* in the form of an open letter to Buber and that the private letter that Benjamin actually wrote was "greatly toned down."[1] One can only wonder what Benjamin had in mind for the never-written open letter. The one he did write, characteristically, touches only initially and briefly on the concrete political and ethical differences between him and Buber and passes quickly on to an impassioned appeal for an understanding of writing with a critical intent, and a relation to action grounded in purely metaphysical categories:

> There is a widely accepted, indeed almost commonsensical opinion that writing is capable of influencing the ethical world and human actions, insofar as it can provide actors with motives. In this sense, then, language is a mere means for a rather suggestive preparation of certain motives, which then determine action within the interiority of the soul. It is characteristic of this view that it is wholly incapable of conceiving a relation between language and deed [*Tat*] in which the former would not be the means to the latter. This relation presents language and writing as powerless, and demeaned to the role of a pure medium; thus a weakened act whose source lies not in itself, but rather in this or that speakable, expressible motive.

This rejection of any use of language as a means to establish a political or moral effect brings Benjamin to an affirmation of the "essential Being" of writing and language itself:

> I can understand writing in general, whether poetic, prophetic, or objective in its effect, only magically, that is, only immediately. Every sound and healthy effect of language—indeed, every effect that does not represent a self-demolition of language, touches upon mystery (of the word, of language). Whatever the form in which language is capable of proving itself effective, this cannot be through the communication of contents, but rather through the purest revelation of its own worth, and its own essence.[2]

Benjamin thus presents a mystical and romantic conception of language, whose "purity" and "essence" stand in an unresolvable conflict with the instrumental use of language as a medium of the communication of contents. Implicitly, language itself extends beyond the boundaries normally ascribed to human words and posits a realm of the unsayable (*das Unsagbare*), which is allocated a special status over against the "sayable, expressible" realm of communicated content. Language itself contains a domain of "objective" meaning that the human word fails, a domain that is at least partially indicated by the poetic dimension of language. This conception of the duality of human language carries with it an intuition of an alternative relation between language and action—*logos* is no longer a means for *praxis;* on the contrary, the activity of *writing*, once liberated from its enmeshment in the instrumentality of communication, is shown to be a mode of revelation of the spiritual content of the realm of language itself. Indeed it is this form of writing that, for Benjamin, must be considered political in the highest degree, since this form of "grammatopraxis" aims at its own overcoming of self, at the frontier of the sayable and the unsayable: "My conception of straightforward and at the same time highly political style and writing," Benjamin's letter to Buber concludes, "is to indicate that which fails words; only there, only where this sphere of wordlessness reveals itself in its unspeakable pure power, can the magic spark between word and deed arise."[3]

Under the weight of such a response it is understandable why Buber pursued the matter no further. On one level, to be sure, Benjamin's refusal can be seen in its own political context. For those who physically escaped it, the war proved to be a bitterly divisive force within the milieu of German Jewish intellectuals, and the task of formulating a coherent opposition to the war and the forces that the war represented was not a light one; Benjamin's resolute esotericism, so evident here, represents an effort to come to some understanding of a form of resistance to a barbarism that extended to the structure of human language itself.

This political context is especially significant in Benjamin's case. His break with the youth movement, while coming as a direct response to the enthusiastic support for the war by the rank and file of his peers (as well as his mentor, Gustav Wyneken, and Buber), was the inevitable outcome of Benjamin's continuing opposition to any introduction of practical political motives into the self-understanding of the youth movement. Such motives could only force the movement to deviate from the rigidly abstract and spiritualized conceptions of youth, ethics, and community, which were for Benjamin the ultimate values of the youth movement, and whose realization was the movement's only valid "political" goal.[4]

There was, to be sure, a dimension of theoretical vigor in Benjamin's involvement with the youth movement, consisting in the task, common to many in Benjamin's milieu, of formulating a vision of a spiritualized politics; an explicit rejection of the pernicious effects of the commodification of culture and the decay of experience, an extension of experiential possibility so vast that "youth" became the project of the realization of the "abstractness of pure Spirit" itself.[5] "Youth" would stop at nothing less than a communal realization of an ill-defined idea of the unconditioned, and politics assumed the task of the reconciliation of spirit and nature. In this sense, Benjamin was one point in a constellation of voices of synthetic, creative reaction to the experience of political exclusion and alienation, to the shallow and bankrupt culture of the older generation. It was a constellation that, by a variety of different strategies, was attempting to explore the implications of an attempt to relate the intensely otherworldly and metaphysically remote attitude of the *Intellektueller*—itself a relatively new term in German, dating from the German response to the Dreyfus affair—to the practical realm of engaged politics. Such an attempt, visible in such pre-Weimar figures as Landauer, Kurt Hiller, Herzl, or Buber, revolved around the question of the political role of the intellectual; how the intellectual could effect a relationship between the ideal realm of spiritual purity, which was philosophically or poetically accessible, and the realm of pragmatic political power. Answers to such questions pointed in the direction of a "spiritualized" or *geistliche* conception of political action, *Tat*, or deed, whereby the intellectual would break out of poetic isolation, become "active," enter into politics both negatively—by offering critiques of the decadence and spiritual bankruptcy of society—and positively, by pointing to a realm of utopian self-realization in which the spiritual and the concrete would achieve a living mediation.

For the predominantly Jewish followers of Wyneken's branch of the *Jugendbewegung*, the attempt to articulate the role of the intellectual gained an additional polemical vigor as a revolt against the futility and hypocrisy of assimilationism, and its corresponding ideology of tidy historical progress, an ethical conformism based on an artificially narrowed conception of experience and an inveterate blindness to "ultimate values." Seen in this narrower, Judaic sense, such a constellation included Zionism, of course, but also Marxism, or the occasional and fragile attempts to synthesize these two movements, as well as Benjamin's wing of the youth movement.[6]

Seen in this way, Benjamin's early writings appear as particularly extreme examples of a more general process, the task of discovering a radically new political-ethical vocabulary that, on the one hand, would prove itself adequate to the special historical and social experience of "youth," but on the other hand would also be capable of expressing the essentially metaphysical task of politics as such: the realization of abstract spirit in the context of a morally pure community, the achievement of a sort of communal perfection that, abstracted from the inherently messy realm of "politics" in the conventional sense—the realm of competing interests, consensus, and compromise—was in the end to be understood in the predominantly religious-aesthetic terms of expressibility, integrity, and unity. Such a conception of spiritual politics of course demanded the progressive and critical rejection of the political and cultural values of conventional society; a completion of the process of exclusion that society itself had already begun.[7] More significant, however, it also demanded a steady redefinition of standard elements of political rhetoric, in order to render them serviceable to a new and rather rigidly impractical political sensibility.

The consistent opposition in Benjamin's early writing between the dimension of spiritual or cultural purity, the realm of the intellect, and the political dimension produced a marked need to transform terms that would otherwise have referred to the latter realm into expressions that could find a metaphysical referent only in the former. The great predilection for terms such as *deed, action, decisiveness, beginning,* and *freedom*—common to the entire intellectual milieu but endowed with a particular edge in the political speculations of postassimilationist Jewish intellectuals—derives from this need for a vocabulary of spiritualized politics; moreover, the terms are part of an essential redefinition of the meaning of political *praxis*. Abandoning all interest in a political rhetoric dedicated to pragmatism or gradualist reform, such a redefinition sought to revolutionize political sensibilities in order to revolutionize politics, to struggle against social injustice and demand a revitalization of German culture, even if, as was often the case, the precise terms or strategies for such a revitalization remained disturbingly vague.[8]

Although it is true that Benjamin's early writings place him within such a broader redefinition of the meaning of political *praxis*, he is distinguished by his insistence that, however *praxis* was to be redefined, it must not sacrifice its strictly spiritual essence and must thus remain determinedly aloof from concrete political motives. Indeed, his position throughout his involvement with the youth movement remains remarkably consistent: in opposition to virtually all of his intellectual colleagues, Benjamin insisted that "politics," whether regarded in terms of Hiller's "Activismus," Zionism, or the cultural yearnings of the youth movement, be understood in a rigorously and uncompromisingly abstract manner. Any immediate relation to pragmatic politics, any attempt to relate *praxis* to concrete action and change, was subordinated to the project of an intellectual intuition or comprehension of the world. In fact this insistence, as much as any factor, marked Benjamin's relative theoretical isolation amongst his own intellectual milieu.

Adorno is surely right to point out that in the youth movement, as in so many other political movements, Benjamin was painfully out of place and that he managed to ignore, perhaps for too long, the palpable inferiority of his colleagues in the movement (and the increasingly fatuous and bellicose ideology that the movement in general acquired in the years leading to the war) only because the movement itself offered a "psychic compensation," however unsatisfactory, for Benjamin's own personal and intellectual isolation.[9] But it is also surely the case, as Bernd Witte has argued, that all existentially pressing needs notwithstanding, Benjamin came to the youth movement in search of a vocabulary to express his own nascent vision of historical criticism, and thus brought to the youth movement certain inflexible postulates concerning the nature of historical time that, in concert, could not help ruling out from the start anything but the most esoteric conceptions of political activity. While Witte is thus surely correct in seeing Benjamin's involvement in the youth movement as a curiously oblique means for the articulation of certain notions that were alien to the movement itself, it is probably not quite right to argue that the spectacular failure of the movement—which in any case Benjamin had sensed far before the war—obliged Benjamin to develop a theory of criticism as an ersatz form or compensation for a now impossible social-political *praxis*.[10] From the start, *praxis* for Benjamin was to be defined in strict opposition to the determination of concrete—profane—political movements and motives. Rather than an ersatz form of *praxis*, critique constituted the only form of historically possible meaningful action on the part of the subject.

Benjamin's early writing thus tends toward an already dimly visible goal: the formulation of a conception of critical thinking and writing that, by the purity of its ideas and the rigor of its method, could represent the purity of a transcendent, messianic truth within the realm of immanent, historical experience, and further, to direct this critical energy into the heart of contemporary society in a transformational way. Indeed, surveying Benjamin's work even in this early period, what distinguishes it from that of other figures is, first, the tendency to understand contemporary cultural or political crises only insofar as they fragmentarily reflect universal-historical, that is, messianic truths; and second, the related tendency to infuse the expression of such contemporary cultural diagnoses with a mournfulness or a sense of historical dejection that seems to be generated not from the crisis itself, but from some esoteric, hidden source. Even in his earliest work, Benjamin's thought is distinguished from that of his peers by an almost prescient sense of the radically restricted range of the politically possible and a concomitant heightening of the sense of the mournful, historically exiled, and imperiled contents of human experience. Thus Benjamin's earliest critiques of cultural impoverishment, of a crisis of values and the need for spiritual renewal, are consistently framed in terms of a historical conception that, from its beginning, treats the categories of *Tat* or *Handeln* not primarily as gestures of self-assertion against a bankrupt present, but rather as interruptive actions against a meaningless historical continuum.

Thus Benjamin associates youth with a certain "Hamlet-like consciousness of the sheer badness of the world,"[11] and a resolute unwillingness to allow ideals to dilute themselves in the historical "*Immergleiche*," the realm of the "meaninglessness" and "brutality" of life, got up as "experience" by the adult generation.[12] For youth he will claim the will to smash a bad present in order to release the grip of the past: "School makes us indifferent; it wants to tell us: history is the struggle between good and evil. And sooner or later, the good will come through. So there's really no hurry to act. The present is, so to speak, without actuality—time is unending." Benjamin wants to pierce through this adult ideology: "To us, however, history appears as a stark and gruesome struggle. Not for values that already exist—not for good or evil.

Rather, we struggle for the possibility of values as such, that is, for culture, which lives in eternal crisis."[13]

Benjamin's own turgid formulations of "spirit," "youth," and "life" are in this way often tinged with other, less unambiguously transcendent "categories": loneliness; the absolute necessity of spiritual solitude; silence; the fragility of virtue; temporality as a continuum of mythic, deadly repetition; history as a continual crisis of culture; the world as a source of pain. The earliest of Benjamin's writings already work toward a troubled synthesis of the more emphatic spiritualisms of the neoromantic youth movement with Benjamin's own, darker vision of the nature of historical time and the fate of subjectivity within it. Even before Benjamin's rejection of the youth movement, then, his writings provide early glimpses of his critical sensibility, and his sharp disappointment with the political fate of the youth movement clearly sharpened the messianic and mournful tone of his critical writings and allowed a nascent historical sensibility gradually to achieve a prominent role in Benjamin's earliest conceptions of criticism.

This process is particularly visible in "Das Leben der Studenten" (1915), in which Benjamin begins with the now familiar early evocation of his messianic historical vision:

> There is a conception of human history which, proceeding on the faith in the endlessness of time, bothers only to distinguish the tempo at which men and epochs roll down the highway of progress. To this view properly belongs the incoherence, the lack of precision and force of the claims which this view is capable of presenting to the present. The following reflections, on the contrary, are based on a peculiar state in which all of history is collected into one focal point, as in the historical image of the utopian thinkers. The elements of the end of time [*Endzustand*] do not lie evident as formless tendencies toward historical progress, but rather, they are embedded deep in the present, as its most endangered, ridiculed and scorned creations and thoughts. To render the immanent state of perfection in its absolute purity; to direct it visibly and powerfully into the heart of the present: this is the historical task.[14]

The passage already contains in crystallized form much of Benjamin's later critical sensibility: the task of the critic, no longer conceived as relating directly to the organization or development of a spiritual community in the present, is now understood as a "historical" one, which emerges from an essentially messianic and therefore opposition sensitivity to the movement of spirit within time. Only by definitively rejecting a harmonizing and totalizing vision of historical continuity and progress does the critic come to recognize that the utopian elements of the messianic end of history—its destruction, not its developmental outcome—lie precisely in those fragmentary and discrete events buried in the heart of the present. This bestows on the critic a peculiarly ambiguous status in relation to the past since, on the one hand, the critic acquires by virtue of this insight a responsibility for advocacy for those imperiled thoughts and creations that, without critical interventions, would be consigned to the "endlessness of time." On the other hand, these fragments of messianic experience, "collected into one focal point," that is, removed from their embeddedness in one dominant conception of historical happening, take on a new meaning insofar as they now stand in a different light. This, the light of criticism, has in this sense no immediate political role. But the *historical* task of criticism consists in a curiously dual activity: The utopian "immanent state of perfection" encoded within the fragmentary data of critical illumination is to be arranged or formed (*gestalten*), presumably by an arrangement of the elements of the *Endzustand*. Such an arrangement also must be made visible, and thus to prevail (*herrchen*) within the present, a profoundly, if characteristically ambiguous political sensibility.

The ambiguity of the critical position in this very early essay thus consists of a dual relationship of the critic to the fragments of past experience. They are to be rescued (*gerettet*) from their consignment to oblivion, and in this the critic declares an advocacy for the past. Irrespective, then, of the intellectual response to a political present confronted with a modern crisis of values, the critic is also—indeed primarily—confronted with a past whose structure objectively contains elements endowed with a messianic *meaning:* not in the sense that such elements have a didactic effect for contemporary *praxis,* but rather they themselves are messianic, are "elements of the *Endzustand,*" irrespective of the use to which we put them. Yet they are also to be directed to the present, for the sake of its redemption (*Erlösung*). Such a redemptive end of history has nothing to do with "pragmatic descriptions of particularities (institutions, customs, etc.)," however, but rather can only be grasped "in its metaphysical structure, as the Messianic Kingdom or the French Revolution."[15] This tension between an attitude toward the endangered past as deserving rescue for its own sake, and also serving (in a sort of messianic pragmatics) the interest of a redemptive illumination of the present, will remain a constitutive dimension of Benjamin's criticism.

In this early form, the tension produces a similar ambiguity attending the *role* of critical illumination in this process, a dual understanding of critical praxis in which the critic, intervening in both past and present, must not only recognize the messianic "metaphysical structure" that is encoded, objectively, within the fragments themselves, but also must decisively intervene in their historical fate, and forcefully *arrange* or enform them, so that this metaphysical structure can become visible. The faculty whereby the critic is empowered to recognize the messianic dimension in history is not, at least in this first glance, quite the same as the faculty whereby the critic can shape and transform such fragments in order to constitute a messianic meaning from their arrangement. The first is passive and consists of a special, heightened receptivity to the trash of history, as Benjamin would later call it. The second is active and consists in a constructive talent. But what the relation between these two faculties is and, moreover, how the constructive dimension of critique could secure its legitimacy as more than a merely arbitrary arrangement of fragments according to the empirical will, the "authentic experience" of the historical critic, is not illuminated.

In "*Das Leben der Studenten*," this description of the historical task of the critic is all the more surprising insofar as Benjamin, having already definitively rejected his involvement in the youth movement, still attempts to relate the critical activity to his earlier metaphysics of youth, despite having clearly moved beyond it.[16] Youth now is a conception that can only provide a semblance or likeness (*Gleichnis*) of the "metaphysical status of history"; such a likeness, while in itself "effectless," is at least capable of providing a means for the critical intellectual renewal Benjamin held to be possible only through the philosophical system.[17] The system, in turn, would constitute the intellectual grasp of the real through the conceptual representation of the objectively true, the apogee of critical insight into the messianic contents encoded into contemporary (linguistic) experience.

The excessively vague formulations of key terms such as *language*, *deed*, *silence*, and *mystery* characteristic of Benjamin's letter to Buber were, even as Benjamin wrote, themselves undergoing an alchemical refinement. By July of 1916 Benjamin had written to his friend Herbert Belmore expressing his growing sense that criticism alone could constitute effective *praxis* by engaging the mythic forces conjured up by the war and by acting as a spiritual beacon, illuminating eternal truth against the onset of night: "We are in the middle of the night," Benjamin wrote. "I tried to use words in my struggle; I learned then that he who battles the night, who seeks to roll back its deepest darkness, must bring out its own light, and in this greatest challenge of life, words are only a station." The *unendliche Aufgabe* of critical illumination does not, therefore, constitute itself as a mere antagonistic half of a metaphysical dualism. If darkness is conceived as myth, then critical illumination can only "struggle" against the night by the subtlest dialectic in which the form and content of myth and mythical language itself could yield up the messianic originary truth concealed within it. And although words here are, in a strictly nonmetaphorical religious sense "only a station," and would ultimately have to give way, in the completed doctrinal system, to an as-yet only intuitively glimpsed form of pure, postconceptual cognition, such a station was still strictly necessary in order for it itself to be transcended: "True criticism," the letter continues, "does not go against its object. It is like a chemical substance which reacts against another substance only in the sense that, through its dissolving power, it reveals the inner nature of the substance without destroying it. The chemical substance which reacts to spiritual things in this manner (dialectically) is light. This does not appear in language."[18]

Yet, if criticism's vanishing point is the mystery in which darkness distills from itself a spiritual, healing light, and if this mystery, like all mysteries, exceeds even the most spiritually pure and immediate language, then what relationship exists between language and criticism? How can one attain a critical writing whose *effect* could magically "touch upon mystery," itself beyond language and history, by a revelation of the essence of language itself? Benjamin's answer, as he concluded his letter to Belmore, had already taken more definite theoretical shape. In rapid succession he had written five short essays that, taken as a series, mark a first significant attempt to articulate an esoteric theory of criticism: "Das Glück des antiken Menschen," "Sokrates," "Trauerspiel und Tragödie," "Die Bedeutung der Sprache in Trauerspiel und Tragödie," and "Über Sprache überhaupt und über die Sprache des Menschen." In reading the last of these essays, my concern here is not so much to offer a full and detailed account of the genesis of Benjamin's conception of literary criticism; this is beyond the scope of this work and has been admirably accomplished elsewhere.[19] Rather, I want to see how Benjamin's essay "On Language as Such and on Human Language" already demonstrates a dependence on a conception of mourning or *Trauer,* and how this conception, in turn, leads to a series of odd ambiguities concerning the nature of critical—and mournful—subjectivity.

"On Language as Such and on Human Language" was Benjamin's first significant theoretical writing. The mystical theory of language and naming developed in it was clearly intended as a significant, indeed systematic effort to clarify the underlying premises for a theory of criticism;[20] insofar as the essay succeeds in doing this, it establishes conceptions of nature and history, and of the critical sensibility in them, that remain remarkably intact throughout Benjamin's work, above all in the *Ursprung des deutschen Trauerspiels* published eight years later.[21]

The mystical, often fantastic conception of language as a medium of the communication of "spiritual content" developed in the essay is closely related to the vision of the sharp distinction between conventional and critical uses of language drawn in Benjamin's letter to Buber. Moreover, the intellectual pedigree of this conception is equally clear, constituting a creative (and often imaginative) synthesis of the long German tradition of language mysticism or ontologies of linguistic being stretching from Boehme through Hamann, Schlegel, and Humboldt, all of whom Benjamin had been actively studying for some time,[22] and the Jewish sensibility—reactivated through the filter of German romanticism—of language as the inexhaustible field of encoded messianic truths. (One could also point to the influence of the symbolist poets, above all Mallarmé.)

And yet, as Winfried Menninghaus has argued, the essay's curious tendency to oscillate between the forbiddingly esoteric, indeed occult notions of the hidden spiritual content of objects and the direct and unabashed use of the story of Genesis as a foundation for such notions ought not blind us to the fact that the essay nevertheless points toward linguistic conceptions, practical interpretive outlooks, and critical strategies that are in themselves not necessarily "mystical" or based without mediation on theological categories.[23] Indeed, Benjamin is clearly "up to something" in the language essay—not a "linguistic theory" in any conventional sense, but rather a general systematic doctrine of the production and dissemination of meaning, which not only would account for relevant contemporary problems of critical epistemology, but which would also ground a conception of historically attuned criticism.

"Every expression of human spiritual life," the essay begins, "can be understood as a form of language, and this understanding, in the manner of a true method, everywhere raises new questions." The new questions proceed from the insight that language is a universal medium of the expression of the spiritual content not only of human—cultural-historical—life, but also of all created being. The expressibility of the spiritual essence of created being constitutes the existence of being itself—thus that which exists exists insofar as it continues to bear within itself the communicability of its spiritual essence. Understood as the universal medium of the expression of spiritual content or "spiritual essence" (*geistiges Wesen*), language thus becomes fully distinct from the conventional sense of a means or a medium of the communication of a subjective "meaning" between speaker and hearer and emerges as the ground of being itself: "What does language communicate? It communicates the spiritual essence corresponding to it. It is fundamental that this spiritual essence communicate itself *in* language and not *through* language."[24]

Insofar as the spiritual essence of humanity consists in the faculty of naming, it differs qualitatively from the remainder of linguistic being. The communication of this spiritual essence is the Adamic act, is "pure" human language, and in this way human language distinguishes itself from language as such. By raising nature from the anonymity of its own language, Adamic language both repeats and completes the original creative act of God.

Adamic naming constitutes the translation of spiritual essences of divine nature (that is, the language of things) into the ordered realm of names, and in this sense constitutes the idea of knowledge, establishing Adam as the first and true philosopher. "The translation of the language of things into the language of man is not only a translation of the mute into the sonic; it is also the translation of the nameless into the name. It is therefore the translation of an imperfect language into a more perfect one, and cannot but add something to it, namely knowledge." Insofar, then, as the Adamic name thus takes on a *cognitive* dimension, it is one in which the "normal" problems of dialectical epistemology have no place. The knowledge of Adam, by which he was able to assign to all created being its *true* name, is one in which no concept mediates between a faculty of the knowing subject and the manifold of sensory intuitions presented to it; nor does the ideal content of the object require a corresponding event of understanding on the part of the knowing subject in order to approximate fragmentarily this ideal content in terms of discursive concepts—in this utopian epistemology, there are no concepts.

> God rested when he had left his creative power to itself in man. This creativity, relieved of its divine actuality, became knowledge. Man is the knower in the same language in which God is creator. God created him in His image, he created the knower in the image of the creator. Therefore the proposition that the spiritual being of man is language needs explanation. His spiritual being is the language in which creation took place. In the [divine] word creation took place, and God's linguistic being is the word. All human language is only reflection of the word in name.[25]

As a derivative of God's creative word, (naming) knowledge can only imperfectly be expressed as the achievement of a certain adequacy in the cognition of a subject or, dialectically, in the mediated interplay of subjectivity and its objects. Knowledge here is immediacy (*Unmittelbarkeit*). As Winfried Menninghaus argues, just as language does not serve as a medium for the communication of profane contents but rather for the mediation of essence itself, so the Adamic name constitutes a form of cognitive purity prior to all traditional conceptions of representation: in Adamic naming, the idea is immediately present in the name; it is represented not in the sense that the name erotically-anamnestically strives for a unity of cognitive act and intended object, but that the name *is* this unity perfected in the new form of (sonic) deed.[26]

This vision of precognitive immediacy implies that Benjamin's utopian epistemology also extends to a utopian theory of meaning. In the essay, Benjamin takes pains to make clear that the immediacy of language—its "magic"—consists in the presence of the communicable linguistic being of things, in distinction from the collection of "verbal contents" defining the crudely conventional notion of language as a means for communicating factual information. Adamic language communicates its own essence, but only in the sense that "in naming the spiritual being of man communicates itself to God."[27] Such a communication, however, also completes and elevates the mute language of things to the realm of knowledge, and therefore expresses the true meaning of things, not in the sense of the conventional or pragmatic denotative meaning of a name, its *Bedeutung* in the crude sense (and the implicit notion of "pointing at" a thing, *deuten*), but in its significance as an integral and correct expressivity of the thing's status as part of the overall creative effort of God, the thing's *Sinn*. Adamic names are expressions of divine significance, as distinct from conventional (and therefore arbitrary) specifications of pragmatic use.

The Adamic *Ursprache* thus constitutes an originary cognitive-linguistic deed that expresses the initial unity of thing and name, in which knowledge is immediate, absolute, eternal. The creative word of God infuses the mute language of things with a resonance that is fulfilled, completed, and brought to the level of knowledge by the human name. Thus all three—word, name, and being—take their place in the blissfully ordered hierarchy of God, humanity, and nature. Bliss (*Seligkeit*) is thus the feeling that corresponds to the absence of "private" or conceptual knowledge; bliss is a nonarbitrary, an objectively necessary feeling. It is therefore the natural emotive supplement to the image of prehistoric and precognitive immediacy of knowing, and properly speaking cannot be applied merely, or even primarily to empirical subjects. One would speak instead of blissful things, or blissful nature in this sense.

The notion that the *Ursprache* represents a blissful state of preconceptual and hence immediate and perfect knowledge is a very old one and is in this basic sense common both to the Jewish mysticism and to the German romantic theories on which Benjamin draws. Hamann and Schlegel seem to be the primary sources. Particularly for the latter, an insight into the revelatory, noninstrumental character of language as such led to theological-historical speculations about a lost poetic faculty, a lost unity with nature, and a vanished capacity for absolute disclosure. Schlegel referred to the *Ursprache* as "the great collective memory of the human race,"[28] and thereby illuminated what, in the language essay itself, remains predominantly implicit—the sense in which the conception of the *Ursprache* is meant as a critical-heuristic category, a claim that the utopian noninstrumental dimension of contemporary language holds the key to an anamnestic archive of preconceptual cognitive achievements and insights, which a theologically inspired poetry—or criticism—must dislodge, recover, and invigorate.

Yet while clearly developing a strong systematic relationship with the conceptions of language both in Hamann and in the romantics, as Menninghaus claims,[29] Benjamin seems less interested in the notion of the *Ursprache* as an originary poetic faculty than in the special and more manifestly theological relation between the *Ursprache* and human history. The loss of the *Ursprache* is the price paid for by the Fall. Exile, just as much as the beginning of human suffering and human history, marks the end of the immediacy and creativity of Adamic language. With the reduction of the *Ursprache* to the plurality of human tongues, "knowledge," the human expression of the divine unity of name and thing, becomes itself fragmented: "The paradisiac language of Adam must have been one of perfect knowledge; whereas all later knowledge is . . . infinitely differentiated in the multiplicity of languages." Just as the Fall converts human language into a mere means of communication, so the naming faculty, deprived of its divine creativity, degenerates into the endless production of inherently arbitrary assignations of conventional signs. This is the "abyss of prattle [*Geschwätz*]."[30]

The effects of this fall extend beyond merely human language, however. "The enslavement of language in prattle is joined by the enslavement of things in folly almost as its inevitable consequence." Nature, which was once lifted from its muteness and anonymity by the divine immediacy of the Adamic name, is now caught up within the multiplicity of systems of instrumental name giving, and is thereby overnamed. Having too many names is worse than having none; overnaming is "the deepest linguistic reason for all mournfulness and (from the point of view of the things) of all muteness." Nature thus falls into a second silence, one that no longer resides in the anticipation of receiving its true name, but that mutely suffers the arbitrary, instrumental names heaped upon it. The Fall, while bringing humanity into linguistic and epistemological confusion, consigns nature to a mournful silence. Blissfulness had emerged as the objective feeling of joy corresponding to a condition of muteness that is brought into its own fullest self-expression in the name—the "life of man in pure language-spirit was blissful [*selig*]," but things too partook of this bliss, albeit "to a lower degree." In a corresponding sense, the mournfulness (*Trauer*) of human life after the Fall is an objectively necessary feeling and is matched by the mournfulness of nature itself:

> After the Fall . . . when God's word curses the ground, the appearance of nature is deeply changed. Now begins its other muteness, which we mean by the deep mournfulness [*Trauerigkeit*] of nature. It is a metaphysical truth that all nature would begin to lament [*klagen*] if it were endowed with language. . . . This proposition has a double meaning. It means, first: it would lament language itself. Speechlessness: that is the great sorrow of nature (and for the sake of nature's redemption the life and language of man—not only, as is supposed, of the poet—are in nature). This proposition means, secondly: it would lament. Lament, however, is the most undifferentiated, impotent expression of language; it contains scarcely more than the sensuous breath; and even where there is only a rustling of plants, there is always a lament. Because it is mute, nature mourns. Yet the inversion of this proposition leads even further into the essence of nature: the mournfulness of nature makes her mute. In all mournfulness there is the deepest inclination to speechlessness, which is infinitely more than the inability or disinclination to communicate. That which mourns feels itself thoroughly known by the unknowable. To be named—even when the namer is Godlike and blissful—perhaps always remains an intimation of mourning. But how much more so to be named not from the one blessed, paradisiac language of names, but from the hundred languages of man, in which name has already withered, yet which, according to God's pronouncement, know the things.[31]

The "inversion" of the principle of the muteness of nature states that mournfulness is the cause of silence, and not its result. Therefore nature mourns not so much because it cannot express itself; its mournfulness arises from the loss of that world in which it could ever have done so, and silence is a testament to and consequence of its ontological status. Mournfulness—*Trauerigkeit*—is the ontological status of fallen nature. Its linguistic being is silence.

There is disagreement concerning the relevant background of this particular mode of speculation in the language essay. Most interpreters—for example, Witte or Susan Buck-Morss[32]—have proposed that the movement of thought in the essay consists of Benjamin's ingenious, often iconoclastic, and imaginative synthesis of themes and concepts from romanticism and Jewish mysticism; Benjamin's understanding of the theodicic origin of the mournfulness of nature would then be an excellent example of this synthetic process. The open dependence on the linguistics of the early romantics and Humboldt is combined with a clearly Hebraic form of theodicy; Benjamin's reference to the "tree of knowledge" as well as the extravagant and literal use of the story of the Fall signal this.[33]

Nevertheless, it is also clear that the peculiar conception of the mournfulness of overnamed nature is to be found neither in the relevant romantic nor in the Jewish mystical sources, and must count as an original, if initially obscure, dimension of Benjamin's metaphysics of language. It is true that a long tradition of Jewish mysticism refers to the entwined trees of knowledge and of life; Adam's sin was the "cutting of the shoots," that is, the separation of the entwined trees, the separation of the organic unity of living and knowing, and thus the introduction of evil as a principle of difference and separation.[34] Moreover, as Menninghaus observes, the introduction of the theme of paradisiacal language and Adamic naming bears strong affinities to Böhme's notion of the "mysterium magnum" and can be followed into baroque conceptions of "fallen tongues."[35] But the theological interpretation of the mournfulness and the "other muteness" of the realm of things, while arising from an often inventive admixture of romantic and Judaic linguistic speculation, seems also to arise from Benjamin's interest in delineating a systematic foundation for a theory of meaning. This means, in the first place, providing a set of governing postulates to express the relation between language as a conventional sign system that, as a network of purely instrumental relations between sign and signified, can thus be described as arbitrary, as an imposition of subjective judgment. And indeed the imagery evoked by the enforced silence of nature carries with it, as Irving Wohlfarth has argued, a legalistic resonance that relates the fallenness of nature and its paradoxical "court of appeals" in the arbitrary sphere of human language to the conception of mythic law in the "Critique of Violence."[36]

The "arbitrariness" of language as a plurality of instrumental sign systems does indeed bear the mark of myth, and this, applied to nature, takes the form of the bankrupt court, the hollow, dead law that exists not for the sake of justice but for the sake of judgment, for its own perpetuity. Such arbitrariness, as both a descriptive and a normative category, also implies that there is a cognitive recourse to a nonarbitrary dimension of linguistic signification. The conception of an arbitrariness (*Willkür*) of the system of signs thus arises from the prior metaphysical pronouncement that a nonarbitrary immediacy of sign and signified (the *Ursprache*) is lost or withheld; moreover, that this utopian prehistorical unity of sign and signified in the Adamic name is related to a history of values. Arbitrariness of the plurality of sign systems is thus indissolubly linked with the concept of evil. But evil, Benjamin claims, like good, is "unnameable," does not exist in God's creation, arising only with the advent of private knowledge, with the intrusion of pure subjectivity (of Adam) into the unity of living and knowing.

According to an ancient theodicy, Benjamin thus affirms that evil is an illusion and has no reality of its own. Subjectivity is the origin of evil, the source of meaninglessness, of "chatter." In this sense, then, the muteness and mournfulness of the realm of natural things is also related to the subjective deprivation of a nonarbitrary unity of human sign and signified. The spiritual essence of the thing is, as Benjamin had already claimed, one with its linguistic being; that is, the thing is that which is signified, the expression of (divine) signification. The expression of the signification of the thing is precisely the divine event or deed that transpires in the name. The deprivation or the nonoccurrence of this deed thus transforms the thing as expressivity of signification into an entirely new configuration, one in which "signification" is relegated to the arbitrary imposition of subjective, and hence abstract and instrumental, mythical judgment over the sphere of the existing. In this sense, however, "signification" is no longer possible; the "mere sign" is the expression of the perfectly evil, and the sphere of the existing thus merges into the sphere of the nonexistent, evil.

"Objectivity" as such is thus also a dialectical concept. It arises only insofar as the things are overnamed. Consequently objectivity is a concept that is graspable only in relation to the notion of *Trauer*. Instead of understanding objectivity and its dialectical relationship with subjectivity in the language of philosophical idealism, Benjamin already sees the relation between subject and object as the stage of a catastrophic history in which the sorrowful investigation of mute nature is always outdone by the silent mourning of the "objective," that is, the overnamed, meaningless, and forgotten natural thing, which, under the sentence of subjective cognition, is transformed into history's "most endangered, ridiculed, and scorned creations and thoughts." This implies that the transformed cognitive-expressive status of the sphere of the existing thing can be rendered by the following formula: in the arbitrary sign system, the meaning of nature ceases to exist precisely insofar as subjective arbitrary judgment deprives the expression of signification through a language of names. This implies that meaning—the originary expressivity of the named thing—ceases to exist only insofar as subjective cognition imposes essentially arbitrary sign systems upon it. The thing's muteness, in this sense, has no reality beyond this. All reification, as Adorno would later put it, is a kind of forgetting—forgetfulness already acquires, in the language essay, its metaphysical and ethical resonance and points in the direction of an anamnestic criticism.

It is thus evident that, in the context of Benjamin's appropriation of Original Sin for his own linguistic theories, the kernel of experience is the awareness of the deprivation of the originary signification of the things.[37] The recourse to biblical themes appears as the best way to present the theme Benjamin had been working at all along: the thesis of a deprivation of an originary signification appears as the only means to express a critical insight into the arbitrary character of human language and the presence of critically recoverable, concrete linguistic elements within profane speech. Indeed, Benjamin's extravagant use of religion in this context essentially removes his presentation from criteria of rational argumentation and empirical evidence, as many commentators have complained.[38]

Yet by all appearances, Benjamin's "argument" here appropriates the story of the Fall in large measure because the thesis of the deprivation of an originary signification could not be "proved" in any other way and therefore had to be proposed axiomatically and categorically, by recourse to theological postulates that themselves stand outside of the sphere of rational debate.[39] Indeed, Benjamin's notes for the composition of the language essay reveal an attempt to work out the nonarbitrary dimension of linguistic functions such as description, reference, and predication on purely logical grounds, a reflection of the "relation between mathematics and language" that according to Scholem was the original impetus behind the composition of the essay.[40] This attempt seems to have failed in large part because the attempt to delineate systematically the relation between name, sign, and object could not account for the "peculiar nature" of the name, that is, its nonarbitrariness within the use-context of a "spoken and written fixed complex" of language.[41] Thus Benjamin's earliest systematic attempt to ground the objectively existing truth elements residing within quotidian language takes the form of theological doctrine because the arbitrary-nonarbitrary distinction upon which any such attempts must test themselves could not, at least in 1916, be itself grounded without resort to axiomatic and hence indisputable theology.

This state of affairs establishes a peculiar dialectic relationship between the realm of things and the sphere of profane language. It is the intrusion of arbitrary subjectivity—of evil—into the latter that renders the former objective "*trauerig*" and mute. And it is not an entirely equivocal use of terms to observe that *Trauer* thus becomes the *objective mode of being of the objects themselves*, first and foremost, an objectively present status of the things. Thus the idea of *Trauer*, which in conventional usage would be used to denote a subjective emotion or sensibility, now acquires an objective meaning precisely because the subjectivity of speaking and writing humanity imposes itself on the objects by "overnaming" them. The dialectic between subjectivity and objectivity, or subjectivity and substance, instead of unfolding itself in the spiral teleology of the self-discovery of absolute subjectivity, of an identity of identity and difference, depicts the production of subjectivity from the divine realm of the universal and, antithetically, the concentric, inward collapse of the objective into itself—its dialectical self-concealment from profaned subjectivity—until the abyss between subject and object becomes ontologically frozen.

The image of mournful nature that Benjamin paints in the essay is already close to that of "natural history": the realm of created nature, from the point of view of the subject of profane language, appears as a sedimented and petrified continuum. Nature, in its muteness, never-theless is pregnant with this ancient dialectical tension. Were nature endowed with language, its mournfulness would instantly spring forth into an endless lament. Insofar as nature could be imagined to take part in profane language, its mournful silence would find its natural counterpart in lament, understood both as a response to its loss and degradation ("nature would lament language itself") and as a mode of linguistic expression in its own right ("it would lament"). Relieving nature of its muteness does not relieve it of its mournfulness: since lamentation is conceived as a profane translation of mourning into the meaningless chatter of human tongues, it is envisioned as "undifferen-tiated" and hence "impotent."[42] And in fact Benjamin imagines this to be a not entirely hypothetical state of affairs, for the lamentation of nature can be dimly—auratically—perceived as the sounds of nature itself, the "sensuous breath," the sigh of trees and rustlings of plants. Yet if *"Klagen"* is thus also an expression of profane language, there is another, far more obscured critical dimension that resonates in the very structure of the language essay itself: the implicit relation between objective *Trauer* and criticism.

The subjective deprivation of objective signification renders nature into mournful objects—nature is mute, but it mutters. Nature's mutter-ing: the image leads us deeper into the curiously frozen dialectic that structures the language essay. Speaking and writing subjects, people who use language, who discover things in and about it, barely exist in the essay; "On Language as Such and on Human Language," not-withstanding the disturbing mythic image of the world as a twittering cacophony of words, rustles, mutters, and sighs, is a strangely depopu-lated discourse. Benjamin makes no reference to the implications for humans—for thought, for sensibility—of his catastrophic history of language and perception. The essay's own language, the rhythmically intoned sentences, solemnly, somehow ritualistically follow each other, establishing a strangely formulaic, empty region. The emotional, spir-itual dimension of human language as the site of an insatiable drive of an unhappy, yearning humanity for the recovery of a lost, originary blissful union with nature disappears behind the strangely cold—"objective"—incantations of metaphysical truth, as if the unmistak-ably subjectivistic, romantic emotive atmosphere has been pumped out of the essay by the catastrophic weight of nature's mournfulness.

The frozen dialectic structuring the essay can be seen as Benjamin's recognition, first of all, that a philosophical writing that seeks to address the linguistic-theological situation of mournful nature must confront the paradoxical situation of doing so precisely in the profane language that is the medium of nature's sadness. Second, the very structures of subjective inwardness, the darlings of academic philosophy—speculation, inner intuition, autonomy, self-constitution—were the sites of the disappearance of meaning and strategies of intellectual (and political) domination over nature, were themselves mythical. The intoned, formulaic speech of the language essay attempts to enact in the medium of philosophical style what the doctrine of universal linguistic expressivity does in the dimension of ideas: the elimination of the medium of subjectivity from the mode of philosophical thinking and the concomitant concentration of thought on the ridiculed and scorned linguistic object.

In this way the language essay introduces what had already become a central category in Benjamin's critical thinking: the elimination or transcendence of the dimension of subjectivity from the activity of criticism.[43] The process by which "mournfulness" as a description of an emotive state is transferred from subjectivity to the objective realm is matched, dialectically, by the depersonalization of the activity of criticism.

The language essay makes only one veiled reference to the implications of objective *Trauer* for the task of criticism: "Speechlessness," Benjamin writes, "is the great sorrow of nature (and for the sake of nature's redemption the life and language of man—not only, as is supposed, of the poet—are in nature)." Nature's redemption is, in terms of linguistics, the deed by which nature is given voice in such a way that its deep mournfulness is transmuted into bliss, so that nature is illuminated from the standpoint of reconciled nature. Redemption in this sense implies not only a restitution of a lost unity, and therefore an essentially anamnestic act, but also a revelatory function. The originary significance of the things is "remembered" only as it is publicly revealed and proclaimed. Benjamin implies that this redemptive task is the essential task of human language as such and, by strong implication, the ultimate goal of critical language, of "highly effective writing." At least implicitly in the language essay, criticism emerges as the dialectical counterpart to objective *Trauer;* that is, it arises out of the condition of the fate of contemplative subjectivity within mournful nature and directs itself against *Trauer,* to destroy it, but also to redeem it. Yet if criticism is thus to take as its task the dissolution of *Trauer,* how, insofar as critique turns to the literary text, does this project form itself?

The language essay gives few clues as to how this critical writing is to deliver nature from its mournfulness. The creative synthesis of themes of Jewish theology and romantic linguistic theory in the essay creates such a dense web of historical and theoretical references that it is very difficult to sort out just what Benjamin has in mind. Surely he intends a reactivation of theological doctrine in a philosophically effective form and, as Witte argues, aims the critical edge of this philosophical writing at the linguistic instrumentality of bourgeois society, whose amorality and hostility to all values had been revealed in the brutal language of absolute war.[44] Thus critical writing is charged with a double responsibility, encoded in the dual sense of redemption: the fragmentary recovery of the blissful originary purity of the significance of objects releases a historical energy that can be directed toward contemporary linguistic barbarisms in a revolutionary way. This sensibility clearly recapitulates the ambiguity concerning criticism's status over against the objects of criticism (that is, whether they are to be redeemed principally for their own sake or for the sake of the imperiled present). But to clarify the complex relation between *Trauer* and criticism, and to address the questions of subjectivity, objectivity, and melancholia that Benjamin's early work raises, we must look beyond the language essay and explore the central text of Benjamin's early work, the *Ursprung des deutschen Trauerspiels.*

2 *Trauerspiel* and Melancholy Subjectivity

The *Ursprung des deutschen Trauerspiels* in general, and in particular the theory of baroque allegory, acquires its peculiar, almost vertiginous theoretical complexity in large measure due to Benjamin's self-conscious obliteration of the distinctions among form, content, authorial intention, method, and style that structure more orthodox academic writings. As Bernd Witte has convincingly argued, the theory of allegory of the *Trauerspiel* book is itself allegorical in a relevant methodological sense. Benjamin rips passages of *Trauerspielen* out of their context in order to destroy the continuum of transmitted history in which they are embedded and to illuminate the moment of objective truth contained in the genre itself. And it is occasionally quite clear that the very structure of allegorical subjectivity that Benjamin explores is matched, indeed exceeded, by the willfully subjective—that is, private—meanings that Benjamin himself assigns to the "rescued" fragments of baroque text, thereby rendering highly problematic the distinction between critical subjectivity, the object of criticism, and the theological ground upon which this distinction rests.[1]

Such a procedure generates paradoxes that extend to the very essence of critical writing. One can read the *Trauerspiel* study as a fantastically complicated dialectical fugue, exploring not so much the autonomy and dignity of the genre of baroque drama as the possibility of meaning in the continuum of historical time, the relation between subjective speculation and historical experience, and the phenomenon of critical insight and critical writing. The complexity of these issues is already well represented by the relationship between the allegorical form of presentation that makes up the text of the *Ursprung des deutschen Trauerspiels* and the intense messianic idealism expressed by its "Epistemological-Critical Prologue."

As the week begins with a day of rest, in remembrance of its creation, so it is with books. The prologue is this Sunday of books.—Walter Benjamin; Gesammelte Schriften 6

An exhaustive exegesis of the notorious theoretical prologue to the *Ursprung des deutschen Trauerspiels* is beyond the scope of this work; however, a brief look at the prologue is necessary if we are to enter into an interpretive encounter with the *Trauerspiel* book fully apprised of the sources of its structural contradictions. These emerge most clearly if, instead of attempting to reconstruct the tortuously complex metaphysical speculations that compose the prologue, we concentrate on a dimension that is not explicitly treated; one that, indeed, is conspicuous by its absence. Before turning to the prologue itself, then, we might turn to the curious role—or better, lack of a role—of subjectivity in Benjamin's thinking.

The role of critical subjectivity is, as already described in the earliest theories of *Trauer* and criticism, a suppressed topic in Benjamin's thinking. This refusal to speculate on the role of subjectivity in the critical process is in large measure explicable as Benjamin's reluctance to incorporate idealist philosophical baggage into an exploration of the metaphysical structure of truth, which, as he had been convinced from very early on, was objectively present and objectively discoverable in the phenomena themselves. The unwillingness to regard contemplative subjectivity as constitutive in the critical discovery of truth is a philosophical predilection that Benjamin shared with his peers—both Lukács and Bloch, for example, were engaged in critical receptions of Marx, Nietzsche, and Weber, and reactions against neo-Kantian phenomenology. These led to critiques of "subjectivity" as the romantic "*Flucht nach Innerlichkeit*," an ideological construction that betrayed the mission of thinking by reducing the critical encounter with a degraded and imperiled world into a narcissistic withdrawal into the private ego, indeed the reified belief that a "private ego," a preserve of inwardness bearing no inherent relation to its concrete social conditions, existed. Lukács's *History and Class Consciousness* (1922) had revealed the social ground for the idealist commitment to the transcendental subject; the grand revision of the phenomenological doctrine of subjective intentionality into fundamental ontology produced *Being and Time* (1927); the era's outstanding critical deconstruction of the paradigm of subjective inwardness was surely Adorno's *Kierkegaard: Construction of the Aesthetic*, published in 1933.

In Benjamin, however, this rejection of the subject is especially pronounced, so much so that we cannot explain it merely—even primarily—as a part of a broader philosophical critique of late idealist accounts of subjectivity. Benjamin's resolute insistence on expunging elements of subjectivity from the articulation of his thinking is remarkable for its extension from the loftiest theoretical formulations to the most intimate details of his person, or perhaps better, his peculiar impersonality. His comment, in the *Berlin Chronicle*, that his own prose surpassed that of his contemporaries due to the rule "never use the word 'I' except in letters"[2] clearly extended well beyond stylistic credos and touched upon one of the deepest and surest of Benjamin's creative impulses: the critical urge to illuminate a dimension of objective truth not through an act of supreme, autochthonous creativity, but rather by focusing a beam of critical energy onto the already existent historical object, so that his own thought could find in it a structure or dwelling for its own self-expression.[3] This was a merging of the critical subject into a moment of an objective process and required, to an often unacknowledged degree, the deliberate stifling of the energy of selfhood; the blurring of the distinct boundary between the person and the critical act. It could happen, as it did so clearly in the essay on Goethe, that this blurring assumed an uncanny exactness, as though the deconstruction of the distinction between object of criticism and critiquing subject were necessary for the magic language spark between text and mind to arise. Scholem, we recall, makes a similar claim concerning the theory of melancholia in the *Ursprung des deutschen Trauerspiels*.

The ebbing of the vitality of selfhood—what, in other terms, we would call "alienation"—is a virtually inescapable leitmotiv in Benjamin's biography. People who knew him felt it. They seem compelled to use the word *incorporeal* when remembering him.[4] Withdrawn, intellectual to the point of ethereality, Benjamin's occlusion of self, like his famous secrecy and touchiness in all things relating to his

person, underlies, perhaps generates, the enormous capacity for metaphysical experiment that stamps his thinking: a controlled fascination
with physiognomies, a capacity for recognizing the significance of the
fragment and detail, a talent for perceiving the tense relation between
the fragment and the universal moment contained monadically within
it. And if we are not simply speaking of personal idiosyncrasies or
psychological structures, then we can observe that Benjamin's lifelong
fixation on the historical object was related in a complex way to his
virtually ontological distaste for subjectivity. It is as though subjectivity were not so much an existential fact, far less merely an aberration
of philosophers, but instead constituted a sort of entrapment, a mythic
swamp or thicket in which the terrors of inauthenticity—fear of death,
indecision, the self-absorbed flight from responsibility—seemed to be
accompanied by a deeper danger.

The potential endlessness of the process of subjective speculation
might close out for good the receptive capacity whereby the messianic
moments of historical experience could disclose themselves in the
medium of critical thinking. Subjectivity, which is the medium in
which the act of critical redemption takes place, is also the realm of
contemplation, of *Tiefsinn*, and poses the constant risk of an abyssal,
endless descent into the inner recesses of speculation as bad infinity.
As Adorno rightly points out, "as his thinking constitutes the antithesis
of the existential concept of the person, he seems empirically, despite
extreme individuation, hardly to have been a person at all, but rather
an arena of movement in which a certain content forced its way, through
him, into language."[5] Elsewhere, Adorno would claim that "in all his
phases, Benjamin conceived the downfall of the subject and the salvation of man as inseparable. That defines the macrocosmic arc, the
microcosmic figures of which drew his devoted concern. . . . His
target," Adorno concluded,

> is not an allegedly overinflated subjectivism but rather the notion
> of a subjective dimension itself. Between myth and reconcilia-
> tion, the poles of his philosophy, the subject evaporates. Before
> his Medusan glance, man turns into the stage on which an objec-
> tive process unfolds. For this reason Benjamin's philosophy is no
> less a source of terror, than a promise of happiness.[6]

Happiness of the sort Adorno had in mind—what he once referred to
as the "victimless non-identity of the subject"[7]—could in Benjamin's

view only mean "to become aware of one's self without terror."[8] This is one psychic maneuver that Benjamin himself could never manage. It is a short step from profound alienation to the dramaturgical posture in which the self, which otherwise is nothing but a source of terror, is transformed into one of many manipulable objects; indeed one might say that all allegorical thinking returns incessantly to the spectacle of the transformation of subject into object; into corpse or commodity. The *Ursprung des deutschen Trauerspiels* is a study dedicated to the process by which "man turns into the stage" on which the objective process of historical catastrophe mercilessly unfolds.[9]

In either case, a distaste for subjectivity is in no sense incompatible with the most intense degree of inwardness; in fact, the two may well belong together. What nevertheless remains so striking is the circumstance in which this insistence on the extermination of subjectivity from criticism finds its natural critical objects in aesthetic and philosophical expressions of extreme subjectivity; that is, in the hypersubjective contemplative depths of the allegorical vision, to which Benjamin's own critical method bears such deep affinities. It is an affinity that cannot depend on existential arguments for its clarification, of course, but demands a theoretical exposition.

No causal arguments, then, for the relation between the personal and theoretical rejection of the subject in Benjamin—merely an observation that this relationship, complex and contradictory as elements of a real life invariably are, was of central significance for Benjamin's lifelong theoretical task, the formulation of a doctrine, later a method of critique in which the subject could be eliminated. It can be suggested, however, that the project of the elimination of the subject bears an extremely important relationship with the question of melancholia, which occupies such a central position in the *Ursprung des deutschen Trauerspiels* because of its relevance both for the critical object, and for the critic himself.

This absence of the subject, implicit in Benjamin's earliest theoretical writings of 1916, was articulated most clearly in his rejection of the *Innerlichkeit* of the romantic critics and in the "Program of the Coming Philosophy" (1919). There, Benjamin complained that the poverty of the Kantian conception of experience was due in large measure to Kant's inability to conceive of cognition apart from the categories of the subject and its (empirical hence arbitrary) consciousness. Thus, "even to the extent that Kant and the neo-Kantians have overcome the object-nature of the thing-in-itself, there remains the subject nature of the cognizing consciousness to be eliminated." In fact, Benjamin is convinced that the very notion of "an individual, living ego, which receives sensations by means of its senses and forms its ideas on the basis of them" is nothing other than "mythology," and in this sense no different than any other mythic or pagan practices by which a people envisions the generation of experience by relating it to natural processes, and thus cheapening it by equating it with the sensuous character of these processes themselves. The conclusion: like its siblings, the Kantian dream of cognizing consciousness is one of many competing forms of insanity. "Cognizing man, the cognizing empirical consciousness, is a type of insane consciousness." Insofar as epistemological strategies incorporate a conception of subjectivity, and thus are compelled to equate experience with a phenomenon occurring within the empirical subject, instead of the "systemic specification of knowledge," there are only differing types of madness, varieties of hallucination, which, "remote from truth," become ultimately indistinguishable. "All genuine experience rests upon the pure epistemological (transcendental) consciousness, if that term is still usable under the condition that it be stripped of everything subjective."[10]

Benjamin recognized that the task of opening theory up to the exploration of alternative modes of experience directed the motion of the "coming philosophy" toward a negative theology, one that would point to the divine-ideal reality of truth whose representation in the mode of fallen language is the principal task of thinking.[11] It is a move, to be sure, away from epistemology as such. The theory of criticism that Benjamin had in mind had, in addition to its goal of making possible a metaphysics with the "universal power to tie all of experience immediately to the concept of God through ideas,"[12] an expressly historical ambition. Not only did Benjamin wish to illuminate the degree to which Kant's cheapened conception of experience was generated by his historical epoch; but also, like Hegel, Benjamin intended to dissolve the rigid Kantian structure of possible experience into the space of history and to show how knowledge and experience were thoroughly historical phenomena.[13] Thus the task of a future philosophy emerged as the discovery of the mode by which the realm of absolute truth could be represented in historical configurations, and this in turn demanded the articulation of a form of religious experience, one in which the subject/object distinction would be sublated and transcended and that would rest on a conception of knowledge that, "by relating experience *exclusively* to the transcendental consciousness, makes not only mechanical but also religious experience logically possible."[14] This conception found (as in 1916) its only medium of existence in language.

These considerations underlie the broader project, in the *Erkenntniskritische Vorrede*, to rehabilitate the philosophical doctrine of ideas by a revision of its relation to philosophical method. The intrinsic esotericism of philosophical method is the consequence of authentic philosophy's subject matter, represented truth. As antisystem, philosophy in form and procedure acquires a tropism toward the fragmentary, the occluded, and the reflected, insofar as it approaches its ultimate object, the divine idea, by means of indirection or digression (*Umweg*) in representation.[15] Theological conditions, not subjective ambition, produce the philosophical treatise's mode of exposition. The treatise already marks a dispersion of the (mythic) subjectivity infecting the philosophical system; the moment of authority of the treatise is whittled down so that only the "authoritative citation" remains as the permissible intrusion of intentionality.[16] "The absence of an uninterrupted purposeful structure is [the treatise's] primary characteristic. Tirelessly the process of thinking makes new beginnings, returning in a roundabout way to its original object." This methodological rhythm, a "continual pausing for breath," is "the mode most proper to the process of contemplation."[17]

If the philosophical systems of the nineteenth century bore unmistakable affinities to the model of the autonomous artistic genius who conjured up artworks full-formed and independent from the mysterious depths of inner spirit, the new model of philosophical procedure Benjamin had in mind was captured by the activity of mosaic construction:

> Just as mosaics preserve their majesty despite their fragmentation into capricious particles, so philosophical contemplation is not lacking in momentum (*Schwung*). Both are made up of the distinct and the disparate; and nothing could bear more powerful testimony to the transcendent force of the sacred image and the truth

itself. The value of fragments of thought is all the greater the less direct their relationship to the underlying conception, and the brilliance of the representation depends as much on this value as the brilliance of the mosaic does on the quality of the glass paste. The relationship between the micrological processing of the work and the proportions of the sculptural or intellectual whole demonstrates that truth-content is only to be grasped through immersion in the most minute details of subject-matter.[18]

In one sense the image is clear and precise enough to require little unpacking. But closer examination reveals that the interpretation of the image calls forth a question concerning the status of the critical subject. The activity of producing the philosophical treatise is likened to the activity of constructing the mosaic. The philosopher sifts and sorts through the field of the fragmentary, pulling out the correct piece, fixing it conceptually in place next to apparently heterogenous fragments, so that, as an ensemble, an idea may be momentarily represented. There are no longer any epistemological claims to account for this capacity according to the schema of (empirical) subjectivity, which must therefore be illuminated by reference to a sphere of religious experience in which the idea impersonally erupts into the sphere of language. But how are we to account for the capacity of the philosopher to construct these disparate fragmentary pieces?

Benjamin's own answer brings us deeper into the profound Platonism of the prologue. The mosaic artist has some insight into the image of the final product and can muster technical skill in order to represent it by a construction of material fragments. In this sense the artist becomes the stage for the ironic and necessarily imperfect manifestation of the idea within the physical—not merely in the Kantian sense, in which the aesthetic genius is specially endowed by nature with the capacity for the manifestation of noumenality within the symbolic artwork, but much more in the Platonic conception of *techné*, with its insistence on the anamnestic character of the idea, of the objective, unquestionable presence of truth, existing (for consciousness) in encoded form.

The philosophical writer presumably operates according to the same procedure. The talent whereby the writer brings together otherwise disparate fragments into a constructed whole is no *epistemological* one, if by this term we mean the conceptual knowledge ascribed to an empirical subject: "Truth, bodied forth in the dance of represented ideas, resists being projected, by whatever means, into the realm of knowledge. Knowledge is possession. Its very object is determined by the fact that it must be taken possession of—even if in a transcendental sense—in the consciousness."[19] Thus the representation of the writer is the dialectical counterpart of the possessiveness of the traditional philosopher. The object of knowledge, indeed, is the exact negation of the preexistent, transcendent idea, and the abandonment of the former is a precondition for the representation of the latter. This insight strengthens the inherent Platonism in the analogy between mosaic artist and philosophical writer. Philosophical writing takes the character of a description of the order of ideas, a rendering of empirical elements so precise that the representation of divine truth, the moment of disclosure of absolute meaning and absolute beauty, is simultaneous with the moment in which the specificity of the empirical, its consignment to materiality and its existence as disparate and fragmented, is destroyed.

Philosophical (critical) writing, then, allows the self-representation of the idea and at the same time "includes and absorbs" the realm of the empirical particulars. The philosopher, claims Benjamin, thereby assumes an intermediary position between the scientist and the artist. The immediacy of the representational act of the artist is, in philosophy, combined with the rigorous conceptual classificatory interest of the philosopher. The artist becomes the stage upon which the idea appears within the fragment. The scientist seeks to eliminate the empirical by its subsumption under concepts of increasing abstraction, asymptotically approaching a point where the empirical as such is rendered universally conceptualizable and therefore transcended. The philosopher thus shares the artist's interest in representation, while insisting on combining this with the scientist's engagement with the plenitude of the empirical. This is in keeping with the Goethean motto with which the *Ursprung des deutschen Trauerspiels* opens, according to which a fusion of art and science alone can result in the discovery of the whole within the concrete particular, the production of the *Urphänomen*, which Benjamin hoped to transpose from the realms of botany and chromatics to the realm of historiography.[20]

If the philosophical task is to mark the bridge between the world of ideas and the world of phenomena, then the essential contributing factor of philosophical writing—the "glass paste," as it were—is the concept: "Phenomena do not . . . enter into the realm of Ideas whole, in their crude empirical state, adulterated by appearances, but only in their basic elements, redeemed. They are divested of their false unity so that, thus divided, they might partake of the genuine unity of truth." In this sense concepts, no longer dedicated to the production of objects of knowledge, have a destructive and a constructive function: they both dissolve the "false" unity obtaining among phenomena in their fallen, confused state and render the fragments of this shattered false unity into their "basic elements." "Conceptual distinctions are above all suspicion of destructive sophistry only when their purpose is the salvation of phenomena in Ideas." In this way the application of concepts to the empirical—the material content of the literary text— accomplishes both the salvation of the phenomena and the representation of the Idea. Indeed a major goal of the *Vorrede* is to show that these two tasks are in fact the same. "For Ideas are not represented in themselves, but solely and exclusively in an arrangement of concrete elements in the concept: as the configuration of these elements."[21]

It is here that Benjamin introduces the central image of the constellation to clarify—if possible—the relation between phenomena, concepts, and ideas: "Ideas are to objects as constellations are to stars."[22] This image is so rich with implications that it is worth dwelling upon for a moment.

On first reading, the image of the constructed constellation appears as a striking supplement to the previous analogy to mosaic construction and promises a concomitant elaboration on the role of the critical subject in the constructive process. The subject perceives individual objects—as we take in the vast canopy of individual stars. The imposition of concepts upon these disparate elements could have, as in the systematic ambition, the effect of dissolving the individuality of the discrete phenomena into the abstractness of a new conceptual structure; that is, one way to employ concepts is to subsume particulars under them. Benjamin's alternative is the moment in which the application of a concept effects a mediation in the relationship between the particular objects themselves and the higher unity that is implicit within them but cannot be "grasped" or possessed as an object itself.

Looking into the night sky, we experience a primitive urge to understand the individual lights both as separate and as points of an intelligible structure. This structure, the constellation, is not a product of the mere accumulation of lights, nor is it identical with the concept, in this case the concrete image pattern drawn from collective experience, that we impose upon them in order to reveal their meaning. Rather, the constellation emerges—discloses itself—only insofar as the concept divests the particulars of their status as *merely* particular, refers them to their hidden arrangement, but also preserves their material existence. At that point, a meaningful image jumps forward from the previously disparate elements, which from that point onward can never be seen as merely disparate again. In this way the phenomena are rescued from their status *as* phenomenal or fragmentary, without simultaneously sacrificing the phenomena in the name of an abstract concept.[23] The idea is the phenomenon's "objective interpretation." The phenomena are pulled from their consignment to mythic anonymity, but are also spared the procrustean bed of philosophical intention. Nor are the phenomena to be understood as "incorporated" within the idea:

> Ideas are timeless constellations, and by virtue of the elements' being seen as points in such constellations, phenomena are subdivided and at the same time redeemed; so that those elements which it is the function of the concept to elicit from phenomena are most clearly evident at the extremes. . . . Ideas . . . remain obscure so long as phenomena do not declare their faith to them and gather around them. It is the function of concepts to group phenomena together, and the division which is brought about within them thanks to the distinguishing power of the intellect is all the more significant in that it brings about two things at a single stroke: the salvation [*Rettung*] of phenomena and the representation of Ideas.[24]

Orion's sword is a sword; it does not "incorporate" stars; "the significance of phenomena for Ideas is contained in their conceptual elements."[25] The moment of disclosure of the idea—as momentary image—is fleeting and incomplete. Indeed, the introduction of the mediating role of the concept in Benjamin's image is all that saves Benjamin's doctrine of ideas from lasping into an uncontestable mystical pronouncement: the "concept" here is the only mooring by which the relation between phenomena and ideas is held to a philosophical account of the subject, all that keeps it from being a wholly objective, hence unfalsifiable reality.

Of equal importance to the graphic elaboration of the mediating role of concepts is the dialectical relationship between the constellation and the astrological. The image of the constellation is clearly chosen in full cognizance of its relation to astrology, that is, to myth. The emergence of the constellation out of the assembly of stars is the consequence of the imposition of conceptual patterns upon the stars by a community that, in the revealed images, finds not only the decipherment of the once terrifying expanse of the night sky, but also does so in such a way that the images themselves provide orientation and guidance—both literally, for the purposes of navigation, and culturally by the transformation of the night sky into the panoply of gods, beasts, and natural forces, expressing the relationship between humanity, nature, and divinity. The dialectical character of the mythic in general explains the fact that this motion toward encipherment and decipherment of nature contains both an element of myth and its negation. The cosmos is transformed into a realm of mythic gods and astral forces, exerting malign or beneficial influences upon human life, robbing life of its spontaneity and autonomy. At the same time, the very collective effort by which these astral forces are expressed is the same one that renders the mysterious cosmos known and controllable, and produces the first possibility of rational control of natural features and processes.

Astrology, always of great interest for Benjamin, captures perhaps better than anything else the dialectic of myth. Planets and stars are allegorized, named and overnamed, and in this way humanity falls sway to the illusion of astral forces. Thus the astral becomes the image of fixity, of the eternal loss of human autonomy and responsibility. At the same time, however, the very act by which we name planets and stars and imbue them with power over us is a repetition of an originary insight concerning a paradisiacal relationship to nature that was marked by immediacy, harmony, and organic unity, and thus free from conceptual knowledge and the distinction between subject and object. Hidden at the kernel of the most mythic conviction—the occult belief in astral forces—is the most messianic memory, that of the originary unity with nature and the human encounter with nature as a wealth of sensuous and nonsensuous mimetic correspondences.[26] For this reason, it is the image of the astrological that contains, as a negative image, the highest degree of messianic power.

According to Scholem, Benjamin maintained, even prior to the 1916 essay on language, that a "spectral" age of organic unity with nature had preceded the age of myth and that "the real content of myth was the enormous revolution that polemicized against the spectral and brought its age to an end." This, recalls Scholem, underlay Benjamin's lifelong effort to recover a form of perception "as a reading in configurations of the surface, which is the way prehistoric man perceived the world around him, particularly the sky. . . . The origin of the constellation as a configuration on the sky surface was, so he asserted, the beginning of reading and writing, and thus coincided with the development of the mythic age."[27]

This discussion of the constellation may help to focus more precisely the relevant question here. Throughout his work, but nowhere more manifestly than in the prologue, Benjamin understands the critic to operate at the dialectical crossroads between the mythic and the messianic. The critic is the conduit through which moments of messianic truth are able, however fragilely, to burst through the temporal continuum. The critic is able to serve this function by the conceptual-constructive rigor of thinking, by the representation of the idea through the construction of fragments of experience. Thus the active, essential contribution of critical intelligence involves not only the construction of the mosaic-constellation, that is, the process of juxtaposing and rearranging discrete elements so that they merge suddenly into a momentary representational image of their messianic idea, but also— and just as significantly—the prior, *destructive* moment in which critical intelligence is capable of producing the very fragments from which the constellation is constructed, by destroying the false image of beautiful unity, harmony, and totality of the mythic *Scheinwelt*, that is, by reducing this mythical image to rubble.

The critic produces images; images "spring forth" from the critic's productive activity. Such images are images of redemption. "Origin," the central task of critical construction, is, as an "eddy in the stream of becoming," an exact representation of the idea, which does not compromise the individuality of the discrete fragments of construction.[28] Origin is the image that, springing forth from the juxtaposition of fragmented mythic nature, both contains the anamnestic yearning for the lost unity of subjectivity and nature and points, with hope, toward the restorative, apocalyptic advent of the Messiah. Origin is an image in which the linearity of mythic time is doubled back upon itself, in which the category of anticipatory hope is cast upon the past, in which the category of recollection is imposed upon the future.

Truth, however, is the death of intention. The origin, the represented idea, is not itself a willful creation of the critic; it is a "discovery" or a "recognition."[29] The question becomes this: how, precisely, are we to understand the activity by which the critic can impose his own conceptual faculties upon the mythic world, can wrest from this world the origin, and yet at the same time, can be understood not to "make" the origin, but to "find" or encounter it? If the critic's role is to stand at the dialectical crossroads between mythic and redemptive time, between archaic and dialectical image, then what assurance does the critic have that the image that "springs forth" from the activity of destruction and construction is itself *truly* the origin, and not merely another archaic or allegorical image?

The suppression of the role of the subject in Benjamin's thought, above all in the prologue, sharpens this question. Yet the exclusion of subjectivity from the prologue has the result that the idea of conceptual construction is dismissed as a faculty for discovery or recognition. The discovery of (divine) meaning is distinguished from the imposition of (allegorical) meaning only by fiat. And this decree is even more peculiar when one considers the profound affinities between the method of Benjamin's own critical project in the *Ursprung des deutschen Trauerspiels* and the allegorical procedure that is Benjamin's *object* of criticism. The former is to represent the origin of the genre, and this means to capture a moment of messianic truth from within the fragmented field of the genre itself. The latter, however, is allegorical, and this, as melancholy, remains caught in the structures of subjective, hence arbitrary impositions of meaning upon fragmented nature. As we now turn to an examination of the *Ursprung des deutschen Trauerspiels* itself, the tension between critical subjectivity and the objects of criticism will emerge ever more sharply. They emerge as the problem of melancholia.

"Trauerspiel und Tragödie," the first division of the *Ursprung des deutschen Trauerspiels*, returns explicitly to the problem that Benjamin had already explored in his 1916 essay under the same title:[30] the critical task of representing the idea of *Trauerspiel* requires that the formal distinctions between *Trauerspiel* and tragedy be shown to arise from entirely different aesthetic, historical, and theological postulates.

At the beginning of the *Ursprung des deutschen Trauerspiels*, however, Benjamin is clearly in no hurry to present these postulates themselves. The representation of the idea of *Trauerspiel* is to be reserved for the theory of baroque allegory. Here, Benjamin is more interested in establishing the conditions for a formal distinction between the two genres within the traditional vocabulary of aesthetic theory. This treatment buttresses the book's status as an expert, scholarly apparatus—or, perhaps, deepens the illusion that it is—and also demonstrates the limits of the usefulness of contemporary aesthetic theory and art history for capturing the distinction between the two genres. Thus, while ostensibly remaining within the sphere of art, the first section of the work consistently points in the direction of history; not only in the destructive historical "commentary," which Benjamin had identified as the necessary propadeutic to redemptive criticism in the essay on Goethe's *Wahlverwandtschaften*, but also in a manner that unmistakably moves beyond commentary and into criticism.

The *Trauerspiel* is so thoroughly taken up with the specter of history and historical time that, as this first section demonstrates, the project of representing the historicity of the ruined genre itself merges into a forceful, if perhaps theoretically premature, incursion into the theology of the experience of time. The opening section of the book thus begins with an expanded treatment of the central argument of the 1916 essay on *Trauerspiel* and tragedy. The genres are to be distinguished by the manner in which their differing relations to the experience of historical time impose themselves on aesthetic production. Tragedy arises from myth; *Trauerspiel*, however, is embedded thoroughly within historical time, and this embeddedness, so complete that it rarely need be expressed manifestly by the baroque dramatists themselves, underlies and generates the catastrophic violence and lamentation so characteristic of the genre.

Benjamin quotes Opitz's observation that "*Trauerspiel* is equal in majesty to heroic poetry, except that it seldom suffers from the introduction of character of lowly estate and ignoble matters: because it deals only with the commands of kings, killing, despair, infanticide, patricide, conflagrations, incest, war and commotion, lamentation, weeping, sighing, and suchlike." This remarkable definition of *Trauerspiel* already contains the essence of the genre's peculiar relation to history and historical time. Benjamin writes,

> It may be that the modern aesthetician will not value this definition too highly, because it appears to be no more than a description of the subject-matter of tragedy. And indeed it never has been regarded as significant. This appearance is, however, deceptive. Opitz does not actually say so—for in his day it was self-evident—but the incidents listed are not so much the subject-matter as the artistic core of the *Trauerspiel*. Historical life, as it was conceived at that time, is its true content, its true object. In this, it is different from tragedy. For the object of the latter is not history but myth, and the tragic stature of the *dramatis personae* does not derive from rank—the absolute monarchy—but from the pre-historic epoch of their existence—the past age of heroes.[31]

The embeddedness of the *Trauerspiel* within historical time means that the genre becomes the aesthetic expression of the reality of historical catastrophe, above all the unparalleled physical violence and devastation, and social and political chaos, of the Thirty Years War. The *Trauerspiel* does not offer some manifest commentary on these historical events. Rather, the experience of historical catastrophe itself is incorporated into the structure and the content of the work, becoming the controlling premise of dramatic action, the fixed metaphorical referent for the generation of dramatic language. Lamentation is thus not merely the subject matter of the *Trauerspiel*; it *is* the *Trauerspiel*. It is not a matter merely of the conscious comprehension of the practical meaning of contemporary events within the minds of playwrights; this didacticism, as Benjamin will later argue, while surely present, is not of the essence. Far more significant is the phenomenon in which an aesthetic expression enters into a relation with historical time so dialectically deep that time itself comes to dictate the actual procedure and contours of aesthetic production.

This phenomenon, indeed, underlies the peculiar messianic dimension that Benjamin perceives in the *Trauerspiel*. As a completely "temporal" art form, the *Trauerspiel* is especially ephemeral and transient, consigned to ruins, insofar as its relation with its historical present is so close that it has no chance of establishing itself in the canon of "enduring" art. But this tendency toward historical ruin, in which the artwork is reduced from timeless transcendent beauty to profane rubble, is precisely the moment in which the *Trauerspiel* reveals its own idea, its own truth. From its very inception, the *Trauerspiel* acquires the character of the "eternal and total passing away" of natural history itself, the messianic rhythm of nature, as Benjamin had described it in the "Theologico-political Fragment."[32] It remains to be seen how the image of rhythmic temporal repetition of nature, which in the "Fragment" of Benjamin had identified as happiness itself, wins in the baroque play of mourning its dialectical negation. But that *Trauer* and messianic bliss are intimately related is clear enough from the dialectics of theology and language. The *Ursprung des deutschen Trauerspiels* will follow the phenomenology of this dialectic through to its conclusion by an immersion in the very material of profane, fallen history. And for this, the *Trauerspiel*, the translation of the muteness of fallen nature into the chatter of human tongues, is Benjamin's critical Rosetta stone.

The first stage of this critical deciphering thus consists of a rigorous analysis of the dramatic contents of the *Trauerspiel*. This analysis reveals that the central role of the sovereign is the first site in which the experience of catastrophic historical time finds its characteristic aesthetic expression.

Here again the differences between the *Trauerspiel* and tragedy help to illuminate Benjamin's task. In *Trauerspiel*, the sovereign is king, holder of temporal power, responsible for the establishment of order and stability within the course of historical time. In tragedy, the hero's royalty often serves as a mask, or as a prop through whose agency his tragic fate is revealed and fulfilled. The hero's relations are with gods; his struggles and fall reflect upon the divinely ordered, humanly disrupted hierarchy of cosmic signification. Conflict, in this sense, is rendered inherently significant, articulated through a preinterpreted mythic worldview. The king of the *Trauerspiel*, on the other hand, has no such access to an inherent ordered hierarchy in which even the terms of conflict are related back to a preunderstanding of cosmic hierarchy and order. Order and meaning are precisely what is lacking.

The sovereign of the *Trauerspiel* is produced as a dramatic character by virtue of his sovereignty, which, unlike the tragic hero, is possessed

passively, as a state rather than a performance. Sovereignty thus consists of nothing more than the flimsy convention by which a mortal
claims the capacity and duty to hold absolute power within a historical
continuum of catastrophic violence. History makes a mockery of this
claim to sovereign authority. The king's sovereign status proves no
match for it; the scepter and the robe, the accoutrements of his temporal power, prove to be lumps of metal and tatters of cloth, outward
physical signs of an inward spiritual vanity and self-misconception.
The sovereign becomes "the principal exponent of history," indeed
"almost serves as its incarnation,"[33] because nowhere more than in his
figure is the contradictory status of human agency within the continuum of historical time encapsulated: the simultaneous demand for a
capacity for meaningful, decisive action, on the one hand, and on the
other, the helplessness of the creature in the face of a history that
seems designed to reduce all human striving for meaning to so many
piles of rubble.

"The sovereign is the representative of history. He holds the course
of history in his hand like a scepter."[34] Here, Benjamin argues, the
baroque depiction of the absolute power of the monarch arises from a
broader crisis in the theory of sovereignty in the seventeenth century.
The decay of a religiously guaranteed authority of the temporal monarch led to a debate concerning the ultimate legitimation of sovereign
power, and in particular over the relation between sovereign authority
and physical violence. Benjamin had already recognized the relevance
of questions such as this not only for his own political reality (one need
only think of the relation between the Weimar government and the
Freikorps and the role of assassination in contemporary political life),
but also for the notion of law in general, in the "Critique of Violence"
as well as "Fate and Character." These reflections are clearly still very
much on Benjamin's mind as he reconstructs this older debate, in
which the baroque dramatists themselves, particularly Gryphius, were
often prominent participants.[35]

Benjamin, however, turns to a new source for his treatment of the
matter: Carl Schmitt, whose *Political Theology* had appeared in 1922.
Borrowing heavily from Schmitt's analysis, Benjamin observes that the
seventeenth century witnessed a transformation of the entire conception of sovereignty, such that the role of the king came to be defined as
the capacity—and the responsibility—to declare a "state of emer-

gency" and to exercise any physical force necessary to maintain order.[36]

Benjamin could have found much the same theory in a more secular voice in Hobbes; Schmitt, however, provides a rich examination of the extent to which the "state of emergency," political chaos, and the constant threat of civil war entered into the very form of political debate in the seventeenth century and resulted in a deep and in some sense permanent distrust in the process of quotidian politics.[37] The ideal of the seventeenth-century sovereign thus became the capacity for maintaining order and stability within an inveterately disorderly and violent state. Sovereignty itself is turned into a concept whose meaning can only be grasped by the departure from normalcy; it is an extreme concept.[38]

Schmitt's theory is decisionistic. The sovereign must mobilize the power of effective decision, must decide when to declare emergency, must decide upon ruthless measures for its control. Borrowing this notion of the decisiveness of the sovereign, Benjamin thus identifies the king as "the representative of history" insofar as the king stands at the intersection of the collective yearning for peace and the recognition of the world as a realm of violence and death. The sovereign represents the antithesis between restoration and catastrophe. In this sense, the downfall of the king—above all, of the tyrant—represents the futile struggle of humanity to effect a meaningful existence within the continuum of historical time: "If the tyrant falls, not simply in his own name, as an individual, but as a ruler in the name of mankind and history, then his fall has the quality of a judgment, in which the subject too is implicated."[39] The steps of the tyrant's demise operate as stations along a path of destruction that, while wholly immersed in a concrete collective apprehension of political reality, wins a universal applicability.

This judgment leads to a feature of the *Trauerspiel*, which illustrates well the merging of history into the production of dramatic action. At the moment of temporal crisis the tyrant, whose status is crystallized around the capacity for decisive action, is suddenly rendered incapable of making a decision. This tendency to lose the power of decision at the moment of emergency is related to another consistent theme: the slow descent of the tyrant into madness. Confronted with the urgent necessity of restoring order, the tyrant responds by losing his wits. The confrontation between order and disorder, human meaning and the meaninglessness of the natural continuum, receives in the *Trauer-spiel* a characteristically graphic "resolution": the tyrant responds to the threat of disorder and the need for decision with a mad, self-destructive, meaningless spasm of violence himself, ranting, lamentation, indecision, excessive mournfulness, paralysis, suicide. As he destroys himself, the tyrant fulfills his role as the incarnation of history by being turned—along with his court—into a corpse. "At the moment when the ruler indulges in the most violent display of power, both history and the higher power, which checks his vicissitudes, are recognized as manifest in him."[40] In this way, the tyrant's bloody finale operates as a ruthless illustration of the historical resolution of the conflict between the human capacity for significant action and the brute capacity of history for meaningless violence, the universality of death. History wins every time.

More significant, however, than even the tyrant's inevitable downfall is his inability to decide, and this, indeed, is what draws Benjamin's sharpest attention in this opening analysis. Benjamin cites several examples of mournful monarchs who display nearly comic indecision in the face of emergency: "The prince, who is responsible for proclaiming the state of emergency, reveals at the first moment that he is incapable of making a decision." It turns out that his actions all along "are determined not by thought, but by changing physical impulses"; that is, the tyrant's power, rather than a sign of some moral autonomy or character, is merely the effect of some prior physical change, thus revealing even more deeply the extent to which the tyrant is still in the thrall of the forces of the creaturely, of magnets and tides, passions and stars. His actions arise from nothing more than "the sheer arbitrariness of a constantly shifting emotional storm."[41]

We have seen that, from Benjamin's earliest writings, a link exists among decisiveness, morality, and the political/critical victory over the specter of empty or repetitive time, theologically conceived as fallen nature. Conversely, melancholy indecisiveness is taken as a cipher for the absence of a truly moral state of character, and this in turn can be expressed as a sort of spiritual and physical paralysis, as fate, in which the subject is revealed as a creature under the thrall of physical or astral forces.

Benjamin was convinced that a critical encounter with tragedy and

Trauerspiel would reveal the ability of each aesthetic form to express the human struggle for significance in the face of mythic fate, expressed as the triumph over law and legend in tragedy, or as the immersion in the continuum of historical repetition in the *Trauerspiel*. The former presents the image of the hero's silent decision, which shatters the dominion of the mythic gods and transfigures the hero's death into a symbolic instant of immortality. The movement of the tragedy is thus always toward the transcendent. Drawing heavily from "Fate and Character," Benjamin thus argues that tragedy arises from the experience of sacrifice to mythic law; as the hero fulfills his tragic fate, and thus becomes himself the sacrificial moment, his silence signals his realization that he is superior to the gods. The sacrifice of the hero, as the schema of victory over mythic fate, thus constitutes an excursion into pure selfhood; not as "subject" but as character. As an excursion from the sphere of the fated, it is also an exit from the *polis*, from the political life, and thus a rebirth of the hero as a moral infant, an individual. The "unwritten" law of the pagan gods is transgressed; the silent cry of the sacrificed hero shatters the hegemony of the codified, ritual proceedings of trial and retribution. Tragedy fulfills, and therefore shatters legend.[42] If subjectivity is held up as a synthetic power, then individuality or character is in essence destructive. Mythic fate is overcome only by the shattering of mythic law.

But the *Trauerspiel*, in contrast, is characterized by nothing so much as its resolute immanence, its refusal to depict the struggle between human subjectivity and historical fate in any other terms than the godforsaken wretchedness of the earthly condition. *Desolate* is the word that hovers in the background behind every speech and action in the *Trauerspiel*. The vaguely claustrophobic feeling of the tragedy, the unspoken throng of the political community, falls away in the baroque drama, as if, in the inscription of the dramatic action in the space of the royal court, the abyss could be glimpsed at the edge of every dramatic space, speech, or action.[43]

This feeling of desolate emptiness extends to the depiction of sovereign fate in the plays. The moment of divine sacrifice characteristic of tragedy finds its counterpart in the martyrdom of the sovereign. There is, in the *Trauerspiel*, no possibility of ennoblement through suffering. The tyrant-martyr remains utterly enmeshed in the worldly affairs that do him in, and his grisly death is equally free of any "higher" metaphysical meaning. From power and majesty to miserable death, the sovereign remains entirely within the estate of the creaturely and the dying. For readers who expect a measure of moral didacticism, a moment in which the resolution of conflict, however fragile, points even obliquely to a broader insight into the human adventure, this fact contributes greatly to the oddly empty feeling occasioned by the end of the *Trauerspiel*. Unlike a more "acceptable" dramatic form, in which, at the very least, the extinction of the cast is accompanied by some evocation of the relevance of life and death, some moral, some point, the carnage of the *Trauerspiel*'s bloody end is exactly what it seems to be: death. Apart from references to the *vanitas* of those in power, the conclusion is frightening in its literalness, disturbingly lacking of any didactic power. This makes the *Trauerspiel* an artwork "about" fate in a peculiar sense.

The plays attempt the literal depiction of the absolute subjection of humanity to the tug of natural history, the precise representation of the natural phenomenology in which subject is translated to corpse. "Fate," as in the Goethe essay, is present not so much as the ensemble of pagan, demonic astral forces and influences but, in its Christian translation, as the guilt context of the living. "Natural history" thus captures the meaning of fate in the baroque drama:

> For fate is not a purely natural occurrence—any more than it is purely historical. Fate, whatever guise it may wear in a pagan or mythological context, is meaningful only as a category of natural history in the spirit of the restoration-theology of the Counter-Reformation. It is the elemental force of nature in historical events, which are not themselves entirely nature, because the light of grace is still reflected from the state of creation. But it is mirrored in the swamp of Adam's guilt.[44]

The implicit reference to the 1916 essay on language indicates the extent to which Benjamin's treatment of the "material content" of the *Trauerspiel* is guided by unswerving theological postulates; indeed one needs to be familiar with the earlier, doctrinal development of these postulates in order to comprehend how "natural history"—as fallen nature, invading and petrifying from within the course of human action—could nevertheless distinguish itself as a dialectical vision by the remembrance of divine bliss reflected from the basest, most corrupted "swamp," captured in the conception of Original Sin.

Adam's sin was the introduction of private, subjective motives into the conduct of life. The price of this sin was remoteness from God, the confusion of created being that required knowledge, and the translation of the meaningful order of God's realm into a realm of death, the form of being of meaningless nature. The historical graphicness of the "ruined" *Trauerspiel* accomplishes the invaluable service of depicting precisely the state of humanity and nature as fallen. This graphicness undermines and ruins the mythical enchantment in which this state appears through the mist of astral forces, mythological meanings, or pagan superstitions. Ruin operates as a mode of enlightenment. The world, in the *Trauerspiel*, is brought into merciless focus, and in this way even fate loses its mythic appearance, stands naked before the viewer as universal death.

Nature as meaningless because fallen: this is what the *Trauerspiel* depicts. But the depiction, by virtue of its radicalness, is capable of containing within itself its own negation. As a mode of expressivity of this ontological confusion in human speech, the *Trauerspiel* is capable of encoding the negative image of God's presence; that is, by expressing the subjection of humanity to the meaninglessness of fate—according to the theological spirit that characterized the baroque—the *Trauerspiel* offers an encoded retelling of the story of creation, awaiting its completion by critical illumination.

As in his earlier critical efforts, Benjamin once again returns to the conviction that the essential core of this encoded story is death. Death is the theme common to all the historical-literary variations Benjamin studies and is recognizable as the ultimate expression of the meaninglessness of fallen nature and human fatedness. Here, as in the Goethe essay, "fate leads to death. Death is not punishment but atonement, an expression of the subjection of guilty life to the law of natural life." Once again borrowing from Lukács's "Metaphysics of Tragedy" as well as his own "Fate and Character" and "Trauerspiel und Tragödie," Benjamin argues that the process of immersion within natural fate depicted in the *Trauerspiel* deepens the fatal connections between different characters, moments, and locations on the baroque stage until even the stage properties become engulfed. Things, not just people, come under the thrall of universal death, since "once human life has sunk into the merely creaturely, even the life of apparently dead objects secures power over it. The effectiveness of the object where guilt has been incurred is a sign of the approach of death." For this reason, the world of things "towers oppressively over the horizon of the *Trauerspiel*";[45] in the baroque's own characteristic reification, the individual characters are thus dragged down to the level of objects, as the mute objects come to reassert with a vengeance their ancient judgment.

Whereas the singular, nonrepeatable death of the tragic hero constitutes a moment of individuality in which the hero for the first time discovers his own autonomy as a moral individual, the collective death of the *Trauerspiel*, as the sheer "thereness" of universal death, dispenses the same sort of grim anonymity upon the characters that Benjamin had discovered in his reading of the *Elective Affinities*. In both cases, subjection to the deathly is the fall back into the realm of unredeemed, mute nature and causes the loss of "name-bearing individuality," the severance of the relation between humanity and language.[46] In this terrifying proximity of the creaturely, Benjamin finds the true contours of what, in the production of the *Trauerspiel*, had drawn his attention in the first place: not merely the drama's fixation on the repeated schematics of natural history, but also its unparalleled ability to transform this fixation into an immanent, earthbound vision, into an obsession with the world of dead and ruined objects.

The vision of history as endless catastrophic repetition is, in the baroque, a consequence of an exhausted transcendental impulse and thus is incapable of leading directly to a theology of hope, to a program of salvation through the individual and collective acquisition and exercise of Christian virtues. Rather, this exhausted transcendentalism denies itself any eschatological schemes and remains an entirely immanent sensibility. Having denied itself any doctrinally guaranteed access to a soteriological faith in the restorative end of all things, which in medieval Christianity acted as the concomitant to a vision of the fallen world as the prelude to the reign of the holy, the baroque mind is left with the hollow shell of what had formerly been an indirect but legible transmission of divine intention, the creaturely realm itself.

A dialectical structure is apparent here as well. The realm of things is, on the one hand, clearly the realm of universal transience, death, and historical catastrophe, and mocks the vain pretension toward the significance of human action. But this same realm is, on the other hand, the only one available for any insight into the ultimate meaning of human life. Thus the paradox:

> The religious man of the baroque era clings so tightly to the world
> because of the feeling that he is being driven along to a cataract
> with it. The baroque knows no eschatology; and for this very
> reason it possesses no mechanism by which all earthly things are
> gathered together and exalted before being consigned to their
> end. The Hereafter is emptied of everything which contains the
> slightest breath of this world, and from [this world] the baroque
> extracts a profusion of things which customarily escaped the
> grasp of artistic formulation and, at its high point, brings them
> violently into the light of day, in order to clear an ultimate heaven,
> enabling it, as a vacuum, one day to destroy the world with
> catastrophic violence.[47]

We can see readily the affinities between this paradoxical baroque
attitude toward the world and that which Benjamin had, a decade
earlier, claimed for himself, or at any rate for "youth." In both cases,
an exhausted metaphysics of meaning—meaning as (divine) significance, *Sinn*—leads, in the most acute mind of an epoch, not to mere
resignation but instead to a sort of immanent transcendentalism, in
which the very absence of meaning is taken as an impetus to gather and
analyze the most profane and reviled fragments of experience, guided
not merely by the urgent need for redemption, but also by a will to
discover the elements of the end of time, of the wholly historically
heterogenous, in the deepest center of the very fragments of historical
experience themselves. The shards that other artistic formulations
pass by as meaningless, the baroque grasps and holds so painfully. The
violence with which baroque art brings these fragments into the light of
day is necessary in order for these fragments, the most reviled and
scorned thoughts and creations, to be led from the context of their own
bad history to the heart of the present with apocalyptic force. Thus the
paradoxical relationship between the aesthetic and religious temperament of the baroque, in which the fragments of historical life are
degraded in order to wrest from them answers, however flat and didac-
tically sterile they seem in retrospect, to the question of the significance of human existence.

It is this tense and therefore highly productive immanent transcendentalism that underlies the baroque imagination's tendency toward
ostentation both in language and in the decorative arts. In each sense,

ostentation is a result of the contradictory will to expose the realm of objects as debased and fallen nature, yet by so doing to effect a profusion of objects, filling up the void produced by the withdrawal of doctrinal answers to the question of the meaning of life and the value of creation. Ostentation, Benjamin argues, is thus an essential characteristic of the aesthetic of *Trauer*, "for these are not so much plays that cause mourning, as plays through which mournfulness finds satisfaction: plays for the mournful. A certain ostentation is characteristic of these people."[48] The theological grounds that would explain this assertion are still only implicitly legible in the development of the *Ursprung des deutschen Trauerspiels* and will emerge in full force in the treatment of allegory in the book's second half.

The fact that this immanent transcendentalism, its tendency toward literalness and exaggeration, its dialectical ambiguity concerning a thoughtful appropriation of the historical fragment, its relation to contemplation, introspection, and esotericism, is intimately related to the deepest sources of Benjamin's own critical talent is also never explicitly spelled out. The intimacy of the relation is no arbitrarily generated critical preference on the part of a critical subject, but rather the establishment of a narrow historical window according to which the *Trauerspiel* becomes an object of criticism at Benjamin's own historical moment. The representation of the idea depends on a critical imagination attuned to the phenomena in which this idea is constructed; generated by a historical epoch, such phenomena cannot be willed into existence any more than the authors of the *Trauerspielen* could choose the manner in which they apprehended the world.

This point needs considerable amplification. Notwithstanding the convoluted methodological demands that Benjamin had imposed upon himself in the prologue, the discussion of the characteristics of the *Trauerspiel* has, thus far, done little to live up to the remarkable metaphysical claims made on behalf of the critical act of representation. Indeed thus far the book seems a conventional, if fascinating, document of "comparative literature." Benjamin has advanced a serious argument for the rehabilitation of the autonomy of a literary genre, has attacked the hollow authority of Aristotle, and has questioned the literary prejudices that conspired to impose heterogeneous standards of aesthetic judgment on the literary baroque. He has buttressed these claims with a comparative characterology of tragedy and the baroque *Trauerspiel*, insisting that the role of sovereign in the latter, rather than representing a corrupt or decadent translation of the tragic hero, constitutes a distinct relation to historical time in which the specter of the repetition of historical catastrophe, as opposed to the mythic emergence of the tragic individual from it, invades the deepest sources of literary production. Benjamin has indicated that the emergence of this genre, and its peculiar relation to historical time, is itself intimately bound up with the particular political and spiritual crises of the baroque era; and he has argued that a distinctive attitude of theological despair, an immanent transcendentalism, underlies the production of the *Trauerspiel*, an argument that, while persuasive in many senses, nevertheless seems to place the work of art in a somewhat more simple relation to its historical epoch than one would have been led to expect from the prologue and the theory of "redemptive" criticism that Benjamin had been developing for nearly ten years.

We might observe a certain intriguing parallel in the development of the critical text between the *Ursprung* study and the essay on Goethe's *Wahlverwandtschaften*. Having now effectively completed the "historical" analysis of *Trauerspiel* by arguing for the distinct and complex roles of death and fate in the drama as opposed once again to classical tragedy, Benjamin has reached a point in the development of his critical presentation roughly analogous with a similar point in the Goethe essay. Previous interpretations of the artwork, based on faulty conceptions of the purpose of criticism and the nature of art in general, have been abandoned. The damage they have done to our understanding of the work of art has been stripped away, revealing a quite different physiognomy than was previously visible. For both the symbolic *Elective Affinities* and the allegorical *Trauerspiel*, a commentary has begun the process of the destruction of the historical coating and revealed the vision of mythic nature, historical catastrophe, and fatality from which these works arise, a vision of meaningless or fallen nature that invades the tiniest capillaries of aesthetic form.

A central commitment to this propaedeutic destruction in the Goethe essay was the argument, directed against Gundolph, that the biographical peculiarities of the author have no role to play in the critical encounter; that such maneuvers could only bring about a mythologization of the author's life and undermine the autonomy of the individual artwork by necessarily suggesting some clumsy, mythic causality between the life of the author and the life of the artwork. Despite this, Benjamin nevertheless insisted on illustrating Goethe's own entrapment within mythic consciousness by pointing to Goethe's status as a melancholic, a *Saturnkind,* and found in this contemporary "half-playful" reference to the influence of the melancholic planet a means for introducing the discussion of the relevant consequences of Goethe's mythic thinking for the structure of the novel: sunkenness in myth results in the immersion in the chaotic plenitude of natural forces; this leads to an insurmountable anxiety in the face of death, and this, in turn, to the loss of ethical autonomy, to indecision, paralysis, flight from responsibility.[49] And this diagnosis of Goethe's own ethical paralysis becomes of central importance in the critical project of showing how mythical thinking expresses itself in the secret structure and motives of the novel itself.

In this way a reference to the melancholy temperament in particular and astrology as the canon of mythical thinking in general, served by its very dialectical nature to refer the constitution of the artwork, with all its tensions, to a broader, more panoramic vision of the interpenetration of mythic and messianic dimensions of historical experience. This vision can become self-reflective and completed only through the critical imagination; the truth content of the artwork discloses itself only insofar as the critic is capable of recognizing discrete, fragmentary textual elements as an encoded record of truth. In the *Trauerspiel* study too, the cataloging of the historical data of the artwork is complete when the analysis turns to the presentation of the relation between the "constitution" of the artistic mind and the objective elements present in the created text. Rather than dwelling upon the individuality of the artist and risking a slide back into the mythic notion of the heroic genius, Benjamin introduces the concept of melancholia as an expression of the dialectical mediation of subject and object, a process in which both "objective" elements of a concrete world and dimensions of innermost subjectivity fuse and intertwine, illuminating in the process the theological grounds upon which the text, and indeed the very concepts of subjectivity and objectivity, "originate."

The great German dramatists of the baroque were Lutherans. Whereas in the decades of the Counter-Reformation Catholicism had penetrated secular life with all the power of its discipline, the relationship of Lutheranism to the everyday had always been antinomic. The rigorous morality of its teachings in respect of civic conduct stood in sharp contrast to its renunciation of "good works." By denying the latter any special miraculous effect, making the soul dependent on grace through faith, and making the secular-political sphere a testing ground for a life which was only indirectly religious, being intended for the demonstration of civic virtues, it did, it is true, instil into the people a strict sense of obedience to duty, but in its great men it produced melancholia [Trübsinn]—*Benjamin*, Origin of German Tragic Drama

This opening to Benjamin's treatment of baroque melancholia seems, at first glance, to be a mere continuation of the argumentative strategy of the preceding pages of the *Ursprung des deutschen Trauerspiels:* the warnings of the *Vorrede* notwithstanding, Benjamin seems to be making a roughly causal argument for the relation between features of a theological and cultural *Zeitgeist* on the one hand, and the distinctive formal characteristic of an art form on the other. In this sense, then, melancholia would seem to constitute nothing more than a useful term for referring to a collective conviction of Lutheran playwrights concerning the possibility (or in this case impossibility) of meaningful action, one that could not help but determine the character of their aesthetic products. Both artist and product, then, are marked by what Lepenies called "*Handlungshemmung*"; while the mournful sovereign remains confined in the stage-court, which "represents the timeless, natural decor of the historical process," the dramatists themselves were subjected to a harsh Lutheranism that relegated the realm of meaningful, self-defining human action to a level of theological insignificance. By denying good works any significant relation to the situation of the soul, Lutheranism presented a vision of worldly existence as a meaningless continuum. "Human actions were deprived of all value. Something new arose: an empty world."[50] Such an emptying of meaning from the world might result, Benjamin argues, in a simple, albeit painful, resignation from certain forms of self-determination through individual action and a passive acceptance of a "traditional" conception of Lutheran piety: uprightness and industry, calm acceptance of the irrelevance of worldly attachments, obedience to authority.

Thus far, a solid if oversimplified sketch of Lutheran asceticism— indeed, Benjamin could have found in Weber a far more nuanced conception of Luther's rejection of worldly attachment, one in which the meaning of worldly activity was indeed problematized, but that avoided the specter of an "empty world," at least doctrinally, insofar as Luther was able to balance the intense and uncompromising interiority of faith with a notion of the secular *Beruf*.[51] Benjamin, however, concentrates on a different set of problems entirely. He is primarily interested not in Lutheran doctrine itself, but in the tendency of this doctrine to serve as an expression of a far older and deeper experience, one reserved for the "great men" of the baroque age. In this reference, in fact, Benjamin reveals the direction of his thinking. By paraphrasing Aristotle's question from the *Problemata*—Why do all great men suffer from melancholia?—Benjamin immediately moves the analysis from a discussion of the affinities between contemporary religious controversies and art forms to the very heart of the *Ursprung* study itself: What is the origin of the *Trauerspiel?*

Dogmatic faith was enough to satisfy the average run of humanity that the devaluation of the active life was amply compensated for by the simple displacement of meaning from the present into the otherworldly future. But the "great men" of the baroque were not able to adapt themselves so smoothly to this new doctrine. They required some cognitive apparatus to support the enormous emotional weight of the new conception of faith. "What was the point of life if . . . not even faith had to be proved?" Indeed, the "point of life" was precisely the problem. The new doctrine of faith was the historical vessel in which the question of the *taedium vitae*, always associated with "richer natures," was contained. Faith can provide only an initial, indeed a superficial answer to the question of the point of life; inevitably,

> those who looked deeper saw the scene of their existence as a rubbish heap of partial, unauthentic actions. Life itself protested against this. It feels deeply that it is not there merely to be devalued by faith. It is overcome by deep horror at the idea that the whole of existence might proceed in such a way. The idea of death fills it with profound terror.[52]

We see immediately the extent to which this claim reintroduces themes from Benjamin's first attempts to delineate a theory of *Trauer:* not just historically situated, anxiety-ridden subjects, but life itself protests, is overcome by a deep feeling of horror at the specter of its own devaluation. Here, the older attempt to describe *Trauer* as an objective feeling of mute, fallen nature combines with the connections between the mythic and the demonic, an insight into a radical meaninglessness of existence, the impossibility of authentic action, and anxiety in the face of death that Benjamin developed in the Goethe essay. In all these cases, subjective states and dispositions, for all their interiority, can nevertheless only be properly comprehended once they are seen as moments of an intricate phenomenology of nature and the holy, one that comprehends the history of the world and that underlies the deeply dialectical nature of historical experience. "Deeper" natures, which life fills with a "deep horror" at its own simple negation, recoil from the vision of an empty world.[53] But this very recoil, Benjamin claims, constitutes not just a withdrawal from the world and a concomitant intensification of subjective interiority, but also leads to an entwined, intensified earthly gaze, seeking an odd consolation in the contemplation of the most creaturely, mortal, and decayed fragments of the world of things.

In a remarkable passage, Benjamin rather abruptly reveals that this entwinement of the objective *Trauer* of fallen nature and the intense brooding subjectivity of the melancholy mind is in fact a kind of relationship that itself bears objectively observable (and apparently invariable) characteristics:

> *Trauer* is the sensibility in which feeling revives the empty world in the form of a mask, in order to take a puzzling [*rätselhafte*] pleasure in its sight. Every feeling is bound to an a priori object, the representation of which is its phenomenology. The theory of *Trauer*, as it emerges as the pendant to the theory of tragedy, can thus only be developed in the description of the world which emerges under the gaze of the melancholic. For feelings, however vague they may seem when perceived by the self, respond like a motorial reaction to a concretely structured world. If, for the *Trauerspiel*, laws are to be found, partly developed, partly undeveloped, in the heart of *Trauer*, the representation of these laws has nothing to do with the state of feelings of the poet or the audience, but rather with a feeling which is released from an empirical subject and bound to the fullness of an object.[54]

The passage is surely among the most forbiddingly hermetic to be found in Benjamin's work. The impressive faculty for imagistic think-

ing so characteristic of Benjamin's thought is missing here. The her-
meticism of this passage arises not only from the introduction of the
ponderous and unfamiliar terminology of "a priori object[s]" and "motorial reaction[s]" of feelings to "a concretely structured world" (which,
I suspect, is the precipitate of late phenomenological moves toward a
Lebensphilosophie, typified by Scheler), but also, indeed primarily,
from the profound dialectical ambiguity attending the description of
"feeling" (*Gefühl*), clearly the key concept here. This ambiguity consists of the relation between subject and object, and the mode of
mediation—"feeling"—that exists between them.

The kind of dialectical mediation that Benjamin has in mind here,
however, in his evocation of a feeling that is "released from an empirical
subject and bound to the fullness of an object," is entirely distinct from
any Hegelian dialectic in which the captured contradiction between a
historically situated subject and its object contains, in miniature, the
complete logic of mutual self-determination and self-constitution that
operates throughout the realm of objective spirit and that tends toward
its own self-fulfillment. Here, the dialectic consists of structured sets of
relationships according to which "objective" states of historical circumstances can with a mechanical reliability provoke a concrete set of
emotive and cognitive responses from empirical, historically situated
agents. The phenomenological representation of this precise tropism—
Benjamin's own task—thus takes as its own self-understanding the
claim that specific historical circumstances can, through the medium
of empirical subjects, articulate themselves in (textual) structures that
because of their extreme historical individuation are able to present
themselves as the objectively invariable material for a representation of
trans- or metahistorical, that is, messianic contents.

As early as 1916, we recall, Benjamin had attempted to lay out the
foundations of a theory of language according to the notion of mournful
nature, as well as to argue that the *Trauerspiel* was a mode of expression
dedicated to translating the feeling of mournful nature into the lamentation of human speech. The question for criticism thus became how
Trauer "as a feeling" could "find its way into the linguistic organization
of art." Benjamin tentatively answered this question by claiming that
the *Trauerspiel* is a form of the "endless lament" of fallen nature. Here,
in what is clearly a continuation and transformation of that original
thesis, *Trauer* can now be understood as a subjective "state of mind"
(*Gesinnung*). Rather than redefining *Trauer* as a subjective rather than

an objective state, however, Benjamin now argues for the essential polarity of the idea of *Trauer*, its ability to encompass both subjective and objective moments. "Every feeling is bound to an a priori object, the representation of which is its phenomenology." Thus the feeling of *Trauer*, looked at in its subjective moment, is related in an essential manner to an objective, real state of affairs; it is, as Bernd Witte has called it, an "essentially present component of human existence."[55] The phenomenology of a feeling, therefore, consists in the representation of that linguistic expressivity arising at the interface between a feeling possessed by a subject and the objective world to which it is bound.

This is what happens in the *Trauerspiel*. The "objectivity" of natural *Trauer* is here transformed into a feeling—of horror, sadness, and despair at the vision of a meaningless world and universal death— whose subjectivity consists not in the arbitrary and ultimately irrelevant "states of feelings of the poet or the audience," but in the nonarbitrary, indeed the lawlike manner in which this feeling is evoked by a particular state of affairs and, in turn, the manner in which it thereby interprets and transforms the world. The "a priori object" of *Trauer* is, as Witte maintains, "the creatureliness of the things, the fallenness of the world," but only insofar as this creatureliness is an objectivity produced by the melancholy mind as a response to a devalued and hence empty world.[56]

This empty world is precisely what *Trauer*, in its *creative* dimension, revives as a mask for its own "enigmatic satisfaction," thus producing the obsessive fixation on the profusion of dead objects, the "relationship between *Trauer* and ostentation, which is so brilliantly displayed in the language of the baroque,"[57] that is, in the "purgatory" of language as incessant lament. The object of *Trauer* is the empty world, the world drained of meaning, a world that is presented to an empirical subject in a continuous multiplicity of historically contingent forms, but that nevertheless constitutes nothing less than a real insight into the ontological status of the world of human experience. To understand the full weight of this notion of mourning and its relation to historical experience, it is necessary to place this hermetic presentation of the metaphysics of *Trauer* in relation to the equally hermetic doctrine of "origin" from the *Erkenntniskritische Vorrede*.

Trauer is a feeling that exists at a constantly historically shifting, nevertheless essential interface between the subject and its perception of nature as meaningless and fallen and the objective status of the world itself, as the ensemble of things that, deprived of their originary unity and significance, reside in mute anonymity. If Benjamin is to succeed in the critical representation of the *Trauerspiel*, it is necessary for him to develop a "theory of *Trauer*" as a "pendant to the theory of tragedy." We know from the *Vorrede* that a theory, if it is to satisfy the true demands of philosophical contemplation, proceeds mosaically. It is composed of the finest, often the smallest and most apparently insignificant fragments of historical experience—the idea, which the ensemble of fragmentary phenomena are ultimately to represent, lies encoded in each shard, but it is the task of philosophy to bring fragmentary phenomena together in a critical constellation so precise that truth will allow itself to appear, however fleetingly, in the mosaic representation itself.

Thus a theory of *Trauer* depends on a representation of its origin. As a historical category, origin, as Benjamin explains, has nothing to do with the genesis or emergence of particular historical structures, but rather with moments in which this same process is disrupted and crystallizes, monadically, into an image in which the entire course of historical happening lies encoded. For the process in which Lutheranism of the seventeenth century produces *Trauer* and melancholy as objective and subjective categories of fallen nature, historical origin thus appears as an image in which the pre- and posthistory of this concrete historical structure are contained. From the Ur-old loss of divine meaning to the very now in which the critic represents and redeems it, this historical crystallization of melancholia structures itself, monadically, as a rupture of the course of "progressive" history:

> There takes place in every original phenomenon a determination of the form in which an idea will constantly confront the historical world, until it is revealed fulfilled, in the totality of its history. Origin is not, therefore, discovered by the examination of actual findings, but it is related to their history and subsequent development. The principles of philosophical contemplation are recorded in the dialectic which is inherent in origin. This dialectic shows singularity and repetition to be conditioned by one another in all essentials. [58]

Philosophical contemplation is a dialectical faculty. It involves the ability to encounter a concrete configuration of historical facticity and to deconstruct and represent it so carefully and precisely that, while losing none of its historical concreteness, the actual images of messianic origin, recapitulation, hope, and remembrance that are contained in the historical elements themselves are given a phenomenological depiction.

Melancholy has, accordingly, both a "profane" and a messianic history. Its profane history consists of the progressive course whereby the word and the syndrome plod through their succession of historical forms. Its messianic history, however, consists in discrete, individual historical moments where, as a result of nonrepeatable, unique sets of circumstances, a "motorial reaction" between subject and objects enacts a dialectic so precise that the critic can recognize within this structure the elements for a redemptive construction. The baroque depiction of the devastating melancholy of a religiously shattered world is one such structure. In the baroque, the relation between the melancholy subject and its a priori objects comes into a particularly pregnant state, insofar as the specific historical conditions of physical and spiritual devastation approach the true state of affairs in human history. Such rare moments—for example, the *Trauerspiel,* the allegory of Baudelaire, the motions of Proustian memory—radiate messianic energy like beacons, because they promise to reveal themselves as sites where critical work can find images in which the whole of historical time, of an epoch, or of an era is compressed.

As a feeling situating itself on the frontier between subject and object, *Trauer* only exists in its historical specificity. Yet, insofar as the dialectic contained in *Trauer* is nothing other than the real structure of human history itself, *Trauer* is itself transhistorical, messianic. Melancholy is nothing other than *Trauer* from the point of view of the historically situated subject. A phenomenological theory of *Trauer* thus demands a description of the world from this point of view. As we can see, the question concerning the *critical* subject—that is, whether the critic himself *must* be a melancholic, or whether this is just a vestige of historicism and demands the strict suppression of any "subjective" states or temperaments by the critic—remains here wholly unanswered.

With these unresolved questions in mind, we can take up the

presentation of the theory of baroque melancholia in the *Ursprung des deutschen Trauerspiels*. As the mediating point between the "commentary" on the structure of baroque drama in the first half of the book and the theory of allegory in the second, this presentation occupies a dialectical crossroads. Accordingly, I want to suggest that this influences the fact that Benjamin's theory of baroque melancholy is in essence a *theory of melancholy heroism;* that is, a representation of the dialectic of subjectivity (the melancholy disposition) and objectivity (*Trauer*) as constituted on the historical stage of the seventeenth century. This representation of baroque melancholy as heroic will oblige Benjamin to take considerable hermeneutical risks. But the ultimate position he wishes to develop concerning melancholy, and above all the theological grounds of melancholy revealed in the allegorical way of seeing, mandate a bold interpretive strategy: by representing baroque melancholy in terms of the paradigm of the melancholy heroism of the baroque playwrights, Benjamin will forcefully impose upon the seventeenth-century baroque an interpretive vision normally reserved for the sixteenth-century Renaissance. Moreover, he will rely virtually exclusively on the work of the Warburg Institute for this imposition. A brief look at the Warburg Institute's work on the model of melancholy genius in Luther, Dürer, and Ficino can help bring out more clearly the issues involved.

Like Benjamin, Aby Warburg's thought from the beginning revolved around the poles of myth and antimyth, order and disorder. Perhaps even more acutely than Benjamin, Warburg followed a call to devise a theory of memory that would accommodate the peculiar anamnestic powers that accrued to cultural artifacts. The defining project of Warburg's life was the documentation of the "afterlife of the antique" in Renaissance art and culture: the processes of social memory in which traces of older collective experiences, imprinted onto the archive of cultural images and shared imagination, were continually transmitted, transformed, and reexpressed in high art, popular culture, ritual, and symbol. Unlike Benjamin's "firm, apparently brutal grasp" of the cultural fragment,[59] however, Warburg's appropriation of the fragment is fastidious. This characteristic tenor has something to do with the collector's instinctive distaste for handling objects too roughly or showing them too readily. But in Warburg's case—and this is the significant point of comparison with Benjamin—it arises even more from a profoundly ambivalent relation to the world of objects itself, one in which a fear of the subject matter bordering on revulsion can coexist with an obsessive love of them.

The poles of myth and antimyth around which Warburg's thought revolved had at least this much in common with Benjamin's thought: Warburg was profoundly disturbed by the mythic worldview and understood Western history as the process in which primal collective fears and passions, expressed in superstitions, barely remembered images and gestures, and magical rites were gradually mastered by the principles of rational individuation and control. Whereas Benjamin tended to view the mutual impregnation of myth and antimyth in terms of a set of creative syntheses, pointing toward the presence of redemptive, messianic dimensions of experience encoded in the most profane fragments, Warburg's own response to the mythical was, while equally complex, marked by an ethical imperative far more powerful and plaintive than Benjamin's. The fascination with the mythic dimension of collective experience was, as fascinations tend to be, composed of an admixture of revulsion and attraction. Warburg's lifelong interests in the art of the Renaissance and in theories of social memory were consistently aimed at analyzing how the high and decorative arts provided the medium in which the gradual victory of rational self-control over the forces of primal fear was played out; indeed one might say that if myth and antimyth were the twin poles of Warburg's thought, fear and memory provided the intersecting axes, mapping out quadrant fields of research in a manner similar to the graphics of thought that Susan Buck-Morss has argued for in Benjamin's work.[60]

Astrology provided Warburg with a central organizing idea around which the story of the Renaissance, with its overflow of concrete visual data, could be brought under representational control.[61] He became engrossed in the process by which the gods, the image realm of classical antiquity, ceased to exist as the anthropomorphizations of—and thus simultaneous gestures of control and submission to—feared natural processes; how these divine images were transmitted into medieval culture, transposed into a rival creed tolerated by the Christian church, into calendar gods who ruled over various dimensions of nature and human life. The pantheon of classical gods grew into a thicket of allegorical interpretations, linking traces of the gods' archaic, demonic origins, their Olympian identities, their connections with Christian virtues and sins, with astrological bodies, properties, passions, and temperaments until allegorical entities emerged that were so densely overinterpreted that, as in the case of Saturn, they seemed to split themselves off from any symbolic immediacy, any meaningful relation to lived experience, and become self-maintaining systems, "demonic beings of uncannily contradictory duality of power." The reception of these figures by the theologians, philosophers, and graphic artists of the sixteenth century thus carried this polarity of "magic and logic": Renaissance geniuses could, without a conscious sense of contradiction, adopt and embrace these astrologically and theologically overinterpreted pagan gods as concentrations of demonic force, thus associating them with astrological influences, prophesies, and magical practices, while at the same time recovering from them that kernel of Olympian rational control that allowed these same ancient fears and passions to be harnessed and transformed into higher expressions of the unity and multiplicity of human experience.[62]

Warburg analyzes how both Luther and Dürer could be so profoundly influenced by the pervasiveness of astrological beliefs and practices and nevertheless triumph in reforging them—specifically, reforging the ancient demonic image of Saturn—into a humanistic doctrine. The image of saturnine melancholia was of central importance for Warburg's analysis—both Luther and Dürer (as Ficino) were linked astrologically to the influence of Jupiter upon Saturn by their contemporaries. Both were regarded as having a natural propensity toward "heroic" melancholy in which the baleful influences of Saturn, counteracted by Jupiter, led to intellectual greatness commingled with intense mournfulness.[63] Luther responded by mastering the superstitious vision of the human relation to the divine that underlay these speculations, and in so doing introduced a faith that depended upon the powers of rational control and individuation, of the development of stable and defined personhood.

In a series of engravings culminating in the *Melancolia I*, Dürer was able to transform the host of allegorically developed astrological imagery into aesthetic material, thus imposing his own controlled personality onto the chaos of the overinterpreted images, out-allegorizing the suffocating allegories themselves. Rather than simply banishing the profusion of allegorical objects associated with saturnine melancholia, Dürer instead renders them with clarity, precision, and control, not avoiding the dark forces that produced them, but harnessing them, bending them to the will of the autonomous artistic genius, transmuting them into moments of the genius's own expressive mastery of aesthetic material.[64] Melancholy thus cures itself of its rootedness in fatalism, despair, a hopeless submission and subjection of the contemplative mind to the primal mythic view of the world as a vale of astral forces. It does not, thereby, cease being melancholy; indeed, the melancholy hero of the Renaissance is to his last breath deprived, by his nature and creative response to melancholy, of an easy enjoyment of life and must remain perilously balanced between inspiration and insanity. But the creative energy that turns the power of contemplation upon the demonic profusion of objects constitutes a triumph of genius precisely insofar as it is a willed imposition of individuality upon fragments of the natural world that, in the historical dance of collective memory, have become allegorically laden with a superfluidity of arbitrary meanings. The heroic melancholy genius, for Warburg, is a genius because he is able to impose his will upon demonic meaninglessness, is able to effect a powerful, form-giving transformation of transmitted fragments into a new aesthetic whole. This constitutes a small but significant historical victory for the forces of reason, a moment in which the freedom of the human condition is able to triumph over its subjection to its own fears.

As for Warburg himself, the very composition of the essay in which this fragile victory of the force of rational control and self-conscious will was expressed seemed to mark the occasion for the victory of his own personal demons; in despair over the spectacle of the German defeat, Warburg slipped into insanity in 1918.[65] The work on Dürer, however, went ahead; in 1923 Warburg's disciples Fritz Saxl and Erwin Panofsky published their own study of Dürer's *Melancolia I*,[66] which expanded on Warburg's work with a far more involved discussion of Marsilio Ficino as an exemplar of the Renaissance genius.

A brief look at this discussion is helpful here, insofar as it illuminates more sharply the Warburg Institute's analysis of "melancholy genius" that becomes so central in Benjamin's theory of baroque melancholia. For Panofsky and Saxl, Ficino was more than any other Renaissance figure responsible for the renovation of the Aristotelian conception of noble melancholia. The extent to which Ficino remained committed to an astrological interpretation of reality, but (true to

Warburg's insight) synthesized these magical views with a logical, systematic analysis of the causes and effects of saturnine melancholy, is revealed in his huge "melancholy" book, *De Vita Triplici*. The principal tasks of this grandiose project were clear from the beginning: to demonstrate the complex astral relations between Saturn and the melancholy temperament, to explain the relation between contemplation and sadness through occult science, and, ultimately, to devise a practical doctrine by which the baleful effects of Saturn could be warded off, while its ability (in conjunction with Jupiter) to lead to a deepened contemplative awareness of reality could be simultaneously heightened. The scientific-practical investigation of the melancholy syndrome thus also served to legitimate melancholia as a cognitive disposition. Divorced from mundane empirical reality, the *via speculativa* is redeemed by showing the "true" nature of mental life.[67]

This project defines the primacy of heightened self-consciousness in Ficino's thought and the desire to connect this internal consciousness directly to objective structures of the spiritually constituted universe. Internal consciousness begins only when common sense is discarded. This liberation is invariably accompanied not by joy—or by the Hegelian "despair" in the face of a path of self-negation—but by a profound sense of mournfulness or grief.[68] Like a gateway emotion, melancholy mournfulness signals the passage of the contemplative mind to its transcendent home. Rather that dissipating with this spiritual ascent, however, sadness is intensified, urging the mind on to ever-higher levels of contemplation, a progressive deepening of speculation. The source of this sorrow is at once most personal and objectively "true," insofar as it is a dimension of interior emotion that is occasioned by the theological position of humanity. As Ficino wrote, "As long as we are representatives of God on Earth, we are continually troubled by nostalgia for the celestial fatherland, even if we are unaware of it, and in this exile no earthly pleasure can comfort the human mind, since it is eager for better things."[69]

Ficino thus works toward a synthesis of the ancient doctrine of melancholia, reinterpreted as a moment of astral (saturnine) influences on the one hand and, on the other, an expression of ecstatic Christian mysticism. He thus achieves a remarkable synthesis in which the ancient connection between melancholy and prophesy is reversed. The heightened spiritual power accorded to the melancholy mind now becomes an anamnestic retrieval of the data of prehistory, of the originary blessedness of the human state.

Moreover, Ficino is able to connect this anamnestic mysticism directly to elements in the older doctrine of humoral pathology, with the result that dimensions of both become synthetically brought together in what Warburg would have called a "polarity." Black bile, the crude earthly substance, "obliges thought to penetrate and explore the center of its objects, because the black bile is akin to the center of the earth. Likewise, it raises thought to the comprehension of the highest things, because it corresponds to the highest of planets." The transcendent mind is thus led to its insights into higher truths by an interrogation of the most earthly of fragments, and the low and the high are revealed to be elements of the interconnectedness of all being in God's divine mind.

As Panofsky and Saxl observe (in their later work *Saturn and Melancholy*),

> Thus Ficino's system—and this was perhaps its greatest strength—contrived to give Saturn's "immanent contradiction" a redemptive power: the highly gifted melancholic—who suffered under Saturn, insofar as the latter tormented the body and the lower faculties with grief, fear, and depression—might save himself by the very act of turning voluntarily to that very same Saturn. The melancholic should, in other words, apply himself of his own accord to that very activity which is the particular domain of the sublime star of speculation, and which the planet provides just as powerfully as it hinders and harms the ordinary functions of body and soul. . . . As enemy and oppressor of all life in any way subject to the present world, Saturn generates melancholy, but as friend and protector of a higher and purely intellectual existence he can also cure it. [70]

The same concentrated dialectic of saturnine melancholia that Warburg observed in Luther and Dürer his disciples illustrate in Ficino, with this difference: less encumbered by Warburg's obsession with the victory of rational self-control over the powers of myth, Panofsky and Saxl understand that heroic melancholy, which turns the forces of Saturn against itself to form a new intellectual empowerment and an elevation of the soul, lies on a theological ground toward which theories of aesthetic expressivity can only point. It therefore demands a treatment that, if not "theological" in any outright sense, nevertheless recognizes the necessity of introducing theological vocabulary into the discussion of the melancholy syndrome itself. Warburg's doggedly humanistic interpretation of the meaning-giving triumph of the melancholy genius recedes. In its place emerges an interpretive evocation of melancholia as a compressed—indeed a monadic—representation of the spiritual situation of humankind. [71]

This brief analysis of the work of the Warburg Institute arose from my suspicion that Benjamin's appropriation of their vision of the Renaissance ideal of the melancholy genius implied a willful imposition of meaning all its own; that is, the transposition of this theory from the Renaissance to the baroque. And indeed, it appears that insofar as Benjamin chooses to depend virtually exclusively upon the phenomenology of the melancholy genius as developed by the Warburg Institute, much is riding on a successful argument that the sources of creative genius that Warburg and his disciples identified as flowing from the creative mastery of a remarkable form of speculative thought would apply in a closely analogous way to the baroque playwrights. [72]

Notwithstanding a healthy skepticism concerning the ultimate relevance of broad characterizations of historical epochs such as "Renaissance" and "baroque," Benjamin must nevertheless argue that the contemplative depths that characterized the melancholy genius of Renaissance heroes such as Ficino and Dürer are essential, originary manifestations of the phenomenology of baroque *Trauer*. He must show that the cosmic speculations of Ficino, like the mastery of graphic detail of Dürer, are historically variegated generations of the same essential reality that, in the baroque playwrights, produces the petrified vision of dead nature, the conviction of the vanity of human endeavor, and the brooding fixity on natural ruin. And for these reasons, he must also argue that the genuinely creative forces that, in the Renaissance, are expressed by the ideal of the melancholy genius or "sorrowful investigator" exist, in distinct but recognizable form, in the rejected and scorned creations of the baroque as well; that both are allegorical geniuses. He must show that, just as the melancholy genius of the Renaissance arises at the moment at which the artist is capable of a willful exertion of personal meaning upon demonic forces that have been frozen by a surplus of interpretations, so too the baroque *Trauerspiel* finds its own moment of genuine creativity in the allegorical structure of the dramas themselves, which, while missing the majesty, the cosmic extension of the Renaissance, convey the theological dimension of the allegorical vision even more clearly.

In the case of Dürer's *Melancolia I*, Benjamin seems to effect this transition from Renaissance to baroque by the mere pronouncement that the engraving "anticipates the baroque in many respects. In it the knowledge of the introvert [*Grübler*] and the investigations of the scholar have merged as intimately as in the men of the baroque. The Renaissance explores the universe; the baroque explores libraries." This anticipation of the baroque leads to a reconstruction of the *typus melancholicus* in the Renaissance. Referring to the "dialectical way" in which the peripatetic *Problemata Physica* introduced the paradigm of the melancholy genius, Benjamin observes that the ancient connection among melancholy, nobility, madness, and prophesy reappears in the *Trauerspiel* as the king's horrified precognitions of his own downfall;[73] from here, it is a short step to the introduction of the astrological interpretation of the melancholy syndrome as well.

Benjamin thus proceeds with a reconstruction of the doctrine of humoral pathology, the advent of astrological speculations, and the creative reception of this synthesis in the Renaissance. His presentation is highly compressed and is derived completely from Giehlow, Warburg, and Panofsky and Saxl. Citing heavily from the latter, Benjamin takes up again the "dialectical trait in the idea of Saturn," that is, the historically established polarity of the baleful and the beneficial, the contemplative and the dejective—or myth and antimyth, timeliness and eternity—compressed within the image of saturnine melancholia. Once again: no dialectic of historical motion, but of infinitesimal, concrete concentration of antithetical properties within the same historically constituted image, the simultaneity of the creature's subjection to the pull of fallen nature, combined with fragmentary elements of the redemptive moment locked within the historical continuum, provides—for Benjamin—the dialectical moment of Saturn:

> The history of the problem of melancholy unfolds within the
> parameter of this dialectic. Its climax is reached with the magic of
> the Renaissance. Whereas the Aristotelian insights into the psy-
> chical duality of the melancholy disposition and the antithetical
> nature of the influence of Saturn had given way, in the middle
> ages, to a purely demonic representation of both, as conformed

with Christian speculation; with the Renaissance the whole wealth of ancient meditations re-emerged from the sources.[74]

Thus far, this is not a significant departure from the reading of Warburg. Benjamin adopts the view that the unfolding of the ideal of the melancholy genius in the Renaissance was a genuine moment of the realization of a dialectical image, rather than the mere appropriation of classical images by a later age. The pagan gods, plunged into the resolute moral allegoresis of the Middle Ages, thence recovered by the Renaissance, bear encoded traces of their contradictory histories within them: the reaper is not only the seasonal god of harvest plenty, of life, but also the image of death; Aphrodite is both eternal beauty and its inevitable corruption by time. And yet the morbidity and historical petrification that attaches to these image fragments, while registering the subjection of humanity to the demonic, as for Warburg also denote for Benjamin the irresistible pull of historical time itself; "the implacable progression of every life towards death." As the moving image of fallen nature, historical time fills out and completes what, in Warburg's analysis, had been the synchronic fascination with mythic fears. And what is so fruitful for this introduction is not just its ability to connect inherently the expressions of the melancholy mind particular to the Renaissance and baroque period, but to do so in such a way that the model of genius is related internally to the idea of historical time through the mediation of the realm of godforsaken, fallen nature— natural history. When Benjamin turns to Ficino, then, it is not the lofty flights of abstract cosmological speculation that concern him, but rather the peculiar relation to the world of objects contained in Ficino's conception of melancholy genius:

> For this age, which was bent at all costs on gaining access to the sources of the occult insight into nature, the melancholic posed the question of how it might be possible to discover for one's self the spiritual powers of Saturn and yet escape madness. The problem was to separate sublime melancholy, the *melancolia illa heroica* of Marsilius Ficinus, and of Melanchthon, from the ordinary and pernicious kind.[75]

In this way, Benjamin bends the interpretation from the spirit if not the letter of the reflections of the Warburg Institute toward a reading of melancholy genius concentrating specifically on the propensity of the melancholy mind toward the fragmentary, the earthly, the decayed. And Benjamin finds in Ficino the point where this already ancient connection is transformed from a complex of medical, theological, and astrological beliefs and practices to a philosophical insight—the deep connection between contemplation and the earthbound attraction to the realm of things: "For the melancholic the inspirations of mother earth dawn from the night of contemplation like treasures from the interior of the earth; the lightening-flash of intuition is unknown to him. The earth, previously important only as the cold, dry element acquires the full wealth of its esoteric meaning in a scientific reflection of Ficinus."[76]

Benjamin argues that while Panofsky and Saxl may have presented the detailed description of Ficino's conception of heroic melancholy, their concentration on the paradigm of the subjective genius caused them to miss the centrality of the earthbound vision on which it depended. Indeed, Benjamin speculates that the inherent connection between contemplation and earthiness and the revision of the cosmological order that it produced "may well be considered as a seed in which the allegorical flower of the baroque, still held in check by the power of a genius, lies ready to burst into bloom." The emphasis upon the distinctive individuality of the melancholy genius, of his unique, form-giving will, may have prevented the Warburg Institute from grasping that the genuine theological impulse that underlies the emergence of melancholia as a mode of creativity is not the schema of the individual at all, but rather consists of the development of a relationship between subjectivity as such and the physiognomy of its object realm; that is, a "motorial reaction" between the contemplating subject and a "concretely structured world." While this claim might deprive the Renaissance model of melancholy genius of its claim to historical distinctiveness, it also reveals that the *origin*, in Benjaminian terms, of the melancholy vision of the world is more readily visible not in the outstanding works of individual geniuses, but rather in the extreme aesthetic forms produced during what otherwise would be rejected as a period of cultural decadence, in the baroque *Trauerspiel*. There *Trauer*, intense mournfulness, penetrates through the model of the autonomous contemplative genius, and in this depersonalization points toward the image of the thinker too as merely one form of earthly mass. In this way, Benjamin insists that Dürer's *Melancolia I* "anticipates the baroque" not by the precisely rendered arrangement of the allegorical objects of melancholy contemplation, or by the transmutation of these objects into material for aesthetic mastery. Rather, and despite the manifest intentions of Dürer himself, the picture represents with dreadful fidelity "the concept of the pathological state, in which the most simple object appears to be a symbol of some enigmatic wisdom because it lacks any natural, creative relation to us."[77] And in the image of the stone, the one object that the Warburg interpreters overlooked, Benjamin finds the key symbol of Dürer's work: the image of the inert mass and the constant reminder that we too are physical objects, still-animated corpses.

Insofar as the meaning of Renaissance genius is reinterpreted in the extraordinary relation between the melancholy vision and the world of objects, the Christian sin of *acedia* or sloth, over whose grip upon the saturnine imagery the masters of the Renaissance, for Warburg, had to triumph, reasserts itself in Benjamin's view as "the genuinely theological conception of the melancholic." *Acedia* is thereby linked to the subjection to dead nature, and this, in turn, provides an additional insight into the dramatic structure of the *Trauerspiel*. "The indecisiveness of the prince . . . is nothing other than saturnine *acedia*. Saturn causes people to be 'apathetic, indecisive, slow.' The fall of the tyrant is caused by indolence of the heart."[78]

Like the tyrant's melancholy sloth, the faithlessness of the melancholy intriguer illustrates the subjection to the earthly. The mechanical precision with which the courtier abandons his indolent king at the moment of crisis depicts "a dismal and melancholy submission to a supposedly unfathomable order of baleful constellations, which assumes an almost material character." The faithlessness to humans is the obverse of the melancholic's faithfulness to the world of things, his rigid fixation on the spectacle of dead nature as the arena of his despair, and simultaneously as the only text in which a knowledge pointing beyond this despair could be contained. The hopeless loyalty to the world of things constitutes, in the *Trauerspiel*, what in the Renaissance emerges as the creative dimension of melancholy genius: both illustrate the dialectic of melancholy as the subject plunges even deeper into the fragments of an empty world in order to produce a profusion of objects for its own contemplation. The loyalty to the world of things has, for the melancholic, "strings attached": loyalty extends only so far as the things themselves are transformed from their sheer facticity into melancholy objects, capable of emanating—or receiving—meaning. And this too points toward a theologically rendered dialectic:

> Loyalty is completely appropriate only to the relationship of man to the world of things. The latter knows no higher law, and loyalty knows no object to which it might belong more exclusively than the world of things. And indeed this world is constantly calling on it; and every loyal vow or memory surrounds itself with the fragments of the world of things as its very own, not too demanding objects. Clumsily, indeed unjustifiably, loyalty expresses, in its own way, a truth for the sake of which it does, of course, betray the world. Melancholy betrays the world for the sake of knowledge. But in its tenacious self-absorption it embraces dead objects in its contemplation, in order to rescue [*retten*] them.[79]

Here, for the second time in Benjamin's treatment of baroque melancholy, theory outstrips completely the confines of historical commentary, breaking free of its material content entirely and precipitously flying into the thinner atmosphere in which the theological foundation of the melancholy way of seeing is momentarily glimpsed. The subject of this passage is clearly no longer merely "baroque" melancholy, but of an essential theological mode, an energized moment of encounter—and a kind of mediation—between subjectivity and its objects, which can be read from its origins, but which can thereby be only imperfectly and momentarily represented through the phenomena themselves. The truth for the sake of which melancholy loyalty remains loyal only by betraying its objects is the truth of the fallenness of the creaturely—but such a truth exists only as the withdrawal of God's presence, for only the absence of God is to be understood by the universality of death and the meaninglessness of life. Faith evaporates, leaving behind the realm of objects, and these, no longer recognizable as the work of God, become allegories, ciphers of the consignment of humanity to fate, and at the same time ambiguous pieces in a puzzle of redemption. The incessant, indeed the obsessive intellectualism that Benjamin ascribes to the melancholy mind is always dedicated to an ultimately negative theology. Its immanent transcendence, which drives the melancholy mind toward the things at the same time as it plunges the subject ever deeper into inwardness, is comprehensible, in the end, only in terms of the utopian will, the hope that by their very consignment to natural fate, by the very meaninglessness that they embody, the elements of the creaturely might begin to radiate with an individual shimmer, a light that directs them toward the redemptive wholeness of the end of history.

Understood as a dialectic—and this is expressly how Benjamin wishes to understand it—melancholia is the schema of alienated messianic consciousness. Melancholia achieves its messianic content precisely insofar as it is at the farthest remove from "faith" in the redemptive power of God, and instead is entirely transfixed by the earthly spectacle of God's infamous absence. The intensity and persistence of the melancholy mind is always described within the negative space of the absent deity. This underlies the dialectical nearness of intense mournfulness and absolute bliss, or of despair and utopian anticipation. If the baroque *Trauerspiel* was never able to come to any expressive moment of recognition of its own dialectic, to grasp it reflectively and thereby bring it to full, controlled development in the aesthetic, then this aesthetic ruin, pointing all the more clearly to the theological ground of the melancholy mind, is presented to the critic as the *original* mode of melancholy speculation, allegory.

3 Melancholia and Allegory

*It requires moral courage to grieve; it requires
religious courage to rejoice.—Kierkegaard, "Journals"*

Writing on the theory of allegorical expression in the second half of the
Ursprung des deutschen Trauerspiels, Bernd Witte referred to the intimacy of "allegorical criticism" and "absolute subjectivity." Two insights are contained within this description: First, the notion that, in
his study of the *Trauerspiel,* Benjamin effects a deliberate blurring—or
transcendence—of any canonical distinctions among subject, object,
and theological ground of the critical act, a radicalization of the
already radicalized transformation of romantic literary criticism developed in the Goethe essay. Witte observes a tripartite, mutually determining analogical structure emerging in the theory of allegory. Among
critical object, ground, and critical form, the principle of synthetic
unity is a methodological one, the "bringing together of discrete and
meaningless fragments into a new whole."[1] The critique of allegorical
artworks consists in the mosaic fitting together of phenomenal fragments—discrete linguistic elements—violently wrested from their
embedded context in the historical material of the degraded text. For
Witte, this makes the *Ursprung des deutschen Trauerspiels* itself an
allegorical artwork, as Benjamin expressly declared in the Goethean
motto of the study, wherein science and art must, for the sake of their
mutual object, fuse into one balanced totality.[2]

The validity of Witte's position cannot be refuted. But in its undialectical stasis, the claim that the *Trauerspiel* study "is" allegorical is

as much an abstraction as the claim that Benjamin "was" himself a melancholic. In either case, the copula expresses a dialectical history of subjectivity and its objects, an encoded text of concrete images.

Benjamin himself spoke often enough of the delightful process of accumulating his own fragments; the "craziest mosaic technique one can think of."[3] As allegorical reading of allegory, as construction of fragment and imposition of meaning upon this same activity on the part of critical object, Benjamin's theory of baroque allegory establishes a hierarchical progression of theoretical contradictions, revolving around the relationship between the mosaic technique of critical representation delineated in the "Erkenntniskritische Vorrede" and the desperate intensity of assignation of meanings, which he describes as the essential mode of expression of the baroque *Trauerspiel*. As I argued above, this contradiction itself rests upon a question concerning the possibility of meaning and the ability of the subject to discover, create, or participate in moments of divine significance in the context of a historical continuum in which meaninglessness, as godforsakenness, appears as the mode of transmission itself. Much depends, therefore, on the sense in which the allegorical structure of Benjamin's presentation of allegory is itself allegorical by virtue of its method, whether the methodological correspondence of critical form and critical object does not establish the boundaries of a tension between *invented* and *discovered* meaning out of the textual fragments of experience.

Witte's argument notwithstanding, Benjamin clearly believes that he is discovering, not assigning, meaning upon the fragments, and the allegorical activity that he exercises upon the allegorists would, on his terms, differ not in the activity itself but in the success of allegorical construction to disclose the originary points of encapsulation of messianic memory and anticipation within historical time. Thus the inherent tension between object and form of allegorical critique (that is, between the allegoresis of the *Trauerspiel* and the critical text "about" it) consists in the claim that the two are essentially distinguished by the arbitrariness of the former, and thus its sunkenness into the creaturely depths of historical time and the objectivity of the latter, thus its explosive messianic dimension. The critical text would then "complete" the ruined artwork, would represent and thereby indicate its relation to redemption, by revealing and fulfilling the theological

ground upon which the arbitrariness of the former rests. The meaninglessness of the assignation of subjective meaning must itself be
represented as the negative image of absolute or divine meaning.[4] But
how could such a claim be made? How would the *critical* act of
construction be so theologically secure as to avoid entirely the same
moment of arbitrariness (with its internal link to overgrown, mythic
subjectivity) that characterizes the critical object?

This state of affairs leads to the second implication of Witte's observation. The development of an "allegorical criticism" is related to a
form of "absolute subjectivity." For Witte, the allegorization of the
mode of criticism places subjectivity in center stage. Just as baroque
allegory leads to the intensification of the subjective—hence arbitrary—creation of meaning, so the composition of the critical study is a
supreme act of allegorical creation in which the subjectivity of the
critic himself reaches a zenith. This is quite the opposite of the
consistent suppression of the role of the critical subject that was
ascribed to Benjamin in the last chapter. For Witte, this absolute
critical subjectivity marks the coincidence of form and object of criticism on another level as well: by assuming total responsibility of
meaning by the critical subject, Benjamin reveals that the *Trauerspiel*
book is nothing other than a translation of Schmittian decisionism from
the realm of politics to the realm of literary criticism. The critic
extends his power of decision over the fragments; he declares the "state
of emergency" of meaning, and by so doing takes command over it.
This "paroxysm of subjectivity" links Benjamin's book to Schmitt's as
"documents of their time." Both reveal what Arnold Gehlen described
as the subjectivist extremism arising from the anomic dimension of
industrial capitalism in the early twentieth century. Allegory as absolute subjectivity; allegorical critique of allegorical artworks as contemporary (read modernist, hence anomic capitalist) forms of subjec-
tivization: a heavy charge against Benjamin, who was supposedly so
concerned with the messianic, metasubjective possibilities of literary
criticism. For Witte, then,

> The critic too is an allegorist, by all means one with the specific
> historical experiences of an intellectual of his time. For him, an
> insight into the accursed state of the world is no longer present as
> the vision of nature and the course of worldly events, as it was for
> the baroque poets, nor in historical speculations, as for the

romantics. For the private scholar from Berlin, who is as isolated from any social praxis just as much from an immediate relationship to nature, all these regions of experience have become secondary. Rather, the mass of past experiences of nature and history, sedimented in the literature of previous epochs, and archivalized—but never really worked through—by the historicism of the nineteenth century, is material that stands ready for his use, from which he breaks out the elements for his own allegorical construction.[5]

If Witte is essentially correct in this charge—and if, as Hans Robert Jauss has argued, this observation applies equally to the critical reception of Baudelaire and the grand construction of the *Passagenwerk*[6]—then this has profound implications. Notwithstanding his own theologically grounded claims to the objectivity inherent in the critical process, let alone the resoluteness with which he sought to eliminate the category of subjectivity from criticism, Benjamin's own criticism, as allegorical, would emerge as expressions of a prominent subjectivism and therefore open itself to the charge of ultimate arbitrariness. Whether this arbitrariness seriously undermines the status of Benjamin's criticism, as it does for Witte, or constitutes a necessary break from the false and dogmatic "objectivism" of crassly political writing, as it does for Jauss, is an important but secondary matter.

Any satisfactory answers to these sorts of questions concerning the subjective-arbitrary as opposed to the objective-receptive status of Benjamin's criticism would, insofar as they concern the relation among form of criticism, critical object, and critical subject, be answerable only by an analysis of the theological ground of criticism. Moreover, it is a necessary but by no means sufficient beginning to insist, as does Witte, upon the historicity of Benjamin's own allegorical subjectivity. The dimensions of Benjamin's treatment of the intensification of the subject characteristic of allegory are composed of historical images, and these images are arranged according to fixed conceptual points: myth, *Trauer*, decisiveness, redemption. But historical arguments, when truncated, slide into historicist ones by adopting an inconspicuous commitment to historical causality. The relation between the historical situatedness of the critical subject and the objects of critique exhibits a complexity in keeping with the image of history from which both are generated.

Finally, the ambiguous relation between allegory and subjectivity, which appears so central in the formulation of these questions, can only be descriptively captured by recourse to the idea of melancholy. Melancholy is the quasi-objective mode of subjective contemplation in which the theological ground of criticism enters dialectically into the mode of subjective perception and speculation itself. As a mode of *deepened* subjectivity, as the "motorial reaction" between mournful world and subjective concentration, melancholy provides a schema through whose application the relationship between allegory and subjectivity can become clearer, and vice versa: through the theory of baroque allegory, the central mediating role of the concept of melancholia is also illuminated.

The distinction between symbol and allegory with which Benjamin begins his analysis parallels that between tragedy and *Trauerspiel* in the first section of the study: now on the level of underlying modes of expression, the theological distinction between tragedy and *Trauerspiel* and symbol and myth refers back to the tension between myth and history. Benjamin musters scholarly sources to demonstrate the misinterpretations of a prejudiced form of expression. Classical and romantic aesthetic theories, by an irresponsible transmutation of an originally theological "genuine idea" of the symbolic, came to understand the symbol as the immediate sensual unity of essence and appearance. The theological symbol is by its very nature paradoxical; the sensuous unity of spirit and matter makes both a cognitive and a normative claim. It asserts that a meaningful, if always paradoxical, transcendence of polar opposites exists. In this way symbols function as the organizational matrices for religious communities.[7]

The aestheticization of this theological expression has, for Benjamin, a series of unfortunate results. It defuses the originary power of symbolic expression by transferring the metaphysics of disclosure of spirit into the language of beautiful appearance. This prejudice, which Benjamin already observed in Goethe, resulted in the transposition of the inherently *mythic* character of symbolic expression from religious to literary expression, in the secularized image of the beautiful individual. It is for Benjamin a static conception, insofar as it extends essentially unwarranted claims concerning the ability of the autonomous artwork to "capture" and thus eternally preserve an image of the divine in a historically situated text. Moreover, its monopoly on meaning in literary texts consigns the allegory to the status of a decayed or unsuccessful symbol; a symbol clumsily contaminated by the technical traces of artistic intention.[8] This extension, typified by Creuzer, thus described the myth in terms of its ability to lift the symbolic art form, Münchhausen-style, from the historical continuum and thus (as Michael Jennings notes) "makes false claims about the relation between this world and the absolute."[9]

One might say that the secularization of the theological symbol leads to a mythology of presence in an acute sense. Creuzer's introduction of temporal distinctions into this mythology thus became particularly relevant for Benjamin: "the momentary, the total, the inscrutability of origin, the necessary,"[10] are Creuzer's characterization of the symbol against which the allegory could not help but appear as a failed symbol, characterized by the merely inadequate employment of these temporal features. Creuzer thus takes the allegory's repetitiveness, brokenness, conventionalism, and arbitrariness as the expression of the endlessness and displacement of meaning inherent in ancient myth. As Winfried Menninghaus has shown, however, Benjamin neatly reverses Creuzer's distinction between symbolic and mythical modes of expression, which this temporalization of the literary symbol was intended to secure, and argues instead that just as the symbol bears indelible traces of its own mythic origin, so allegory, dispersed into historical happening, comes to acquire a petrifying power capable of "blasting apart myth." By opposing a petrifying and corrosive depiction of historical decay to the sacrificial image of eternity, allegory bears within it a latent critical potential.[11]

For all their professed immediacy and necessity, symbols still partake of the network of secret natural correspondences and forces that, exerting their ghostly influence over human life, plunge it into mythic darkness, the "chaos of symbols," and—as Benjamin insisted in the Goethe essay—rob the subject of the powers of individuality, responsibility, decision, and ethical insight. Under the extension of the mythic symbol into the realm of aesthetic language, a genealogical grouping of correlated terms emerges: appearance (Schein), beauty, distance, aura, phantasmagoria. "The measure of time for the experience of the symbol is the mystical instant in which the symbol assumes the meaning into its hidden and, if one may say so, wooded interior."[12] Like the sacrificial death of the tragic hero described in the 1916 essays, the symbol marks the momentary transcendence of time and thus bears within it the ironic "Idea of fulfilled historical time."[13] This is the extent to which myth is capable of representing the triumph of humanity over its subjection to fate—and this is the moment of resistance built into the very notion of myth.

In the promulgation of myth, however, even this schematism of its transcendence is drawn back within the sphere of the human subjection to natural forces, to the sphere of overnamed nature. The hero's transcendence is, after all, also his own death. The naturalness and spontaneity of the symbol are always part of its status as an expression of the mythic subjection of individuals to natural and temporal processes beyond their control. The image of redemption that flashes fleetingly from the temporal pyrotechnics of symbolic expression bears an indelible trace of "objective mendacity," defined in ethical terms as "not recognizing the situation of decision."[14] It is the image of natural immediacy and completeness, of a divinely ordered and meaningful cosmos, overseen and maintained by superhuman agents. But this image is rendered mythic and deceitful by the objective state of fallen nature. Projected upon fallen nature itself, the beautiful symbol is antithetical to decisiveness and is therefore a political as well as an aesthetic phenomenon.

The first intuition of how allegory could act as a counteractive to myth is already indicated in Benjamin's insistence that the allegorical be regarded as a wholly heterogenous mode of expression and cognition, one that the tradition of Western metaphysics could only reject because of its intense but paradoxical relationship to knowledge and the question of meaning. In contrast to the mythical evocation of unity and simplicity, "the baroque apotheosis is a dialectical one. It is accomplished in the movement between extremes."[15] The baroque writers had neither the interest in nor the capacity for a theory in which the mythical luster of the symbol could take a predominant place: they responded to what they saw.

Insofar as the symbol contains a dialectic, it exists in the simultaneity of the "mountain and plant-like" organicism of symbolic expression and its claim to immediacy; that is, the ironic expression of timelessness within the temporal. The allegorical dialectic, on the other hand, concerns the possibility of meaning itself, subsisting in "the depths which separate visual being from meaning. . . . The violence of the dialectical movement within these allegorical depths must become clearer in the study of the form of *Trauerspiel* than anywhere else."[16] It is not, then, a matter of a literary device in which a conventional association is established between a (visual) object and an abstract meaning, in which one thing stands for another. This is indeed the relevant literary content of allegory, but is only the surface that the classical and romantic discourse had left visible. Rather, allegory emerges as the expression of natural history:

> Whereas in the symbol destruction is idealized and the trans-figured face of nature is fleetingly revealed in the light of re-demption, in allegory the observer is confronted with the *facies hyppocratica* of history as a petrified, primordial landscape. Ev-erything about history that, from the very beginning, has been untimely, sorrowful, unsuccessful, is expressed in a face—or rather, in a death's head. And although such a thing lacks all "symbolic" freedom of expression, all classical proportion, all humanity—nevertheless, this is the form in which man's subjec-tion to nature is most obvious and it significantly gives rise not only to the enigmatic question of the nature of human existence as such, but also of the biographical historicity of the individual. This is the heart of the allegorical way of seeing, of the baroque, secular explanation of history as the Passion of the world; its importance resides solely in the stations of its decline.[17]

The allegorical way of seeing is, by this metaphor, brought back into the sphere of the melancholy vision of the world. By summoning up the image of a cursed history, by placing upon the profusion of images of violence and horror an emblematic face, this response to the spectacle of meaningless historical catastrophe revives the empty world as dead in the form of a mask. Here, as in the metaphysics of *Trauer*, Benjamin is describing a creative disposition composed of objective, emotive, and cognitive elements in which the observing subject, no longer able to sustain the mythic illusion of the unproblematic "objectivity" of meaning in the appearance world, and recoiling with horror from the emptied world that results from this refusal, transfigures the abyss, reconceptualizes it, and by so doing discovers the actual course of historical happening itself. This is the secularized vision of history as the passion of the world; the insight—which Benjamin himself had made years earlier—of the world as the continuum of suffering.

Melancholy vision, then, necessarily precedes allegorical technique. The assignation of meaning onto unredeemed elements of a natural-historical stage, a "petrified, primordial landscape," presupposes the tremendous alienation from immediacy, from the quotidian, that the melancholic experiences. This is another means for reexpressing the ancient connection between melancholy and spiritual insight. Here, however, we observe once again that, while Benjamin does not say so explicitly, a clear connection is also observable between melancholy and criticism, the spiritual insight in which the *Schein* of beauty goes out and the world is exposed, in all its inhumanity, as it is.

In any early article, Hans Heinz Holz distinguished among three moments in the motion of allegorical creativity. *Trauer*, which evokes the nihilism of the *taedium vitae*, constitutes the moment where the subject beholds a world that has been drained of all its "inherent" meaning, where such meaning—as "natural," hence mythic—is emptied. This is the moment of *Entwertung*, of the devaluation of the world of appearance.[18] While Holz does not mention it, the process of *Entwertung* bears clear affinities to what the early Marx had understood by *Entfremdung* or alienation: In both cases, the decay of an immediate unproblematic relation to the sensuous world results in a crisis of meaning. In both cases, too, a creative response is engendered in which the objectively present features of a concretely structured world interact dialectically with a knowing and feeling subject. The response is not only creative but also bears a potential for critique. The devaluation of the world may arise from objective conditions, but at the same time provides for the perception of the true causes of these conditions.

Entwertung or devaluation of the taken-for-granted must be seen as a virtually universal dimension of the melancholy vision of the world. It underlies not only the emotive dimensions of the melancholy experience, the desolation, sadness, and mourning that have always received preponderant attention to the detriment of melancholia's properly cognitive dimension, but it also is related to another consistent feature in the discourse of melancholia: the social and personal isolation of the melancholic, the real or imagined exclusion or marginalization of melancholics from their social milieu, and the flight into interiority so characteristic of the "artistic" melancholy temperament. Understood either as a preliminary condition or as an effect—or both—social exclusion has consistently been viewed as a necessary condition for social criticism, particularly by the tradition of Western Marxism. "Devaluation," then, can be taken not only as a precise description of the initial stage of a phenomenology of baroque allegory, but also as a more general characteristic of the critical imagination. The "great minds" of the baroque, unable to accommodate themselves easily to religious doctrines and political creeds according to which their own experience of general social crisis was to have been rendered comprehensible, perceive with horror the specter of an empty world. This is a destructive moment. But such devaluation leads to a creative response, in art—as in the *Trauerspiel*—or in criticism.

In the allegorical mode of seeing, devaluation is followed by fragmentation. Holz calls this *Verstückelung*, the division of the petrified world into a heap of discrete fragments. Together, devaluation and fragmentation are the propadeutics to allegorical *Konstruktion*, the third, productive moment of allegory. Only through the gaze that sees the homogeneity and repetition of historical time rob the world of all meaning, and thus of all coherence and order, can the allegorist come to construct meaning of his own, by assigning subjective meanings to the fragments.

Allegory is thus a creative cognitive mode inseparably connected to the melancholic disposition: melancholics need not be allegorists, but allegory arises from melancholia. Death as expiration of the creature is inimical to the vision of death as the fulfillment of divine fate; once the world has been transformed into the masklike, into the specter of the melancholy landscape, death takes on a "postmythic" significance. It is the emblem of universal transience, of the subjection of the human subject to natural history, rather than the schema of its transcendence, as in myth and the symbolic artwork. It is no longer beautiful, but stands, stripped of all mythic veiling, as the terrible and sublime. And if existential phenomenology had, from different but comparable premises, reached an analogous point, what separates Benjamin's and Heidegger's conceptions of the density and inescapability of death or the antithesis between death and meaning is Benjamin's resolute refusal to integrate this fragmentary insight into a broader vision of ontology—a "structural totality" as Adorno later called it[19]—in which the history of melancholia would be transformed into the historicity of *Dasein*. If, for Heidegger, the question of the meaning of being renders itself as a question concerning the situation of *Dasein*, and if this questioning illuminates death as *Dasein*'s highest possibility, for Benjamin's analysis death cannot become something "for" the subject. Death cannot be regarded from the light of an ontological project; it is a void that consumes the very atmosphere in which the project—the question—could articulate itself.

In this way, death—the "morbidity" of the melancholic—becomes the central problematic of allegory and takes its place as one pole in the allegorical dialectic, the other being "significance" (*Bedeutung*). The former is literalness itself, the latter, in the ambiguity arising between its existential ("the enigmatic question of the nature of human existence as such") and semiotic dimensions, is, in natural history, indeterminate.

> The greater the significance, the greater the subjection to death, because death digs most deeply the jagged line of demarcation between physical nature and significance. But if nature has always been subject to the power of death, it is also true that it has always been allegorical. Significance and death both come to fruition in historical development, just as they are closely linked as seeds in the creature's graceless state of sin.[20]

The allegorical intention insists upon filling up the space between these two poles (otherwise expressed as "image" and "meaning") with a profusion of objects, to fill up the void, to produce allegorical objects capable of bearing significance. The production of meaning itself thus digs the line of demarcation deeper, and this is where the allegorical intention derives both its restless productivity and its redemptive moment, since "history" as the consignment of the creature to death is precisely the allegorical vision of the depths separating death—as nature—and meaning.

In this way, allegorical production becomes the true expression of natural history. By its form alone, allegory constitutes the moment in which nature and history, and naturally, historically constituted subject and object of allegory express their dialectical interpenetration. And in the profusion of images that results from this form, the theological crisis from which this dialectic of nature and history arises is represented as an encoded text.

The paradoxical notion of a willful production of meaning and the relation between this and the melancholic's fascination with the realm of fragmentary or mortal objects underlies the inherent link between allegory and esotericism. It is closely related to the link, previously developed, between *Trauer* and ostentation. For the allegorical imagination, meaning is almost by definition occult and mysterious; the concept of "fragment" is inextricably bound up with the esoteric conviction that discrete objects or phenomena of the natural world constitute hieroglyphic entities. The production of meaning on which allegory is based is indelibly linked with a frankly contradictory conviction, namely that allegoresis *deciphers* the meaning inherent in fragments and thus constitutes a restorative or redemptive function by recovering, from historical negativity, dimensions of an originary meaning that otherwise would be suppressed and lost from the march of historical "tradition."[21]

Benjamin traces the historical origins of this esoteric will to the Renaissance's fascination with the Egyptian hieroglyph. Borrowing once again from Giehlow's work,[22] Benjamin claims that the Renaissance's project of a "mystical philosophy of nature" led it to receive the Egyptian hieroglyph as a magical mark, an emblem that pointed toward the mysterious occult structure of nature itself—the hieroglyph, still untranslated in the sixteenth century, appeared as the essence of mystery, as a storehouse of secret doctrines. Renaissance scholars, mistakenly following the hermeneutical practices of late antiquity, insisted on the forceful application of metaphysical meanings upon individual hieroglyphs, thus transforming the hieroglyphs themselves from phonetic signs to lexical signifiers and ultimately to occult icons and emblems that, breaking away from the original historical meaning they bore, plunge into an increasingly complex network of interrelated signification, with less and less reference to perceptible reality.

This insoluble, enticing gap, this tense space of mystery established between the materiality of signifier and the occult and spellbinding signified, fascinated the Renaissance speculators. Neo- and pseudo-antique allegorizations of the hieroglyph intertwine with Christian didacticism, with paganism revived as entertainment, with demonology and astrology, into the thorny thicket of allegorized images that the

Warburg Institute tried to hack into. Once again, Ficino is the arche-type. The mis- and overinterpreted hieroglyph leads to the visual image that replaces the grouping of letters to stand for a mystical property of nature, the willfully enigmatic emblem or the rebus.

This "hieratic ostentation," however, found its true home in the baroque, which transformed it into a "natural theology of writing" itself. And in this way the baroque imagination realized the extent to which nature itself is allegorical, is composed of fragments that trans-pose themselves into emblems, that nature itself is transfigured into an interwoven network of occult signs, shimmering with potential meaning but themselves undeciphered and thus quite meaningless on their own. For the baroque, as for Benjamin himself in his earlier essay on language, "nature serves the purpose of expressing its meaning." As the expression of its "spiritual content," nature enters into the allegori-cal intention as the meaningful/meaningless emblem, the true expres-sion of nature's "meaning" in its fallen state, in the image of historical catastrophe. "The transfixed face of signifying nature," which, in symbolic art, is pressed into an immediate, hence false image of uncorrupted transcendent beauty, "is victorious, and history must, once and for all, remain contained in the subordinate role of stage-property."[23] Nature itself thus becomes the sphere of allegories, the pile of runes of the continuum of historical catastrophe. And this again is a further reformulation of the dialectic of natural history. Petrified, transformed into the specter of repetition, history is transfigured into dead nature; mortified, nature becomes the elements of historical ruin and the universality of death.[24]

The very idea of writing bears within it this gap, the essential dialectic of the allegory, between the materiality of the written mark and its occult, divine signified. The gap between emblem and the act of inscription is, on the level of technique, a replication of the gap between deathly nature (Being) and meaning, between whose poles the allegorical intention tirelessly travels. Sacred writing that is read but not understood—that is read and cherished because it is not under-stood—is the schema by which the "eruption of images" of the baroque allegory can be grasped.[25] This eruption of images fills up the void with a pile of enigmatic emblems; the attachment of discrete fragments to moral qualities, to people or places, or to other fragments intertwines ceaselessly.

This is the context in which Benjamin introduces the "antinomies of the allegorical":

> Any person, any object, any relationship can mean absolutely anything else. With this possibility a destructive, but just verdict is passed on the profane world: it is characterized as a world in which the detail is of no great importance. But it will be unmistakably apparent, especially to anyone who is familiar with allegorical textual exegesis, that all of the things which are used to signify derive, from the very fact of their pointing to something else, a power which makes them appear no longer commensurable with profane things, which raises them onto a higher plane, and which can, indeed, sanctify them.

Hence the antinomy: "Considered in allegorical terms . . . the profane world is both elevated and devalued." The object fragmented and rescued from the abyss is rescued *as* hieroglyph, as rune, and is thus revivified as dead, empty, redeemed only as a meaningless image, in order to receive an assigned allegorical meaning. Image emblems pile up; they become material for allegorical construction, which seeks to make a coherent picture from them. This piling up of redeemed but now empty fragments shatters the mythic context of wholeness and completeness in which the fragments were initially presented. But so liberated, they become enigmatic and in this way point even more urgently to the crisis of meaning, the image world of natural history. The fragments become pieces of a mysterious puzzle waiting to be solved. The dogged intellectualism of the allegorical mind asserts itself in the fixity of the goal of knowledge, for the sake of which the fragments themselves are sacrificed:

> In the field of allegorical intuition the image is a fragment, a rune. Its beauty as a symbol evaporates when the light of divine learning falls upon it. The false appearance of totality is extinguished. For the *eidos* disappears, the simile ceases to exist, and the cosmos it contained shrivels up. The dry rebuses which remain contain an insight, which is still available to the *Grübler*.[26]

The *Grübler* (brooder), who will figure so prominently in Benjamin's transposition from seventeenth- to nineteenth-century melancholia, makes his second appearance in the *Ursprung des deutschen Trauer-*

spiels. (Earlier, in the exploration of melancholy in the baroque, Benjamin had referred to the "knowledge of the *Grübler*" that, in the image of Dürer's winged melancholy, merged with the "investigations of the scholar."[27]

Brooding is the image of melancholic *concentration* on "meaningless" fragments, upon pieces of a puzzle. The image of the brooder corresponds with what Holz referred to as the moment of fragmentation or *Verstückelung*, the moment of transition between the destructive devaluation of the world by melancholy and the constructive moment of the allegorical assignation of meaning. The brooder stands midway between the mournful vision of meaninglessness and the creation of allegorical, hence arbitrary meaning. As the propaedeutic to allegorical construction, then, brooding contains within it the schema of the transposition from melancholia as a moment of cognitive-emotive mediation between subject and object and allegory as the activity that springs from this moment. Brooding incorporates the incessant intellectualism of the melancholy mind; the brooder broods over fragments, discrete images that the brooder's own *Trauer* had liberated, however ambiguously, from the "given" world of appearances. This marks the extent to which the very activity of brooding marks a victory over myth.

Brooding itself presupposes that the "false appearance of totality" has been extinguished, that the beautiful illusion of symbolic beauty has petrified; indeed the whole *cosmos*, the mythic image of order, harmony, and correspondence, an interwoven unchanging network of natural forces and plans, has crumbled and blown away under the melancholy gaze. Brooding thus presupposes that, between subject and object, objects of brooding emerge that, thus liberated, appear both as debased and as exalted, as both humiliated and cherished, and contain within them "an insight." They point, however dimly, toward the occluded divinity within them, toward the redemption of the world in which their originary, lost order, like their true names, will be restored and the totality of the world of confused names and historical suffering will be apocalyptically destroyed. The fragments are pregnant with the objective memory of paradise, and this is their "truth," the trace of their originary meaning.

Such pointing toward redemption in the antinomical fragments, however, also indicates the redeemed sphere in which the divisive concept no longer "determines" the mode in which subject and object are related. All redemption points beyond the confines of the epistemic relation of subjectivity and nature. But the paradox of the brooder consists in the fact that the fragments which present themselves, which radiate faint anamnestic glimmers of originary meaning, become meaningful for the brooder only insofar as they constitute discrete elements of an enigmatic text or puzzle; that is, only insofar as they become private clues from which the brooder extracts *knowledge*. But what the fragments actually point toward is the promise of a relation with them in which they are no longer fragmentary; in which knowledge as possession, as subjective intention, has been transcended, and in which the speculative subject and objective nature are reconciled. The brooder wishes to have knowledge of the truth that lies beyond knowledge, and thus becomes enmired in the oldest paradox of philosophical speculation, the necessary and impossible project of producing conceptual knowledge of the ineffable.

This paradox has, in this case, at least two precipitates. It underlies the bottomless frustration that is captured in the word *Grübler*, that bears the connotation not just of brooding, but also of a grumble, a muttered lament. Even before the doomed constructive moment of allegory, the *Klagen* of natural *Trauer* introduced into human speech, the distinctive voice of the *Trauerspiel* is accompanied by its cognitive mode, grumbling. Second, the *Grübler* grubs, concentrates so closely on the earthly fragments that the more he contemplates, the more esoteric and arcane they become. The motion by which the brooder grubs deeper and deeper into the profaned fragment is the same motion—*Tiefsinn*—that carries the brooder farther and farther into the private recesses of inwardness. It is this simultaneous deepening of the intention toward the objects themselves and into subjective interiority that Benjamin sees as the source of the antinomy of the allegorical. Moreover, it is this contradiction that carries the discussion of the metaphysics of the allegory toward its theological denouement. Inwardness, the only ultimate home of the melancholic, is the secret stage in which the allegorical constructions are made, and in which the allegorist wins his ambiguous victories:

> If the object becomes allegorical under the gaze of the melancholic, if melancholia causes life to flow out of it and it remains behind dead, but eternally secure, then it is exposed to the

allegorist, it is unconditionally in his power. That is to say it is now quite incapable of emanating any meaning or significance on its own; such significance as it has it acquires from the allegorist. He places it within [this power], and stands behind [the object] not in a psychological but in an ontological sense. In his hands the object becomes something different and for him it becomes the key to the realm of hidden knowledge, and he reveres it as the emblem of this.[28]

This is the transformation of brooder to allegorist: the brooder is capable of recognizing, however dimly, that the fragments, which in one sense remain meaningless, also begin to radiate meaning. Incapable of reconstructing this meaning, tortured by its elusive glimmer, the brooder begins to fit them together arbitrarily. That is an allegory. In its very arbitrariness, the constructed allegory points toward the messianic meaning that is deferred in the very act of constructing it. This requires more allegories. Deferral becomes not a source of joyful abandonment to the infinite plenitude of writing, but a mournful subjection to the written, to the image of historical delay, the postponement of sensuous bliss that is encoded within it, to an ever-deepening concentration on the gap between meaning and image.

The brooder can be compared to someone addicted to jigsaw puzzles. The brooder's "conventional" image of reality has been shattered by melancholy. The landscape, so intimately familiar, known in every detail, suddenly looks inexplicably wrong; the individual elements that compose it now seem out of place, as though arranged by some unnatural force, and what had previously appeared as natural coherence now is an ensemble of unrelated and discrete pieces, dead ruins. The brooder recoils with horror from this image, but at the same time understands that the inability to oblige the elements of the appearance world to conform to their old, comfortable totality may correspond to a higher truth about the nature of things that had been concealed before: the world, as shattered and meaningless, is truer. Thus the omnipresence of death, of the meaninglessness of the creature, as the truth so conspicuous that it virtually blots out everything else.

This intuition has consequences not only in sadness, despair, and mounting isolation, but cognitively as well. The brooder concentrates on the fragments, not in order to restore their initial context, but because she recognizes that, removed from this context, they are transmuted from fragments to hieroglyphs, to puzzle pieces, bearing hints of color or shape that refer them to relations to other fragments, relations that she otherwise would never have thought possible. Deprived of all other faculties, she appeals to intellect alone to fit the pieces back together into their ur-old, originary image, whose model, no longer present, is dimly felt, is momentarily encapsulated in each individual fragment, in every instance of objective fit. And the brooder, now turned allegorist, begins to sift through the fragments, combining them into new configurations, dedicating every move to an image that is felt but nowhere seen.

The work begins to exhibit a certain attraction. The fear of arbitrariness haunts every move. How should the pieces go back together? How does the allegorist know if the "fit," by which meaning is imposed upon fragments, is an entirely arbitrary one, or one that even in its source in the subjective intention actually corresponds to the true image itself? By knowledge? But knowledge is nothing more than the medium in which the fragments exist as fragments, the medium of forgetting. By a careful "letting be" of the voices of the fragments themselves? The fragments are mute. The allegorist has raised them from their mute anonymity, but has done so only by rendering them elements of her own private knowledge, that is, as valueless, independent of her subjective assignation of meaning—she has, after all, betrayed them for the sake of knowledge, even if she reveres them, and is enthralled by them, and becomes enslaved to them. No option remains open but to press on. The puzzle work continues; fragments begin to overlap, and half-finished or twice-finished connections between fragment and fragment, word and image, concept and phenomenon begin to pile up. The more tentative solutions the puzzler makes, the more frustrating, the more in need of work the puzzle becomes. The number of pieces of the puzzle does not remain fixed, but increases with every move.

The late writer Georges Perec captured beautifully the hidden theological moment of the jigsaw puzzle: "To begin with," he wrote,

> the art of jigsaw puzzles seems of little substance, easily exhausted, wholly dealt with by a basic introduction to Gestalt: the perceived object [the individual puzzle piece] . . . is not a sum of

elements to be distinguished from each other and analyzed dis-
cretely, but a pattern, that is to say a form, a structure: the
element's existence does not precede the existence of the whole,
it comes neither before nor after it, for the parts do not determine
the pattern, but the pattern determines the parts: knowledge of
the pattern and of its laws, of the set and its structure, could not
possibly be derived from discrete knowledge of the elements that
compose it. . . . The pieces are readable, take on a sense, only
when assembled; in isolation, a puzzle piece means nothing—
just an impossible question, an opaque challenge.[29]

This captures fairly well the paradoxical dimension of allegory. The
devalued fragment is devalued precisely insofar as it is elevated as a
part of a higher, originary image of unity; but the act of liberation
itself—and the melancholy from which it arises—are themselves
nothing other than the mournful expressions of fallen nature and sinful
subjectivity, of the forgetfulness of the originary pattern by which alone
the piece could be rendered meaningful. The "readability" of the
piece, like the end of historical time, is deferred. Perec, however,
understands that the very nature of this predicament is theological,
that in posing it, the "opaque challenge" of puzzling answers itself:

One can make a deduction which is quite certainly the ultimate
truth of jigsaw puzzles: despite appearances, puzzling is not a
solitary game: every move the puzzler makes, the puzzle-maker
has made before; every piece the puzzler picks up, and picks up
again, and studies and strokes, every combination he tries, and
tries a second time, every blunder and insight, each hope and
each discouragement have all been designed, calculated, and decided by the other.[30]

A theodicy of jigsaw puzzles—the insight that the innermost heart of
the allegorical predicament is permeated with a messianic energy. The
puzzle solver is never alone. At its most arbitrary, that is, at its most
unsuccessful, the obsessively repetitive attempt to assign meanings to
fragments bears within it a hidden, and thus all the more powerful,
indication of the nearness—the absence—of God.

Baroque allegory, in the form of the *Trauerspiel*, was not able to
realize this nearness, was not able to embrace the complex theology of

backwards hope and visionary memory by which this dialectical theology could embrace and cherish the reviled fragment while also reading it as a cipher of God's nearness. By the same token, this failure makes the theology of the ruined *Trauerspiel* all the more rich for the critic. For the baroque, burdened as it was with the medieval and Renaissance legacies of religious, moral, and scientific interpretation, the repetitive concentration upon liberated, devalued, allegorized, and discarded fragments comes back again and again to the primacy of the written and the schema of the sacred text, and thus the older preference for reading nature itself as a book of moral and religious instruction. The allegorist becomes the source of meaning, but this power is also a defeat, since the allegorist's allegories are dedicated not to the creation of meaning, but to its recovery. And the more allegories the allegorist dedicates to this goal, the more the network of allegorical references multiplies and intertwines, the more distant this goal becomes, the more urgently the allegorist works, and the deeper the allegorist plunges into the well of subjectivity. Just as the tyrant heaps the corpses ever higher, so the allegorist dedicates allegories to allegories, and the midden of dead knowledge grows ever higher. This process is related to the desperation that underlies the garrulousness and ostentation of the *Trauerspiel*. The antinomy of the allegorical, set in productive motion, becomes a *Teufelskreis*, a devil's circle. This circle inscribes within it the same insight that Benjamin had suggested in the language essay: the ultimate identity of subjective knowledge and evil.

The allegory, Benjamin reminds us, was "sown by Christianity." Its historical roots are the adoption of the Renaissance project of exegetical, contemplative interpretations of the image archive of antiquity, wedded with the medieval doctrines of the sinfulness of matter and the transmutation of natural existence into texts of human guilt. Guilt, which in its purely mythic, antique phase is conjoined most clearly with the schema of the fated individual, is reexpressed by the baroque allegory as the human correlate to the transience of nature. This establishes the person as the conjunction of guilt and transience; the person as guilty nature, as flesh. Thus the central allegory for the baroque is the corpse. The corpse is the only fitting allegory of death, the moment of intersection of guilt and transience. Death is the price paid by the guilty; transience secures the universality of death. "And the characters of the *Trauerspielen* die, because it is only thus, as corpses, that they can enter into the homeland of allegory. It is not for the sake of immortality that they meet their end, but for the sake of the corpse."[31] This is the central pattern according to which the "deep horror" of death is rendered into a creative impulse.

The corpse "stands for" death. For all the complexity of the allegorical, its productivity reduces, in the baroque, to this Ur-allegory, a formula stylized to the point of ritual, as though the wealth of puzzle fragments, emblems, and hieroglyphs conjured up by the brooding melancholic, by their very plenitude and by the very repetition of the assignation of meaning upon them revert back to their basic matter. The guilty creature, the dead body, lie at the bottom of the allegorical descent. The corpse is the way that baroque melancholy was able to depict the dialectic between subject and its objects. The subject becomes an object, becomes a body.

The image of the corpse compresses the dialectical extravagances of the baroque allegory into a single image, and this image, stripped of its overthought, overwritten, overinterpreted accoutrements, which contained it but concealed it, now stands as an extreme, as *origin*.[32] In it, the historical genesis of the allegorical imagination characteristic of the baroque is burned away, and the critic is left with the face-to-face between subject and object, which, as Benjamin had already decided in 1916, was nothing less than the theological situation of the world. "The allegorically significant is prevented by guilt from finding fulfillment of its meaning in itself. Guilt is not confined to the allegorical observer, who betrays the world for the sake of knowledge, but it also attaches to the object of his contemplation." The corpse is death: the allegorical meaning, arbitrarily imposed by the "observer," can only at this last point, at its most arbitrary, lose its arbitrariness, because the infinity of possible permutations of meaning conjured up by the mind of the allegorist are exhausted. Only at that point do the guilty body, presented to the allegorical imagination by a millennium of confused images, and the guilt of nature, consigned to history, meet in such a way that the "allegorical" dimension of allegory reveals its theology, hidden to the baroque dramatists themselves, revealed only by and for the critic. If much of this theology is now familiar to us, with our public access to Benjamin's private thought, the melancholic completion of it can only be accomplished at the extreme of allegory, where the image of the corpse springs forth as the origin, as the "eddy in the stream of becoming" in which the continuum of mournful, fallen nature is crystallized:

> Because it is mute, fallen nature mourns. But the converse of this statement leads even deeper into the essence of nature: its mournfulness makes it become mute. In all mourning there is a tendency to silence, and this is infinitely more than inability or reluctance to communicate. The mournful has the feeling that it is known comprehensively by the unknowable. To be named—even if the name-giver is godlike and saintly—perhaps always brings with it a presentiment of mourning. But how much more so not to be named, only to be read, to be read uncertainly by the allegorist, and to have become highly significant thanks only to him.[33]

If the critical insight can, in the image of the baroque corpse, already see a gesture that points beyond the sphere of the creaturely toward the realm in which all matter by its materiality itself contains an image of redemption, the allegory of the baroque, which is obtuse to itself, must complete a few more dialectical reversals before the theology of the corpse reveals itself. The mind of the allegorist is not alone. But at this stage, it is not yet the presence of God but of Satan, embodied in the image of the corpse as evil matter, that accompanies it. "Knowledge, not action, is the most characteristic mode of existence of evil." The evil of fallen nature is the objective mirror image of the evil latent in the very existence of private knowledge. The characters of the *Trauerspiel* are possessed by evil; they are sinful. The allegorical mode of expression, in its tangled web of antique, medieval, and contemporary images and meanings, finds its natural movement in the assignation of sinful qualities to concrete images. Absolute gnosis, pure spirituality—that is Satan, whose fall transforms this spiritual realm into the realm of the perfect, that is, godless materiality. "The purely material and this absolute spiritual are poles of the satanic realm; and the consciousness is their illusory synthesis, in which the genuine synthesis, that of life, is imitated. However, the speculation of consciousness, which clings to the object-world of emblems, ultimately, in its remoteness from life, discovers the knowledge of the demons."[34]

The immediacy of the decayed corpse, the distance from life, the knowledge of the demons—it seems that the phenomenology of the melancholy mind has, despite its dialectical potential, led back to myth. But knowledge of demons is already something quite different than subjection to them; the "false" dialectic between the material and the spiritual, the melancholy "consciousness" belonging to the allegorist, is nevertheless dialectic and is therefore not stable. Mythic subjection, on the other hand, is characterized above all by its changelessness. The end of the phenomenology of melancholia is charged with a transformative power. "In the form of knowledge, instinct leads down the empty abyss of evil in order to assure itself of infinity. But it is also the bottomless pit of *Tiefsinn*. Its data are not capable of being incorporated in philosophical constellations. They are therefore to be found in the emblem-books of the baroque as the stock requisites of gloomy spectacle."[35]

For the baroque, knowledge as the conceptual grasp of the antithetical relation between being and appearance led back again and again to the creaturely immanence of objective nature. This dialectic leads ever downward. Here, however, comes the truly unexpected, the remarkable move in Benjamin's presentation. Having depicted the phenomenology of the melancholy mind in its dialectic with fallen nature to the very nadir—of the sheer presence of the corpse-image, of absolute subjectivity, of absolute meaninglessness, of evil—Benjamin now reveals a breathtaking reversal, a shattering synthesis:

> As those who lose their footing turn somersaults in their fall, so would the allegorical intention fall from emblem to emblem down to the dizziness of its bottomless depths, were it not that, even in the most extreme of them, it had so to turn about that all its darkness, vainglory and godlessness seems to be nothing but self-delusion. For it is to misunderstand the allegorical entirely if we make a distinction between the store of images, in which this about-turn into salvation and redemption takes place, and that grim store which signifies death and damnation. For it is precisely visions of the frenzy of destruction in which all earthly things collapse into a heap of ruins, which reveal the limit set upon allegorical contemplation, rather than its Ideal.

This theological reversal means that the allegorical intention bears within it, for the baroque, a structural limit: insofar as the allegorical is able (or forced) to descend to a certain absolute point, it undergoes a transformation in which the very images themselves are reallegorized: the corpse, as the image of the absolute materiality of the subject, of absolute death, springs under the weight of this matter into its other, and becomes itself the image—of Christ's dead body—in which the promise of eternal life is encoded:

> The bleak confusion of Golgotha, which can be recognized as the schema underlying the allegorical figures in hundreds of the engravings and descriptions of the period, is not just an image of the desolation of human existence. In it transitoriness is not signified or allegorically represented, so much as, in its own significance, displayed as allegory. As the allegory of resurrection. Ultimately in the death-signs of the baroque the direction of allegorical reflection is reversed; on the second part of its wide arc it returns, to redeem.[36]

The allegory, dialectic like the melancholia from which it arises and through which it moves, therefore reaches an extreme formulation, and in doing so negates itself, freezes into image, transmutes itself into its other.[37] "In God's world the allegorist awakens"; the allegories become allegories for the experience of the allegorical, and thereby transmute themselves into their theological antitheses. The death's head becomes the angel's countenance and, observes Benjamin, "this solves the encoded riddle [*Chiffre*] of the most fragmented, the most defunct, the most dispersed":

> Allegory, of course, thereby loses everything that was most peculiar to it: the secret privileged knowledge, the arbitrary rule in the realm of dead objects, the supposed infinity of a world without hope. All this vanishes with this *one* about-turn, in which the immersion of allegory has to clear away the final phantasmagoria of the objective, and, left entirely to its own devices, rediscovers itself, not playfully in the earthly world of things, but seriously under the eyes of heaven. And this is the essence of melancholy immersion: that its ultimate objects, in which it believes it can most fully secure for itself the depraved [*Verworfen*], turn into allegories, and that these allegories fill out and deny the void in which they are represented, just as, ultimately, the intention does not faithfully rest in the gaze at bones, but leaps faithlessly to the Resurrection.[38]

This is the third and final unconcealed statement of the essence of melancholia in the *Ursprung des deutschen Trauerspiels*. It must be read in the context of the metaphysics of *Trauer* at the opening of the treatment of baroque melancholy, and the insight into the "faithless" intellectual intention of the melancholy mind at the conclusion of that section. The *Teufelskreis* of melancholia ceases only at the point that the most depraved—or the most despised, ridiculed, and scorned thoughts and creations—are recovered and cherished by the mind desperate in the face of the empty universe, so that they become ciphers of secret knowledge so mysterious that they drive the melancholy mind to its ultimate face-to-face with its own innermost self, there to discover the image of absolute evil and thence only to discover that absolute evil was nothing other than distance from God, than delusion, than subjectivity itself. Mournful nature and melancholy subjectivity, whose dialectical tension had fueled the phenomenology of melancholia from the beginning, suddenly lose their difference: the allegorist thus loses the wealth of "ruins" churned up by speculation and is left alone with God. Melancholy, at least in this version of the story, ends in faith. Faith, the kind of faith that recognizes the paradoxical nearness of God and the dissolution of the range of existential questions that the perception of God's absence had made possible, renders the destructive-redemptive relation between melancholy and the objects null and void. The latter lose their structure of meaningful-meaningless ciphers, lose their capacity to exhibit, through *Tiefsinn*, their index of redemption. They become a catalog of God's creation and are therefore good—and unnameable.

For a melancholy dialectics, this final face-to-face of subject and object leads not so much to a higher sublated spirit, but to a theological caesura, a cessation of happening.

> Allegory goes away empty-handed. Evil as such, which it cherished as enduring profundity, exists only in allegory, is nothing other than allegory, means something other than what it is. That is, it means precisely the non-being of that which it represents. The absolute vices, as exemplified by tyrants and intriguers, are allegories. They are not real, and that which they consist of they have only from the subjective view of melancholy; they are this view, which is destroyed by its own offspring, while they mean

only its blindness. They point to the absolutely subjective *Tief-sinn*, to which alone they owe their existence. By its allegorical form evil as such reveals itself to be a subjective phenomenon. . . . Knowledge of evil therefore has no object. There is no evil in the world. It arises in man himself, with the desire for knowledge, or rather for judgment. Knowledge of good, as knowledge, is secondary. It ensues from *praxis*. Knowledge of evil—as knowledge this is primary. It ensues from contemplation.[39]

It takes a bold excursion into Judeo-Christian theodicy to reveal the essential truth about melancholia: it is nothing other than hypertrophied subjectivity. On theological terms alone, that is, on the premise of the withdrawal of God's active, forming presence in the created world and therefore the utopian longing for the destructive-redemptive power of the awaited Messiah, the inner identity emerges among melancholia, knowledge, subjectivity, evil, passivity. They are all the human modes of expressing God's absence. As such an expression, of course, melancholia also bears in its deepest recesses its messianic dimension, for the awareness of the absence of God is only possible through the more fundamental conviction of a real, if lost or hidden, realm of divine meaning. Melancholia as (dialectically) both hypertrophied subjectivity and messianic consciousness: this touches upon one of the deepest and strongest impulses in the messianic tradition in Judaism, the vision of the *Tikkun*, which restores the originary flaw, ends the metaphysical *Galut*, and reveals that in the end, all creation was God's creation, all evil was deviation from God's mind.[40]

The existence of evil is, literally, meaningless. This brings us closer to the significance of Benjamin's discussion. In the *Ethic of Pure Will*, Hermann Cohen wrote, "Evil is nonexistent. It is nothing but a concept derived from the concept of freedom. A power of evil exists only in myth."[41] Evil is mythic by its very nature. Myth is, in its essence, mendacious. It is *Schein*. At the heart of myth, its various components—demons, the subject, knowledge, evil—become indistinguishable as elements of the self-deception of humanity, the forgetfulness of divine nature. This insight corresponds precisely with the theology of criticism and the dialectic of myth and antimyth that Benjamin had developed in the 1916 essay on language.

The language essay, it was argued, works toward a general theory of the status of divine significance within the medium of fallen languages, and in this way the notion of *Trauer* became identical with the objectivity of nature itself, constituted linguistically by the arbitrary "knowledge" of fallen subjectivity, captured in the Kierkegaardian notion of "chatter." The sketchy and broad theology of fallen language and mute nature developed in the language essay is supplemented, in the *Ursprung* study, by the argument that melancholy allegory is the mode in which fallen nature and fallen subjects come into dialectical contact, in which they mediate and produce one another, and in which they enter into a phenomenological development. In this sense, the turn to the baroque artwork has been nothing more than a historical vehicle, a mass of phenomenal elements, through which this phenomenology could be represented. At the end of it, we have reached not absolute spirit but absolute subjectivity, absolute knowledge of evil. And knowledge of evil, as knowledge of that which does not exist, is precisely what Benjamin meant by Kierkegaardian chatter in the 1916 essay.

"Knowledge" after the Fall and the fragmentation of the originary unity of God, humanity, and nature could only be knowledge as fragmentation, a knowledge from which subject and object, good and evil, and the diremptions that structure linguistic experience arise:

> This knowledge, the triumph of subjectivity and the onset of an arbitrary rule over things, is the origin of all allegorical contemplation. In the very fall of man the unity of guilt and signifying emerges as an abstraction. The allegorical has its existence in abstractions; as an abstraction, as a faculty of the spirit of language itself, it is at home in the Fall. For good and evil are unnameable, they are nameless entities, outside of the language of names, in which man, in paradise, named things, and which he forsakes in the abyss of that problem.[42]

Once subjectivity grasps objects as mournful constructs and its knowledge of them as moments of its own subjectivity, then subjectivity itself, in its moment of absolute dialectical fixity between the supremely spiritual and the supremely material, is overcome. Melancholia, at the bottom of its descent, transforms itself from absolute subjectivity to the selflessness of absolute faith. Once again, subjectivity stands for the whole breadth of experience of the world as godforsaken and meaningless; the end of melancholia in faith is the self-extinction of the mournful subject, and this means that the allegories, creations of the subject, deconstruct themselves into ciphers of God's presence.

The corpse, or rather the baroque image of the corpse, is still the "origin" of the German *Trauerspiel*, according to the specific terminology laid out in the *Vorrede*. But this claim is only revealed in its fullness now, insofar as the dialectical image of the corpse, exploded by critical intervention, releases the idea of the *Trauerspiel* from within its monadic interior with a terrific divine force: the corpse as hope in eternal life and the image of absolute meaninglessness as the hope in the return of the divine order of God's creation. The complex of melancholy ends by the utterly simple representation of its inner heart: messianic anticipation.

But this end of the story is not entirely the happy ending that one might take it to be. This miraculous self-annihilation of the subject is dubious on two accounts. It represents, it is true, the extreme limit of baroque melancholy. But in the moment of faith, the faithless betrayal of the objects emerges as the price that the brooding subject must pay in order to escape from the devil's circle of melancholy allegory. This is the theological answer of which the baroque was capable: the puzzle motif ends when the puzzler, just at the moment when the "solution" becomes revealed as both necessary and impossible, transmutes the puzzle itself as a sign of its own opposite—walks away from the puzzle altogether. Subjectivity, it is true, is thereby emptied of its entwinement with things, with its ensnarement in *Tiefsinn*, of contemplation and knowledge. It becomes ethereal and empty, a gossamer spiritual instant of God's self-recognition. There is something as *unheimlich* about this vision as there is in the vision of the bottomless *Tiefsinn* of the melancholic. The "miraculous" conclusion of the *Ursprung des deutschen Trauerspiels* cannot be read unambiguously, either as a depiction of the motion of thought toward an encounter with the divine or as a historically naive rejection of this particular baroque theology as "merely" betrayal of the objects, of flight into a Christian conception of selflessness. Rather, the truth lies somewhere in the territory between these alternatives.

Critical receptions of the conclusion to the *Ursprung des deutschen*

Trauerspiels have, typically, opted to stay far closer to the second of these interpretive alternatives. They assume that Benjamin connects the Christian vision of selfless, transcendent faith with the schema of absolute subjectivity, arguing that the eradication of the melancholy subject is nothing other than a facile invocation of subjectivity in another guise, by which the truly messianic encounter with the objects is betrayed. This leads to the conclusion that Benjamin himself is unambiguously critical of the form of faith evoked in the book's last lines; that he recognizes in this baroque flight into abstract spirituality a recapitulation of the idealist betrayal of the realm of the concrete.[43]

This observation is most clearly indicated by Susan Buck-Morss. For Buck-Morss, Benjamin's depiction of the theological resolution to the antinomies of baroque allegory contain "unmistakable clues to Benjamin's own position, which must be read not as an affirmation but as a fundamental critique, one which had political as well as philosophical implications." These political implications consist in Benjamin's understanding of faith as desertion of the objective, in the conviction of the transitoriness and therefore the ultimate irrelevance of the spectacle of world history. Political action, as we have seen, thus becomes inherently, and not just circumstantially, meaningless. For Buck-Morss, the transfiguration of melancholy to faith merely completes this abandonment of the world: like philosophical idealism, allegory "follows necessarily from the melancholic's politics of contemplation rather than intervention" and thus "takes refuge in the spirit."[44]

As in the Goethe essay, active intervention in this world is postponed, transformed into a hope in the hereafter that is intimately linked with political quietism and resignation. As Buck-Morss argues,

> Evil disappears, but at what cost! In order to remain true to God, the German allegoricists abandon both nature and politics. . . . When the allegorists, claiming that the fragments of failed nature are really an allegory of spiritual redemption as their opposite, a redemption guaranteed only by the Word, when they declare evil as "self-delusion" and material nature as "not real", then for all practical purposes allegory becomes indistinguishable from myth. Benjamin criticizes the attempt to get away from the arbitrary subjectivity of allegory, as itself pure subjectivity.

In other words, "Benjamin criticizes Baroque allegory for its idealism."[45] This criticism bears many important implications for our purposes: as promised, Buck-Morss argues forcefully that the conclusion
of the *Trauerspiel* study contains an encoded political critique. In the
structure and development of baroque allegory, we can decipher a
condemnation of the political resignation and apathy, the mournful
withdrawal from decisiveness and political engagement, that marks the
center of Benjamin's ethical-political conviction. Knowledge, indelibly linked with subjectivity, is hostile to *praxis;* conversely, a mode of
metasubjective cognition adequate to the true theological situation
must be developed, in order for a critical *praxis* of decisive intervention
to exercise its redemptive power within contemporary society. This
metasubjective cognitive faculty is sketched in broad doctrinal strokes
in the *Vorrede.*

But while the political implications of this formulation may emerge
clearly, they are rendered murky once again by the far more complex
philosophical implications, and on this subject Buck-Morss is far less
persuasive. While it is true that the end of the *Trauerspiel* study
contains an implicit philosophical critique of hypersubjectivity, and
that this links the end of the book and the *Vorrede,* the relationship
between the critical act and the object and form of critique is far from
tidy. The *Trauerspiel* study, after all, *begins* with a rigorous, magisterial
invocation of a divine, postsubjective doctrine of ideas. It then proceeds with a critical method that, in its fragmentation of the material,
its brooding contemplation upon the liberated fragments, and its construction of constellations of new meaning from them is precisely
parallel to the allegorical method that is its chief critical object.
Benjamin's constructions, unlike those of the allegorists, are ones in
which the idea graphically emerges in an interruptive, uninterpreted
flash of recognition, unknown to the slow and dogged overinterpreta-
tions of the baroque. Benjamin proceeds by inspiration, by beholding;
the baroque remains in the sorrowful, plodding continuum of contemplation, from which it only emerges by betraying the world, and
thus, in faith, falling back into myth.

The problem with this is that the absolutely crucial distinction
between critical act and critical object, between the messianic objectivity of Benjamin's (correctly) constructed constellations and the per-
niciously arbitrary, subjective constructions of the baroque, is secured

by nothing more than the theoretical guarantees offered in the *Vorrede* that this distinction does and must exist. Apart from these theoretical guarantees, Benjamin has little to offer as evidence that his critique of allegory is itself not arbitrary, not itself a product of *Grübelei*.

The philosophical problem that emerges here is, once again, that of subjectivity itself. The *Trauerspiel* study, like the essays of 1916 and the *Programm* essay, declares a transcendence of subjectivity, only to discover that the messianic insights to which it is most powerfully drawn emerge only in the minute examination of hypertrophied subjectivity itself. Thus the suspicion is always present that the critical texts themselves are melancholy; that they constitute moments of melancholy writing in which melancholy comes to an expressive realization of its own nature, discovers enigmatic clues of transcendence in the depths of subjective contemplation itself, and interprets these clues according to the theological convictions and stock of concrete images made historically available to it.

If the problem is one of subjectivity, then we return, in a different form, to the same question: On what basis is Benjamin's criticism not itself an expression of melancholy subjectivity? On what basis does it claim "objective validity"? As stated at the opening of this chapter, the claim that Benjamin "is" a melancholic, like the claim that the *Trauerspiel* study "is" allegorical, is an inadequate formulation insofar as it ignores the dialectic inherent in the idea of melancholy itself. Moreover, any claim to resolve the matter of the "objectivity" or the nonarbitrariness of Benjamin's criticism must ultimately concern itself with not only the theological ground of criticism itself but also more centrally with the specific role of melancholia in the way that criticism relates itself to this theological ground. Now, Benjamin's own development of the theory of melancholy allegory has come a good distance in responding to these issues. We have seen, for instance, that the theology from which allegory arises is the same theology that had underwritten Benjamin's own first formulations of the nature and tasks of criticism, and we have observed that, for this reason, the melancholy specific to the baroque dramatists and the universal and transhistorical *Trauer* of fallen nature itself converge, interfuse, and transform themselves in the image moment of the corpse, the origin that is capable of monadically crystallizing the nature of history, both in its utter fallenness and in its gesture toward its own redemptive end. We have also

seen that this phenomenology of melancholia results in absolute subjectivity and that this absolute subjectivity undoes itself, springs
dialectically open, dissolves its relation with its phenomenal objects,
and its transmuted into absolute faith.

This recapitulation of findings is important in articulating a response to Buck-Morss's claim, which consists in essence of the fact
that melancholy dissolves into idealism and that this philosophical fact
underlies the political impoverishment of the melancholy syndrome.
The problem with this claim, we can now see, is that we are dealing
here with idealism of a very particular sort. In indicting the baroque
melancholic's traitorous flight into the interiority of faith as "idealistic"
here, and by ascribing this indictment to Benjamin, Buck-Morss is
implicitly reading the conclusion of the *Ursprung des deutschen Trauerspiels* through its subsequent interpretation by Adorno. Specifically,
the kind of idealism in question here is that best typified by Kierkegaard, most often described as the most caustic and persuasive critic
of German, particular Hegelian idealism. The claim, which Adorno
made in his study of Kierkegaard, is that Kierkegaard's own phenomenology of melancholy, his flight to abstract inwardness, actually recapitulates the same idealist betrayal of the concrete objective reality
that he criticizes in Hegel.

In a moment, I will return to Adorno's analysis of Kierkegaard. First,
however, it is important to frame the question clearly. Just what position Benjamin himself is taking at the "miraculous" conclusion to the
Ursprung des deutschen Trauerspiels has a great deal—perhaps everything—to do with how he saw the relation between the story of melancholy that is critically represented in the work and the kind of critical
subjectivity that is necessary in order to tell this story. If Buck-Morss is
correct, the baroque *overcoming* of melancholy is in fact to be dismissed not only as a betrayal of the redemptive moment inherent in
melancholy allegory, but also in itself as a contradiction and a failure,
insofar as it merely reintroduces the hypertrophied, passive subject in
a new form. This would tell us that Benjamin saw the relation between
critical subject and object of criticism not in terms of melancholy
allegory, but rather as a relation in which parallels of method, of
theological attitude may have existed, but did not thereby fundamentally imperil the possibility of redemptive criticism itself. If, however,
Benjamin's own attitude toward the self-dissolution of baroque melan-

choly is more complex, more troubled, and more ambiguous, this may indicate that the problem that was *represented* by the critic is also a problem *for* the possibility of critical representation itself.

For Benjamin, melancholy hypersubjectivity is indeed the chief philosophical-political problem. Theoretically, the challenge in the formulation of a critical methodology is how the messianic insights that open up to the melancholy mind by virtue of its dialectical relationship with the object can be preserved, distilled, and rendered theoretically secure, while at the same time overcoming the mournful subjectivity, political paralysis, and contemplative fixity in which these insights are contained. Overcoming melancholia without losing the redemptive relation to the thing: that is Benjamin's real interest. Baroque allegory points toward an overcoming of melancholia, but a traitorous one. In the movement in which absolute subjectivity negates itself in its objectless encounter with God, we find the image of an idealism of a particular kind. Turning to Adorno's critique of Kierkegaard, we may be able to untangle some of the issues arising from the conclusion of the *Trauerspiel* book and the possible significance of this for Benjamin's criticism.

Adorno's study of Kierkegaard, published in 1933, was composed in 1929–1930, while Adorno was under the most direct influence of Benjamin's theory of baroque allegory. Adorno was fresh from his Königstein talks with Benjamin, in which Benjamin was already attempting to think through the projected transformation of the theological criticism of the *Trauerspiel* study into a materialist, politically relevant program. (Adorno had offered his seminar on the *Ursprung des deutschen Trauerspiels* in Frankfurt in 1932.) His study of Kierkegaard, arguably Adorno's most successful sustained critical work, thus can be seen as functioning on two simultaneous levels: as the creative transposition of Benjamin's methodology from seventeenth- to nineteenth-century literary material, and also as an obliquely critical encounter with Benjamin's project.

The Construction of the Aesthetic seeks to represent critically the modalities by which the melancholia characteristic of Kierkegaard's specific historical experience expresses itself. This implies that Adorno took a great interest in the ability of melancholia to contain in encoded or occluded form ciphers of redemptive relationships with nature while at the same time remaining obtuse to itself, embedded within the

concrete set of experiences and images belonging to a specific historical epoch. Thus Adorno's analysis of melancholy, self-consciously
recapitulating Benjamin's, bears a crucial connection with Benjamin's in its critical intent: passages removed from Kierkegaard's own
works are constructed into constellations of tension between isolated
fragment and conceptual context. Recovered textual fragments, cited
against themselves, reveal the truth content dwelling within Kierkegaard's own text, a truth content that becomes legible only when
referred to the mediated social totality in which the text is embedded.
In this way, Kierkegaard's supposed liquidation of Hegelian idealism,
by shunning any vital, mediated relationship with the realm of the
objective and plunging itself ever deeper into subjective inwardness, in
effect recapitulates the very idealism it set out to overcome, falling into
an objectively false, mythical realm in which external reality is merely
a shadowy reflection of inner emotional states, where historical processes are vague and ultimately unreal reflections of the inward path of
the soul in its search for meaning.

Thus Kierkegaard's dialectic of *Tiefsinn* leads, like that of the
baroque allegorists, to a potentially endless freefall, an infinite reflection of reflection in which the world, both as objective reality and as the
subject's own corporeal existence, own body, becomes a mere stage on
the path of inwardness. Like the baroque poets too, this endless
freefall is arrested only at the moment where inwardness transmutes
itself into its other; that is, where the intensity of subjective reflection
becomes itself the moment of Kierkegaard's leap of faith. Subjectivity
itself is transfigured into a reflection of God's grace—but only, as
Buck-Morss has pointed out, by the sacrifice of the subject itself, by its
loss of its own corporeal and historical particularity, as well as its
critical consciousness and its autonomy and freedom.[46]

For Adorno, then, the critical project of a reading of Kierkegaard
involved the representation of the contradictory and ultimately paradoxical implications of Kierkegaard's attempted overcoming of idealism and the revelation of the concrete social conditions by which these
paradoxes became legible. And it is in this way that Kierkegaard's
melancholia assumes a central role in Adorno's study. On examination
of the true relation of Kierkegaard's texts to their social context, his
melancholia emerges in its own dialectic. It is at once the spiritual
affliction arising from an objectively false inwardness and the mediat-

ing moment between subject and object, which, while misunderstood by the subject, becomes rescuable by critical intervention, laden with utopian energy. Like baroque dramatists, Kierkegaard's melancholy arises from the creative production of images of meaningless or dead nature, conjured up from the depths of alienated subjectivity in its desperate attempts to fill up and deny the abyssal vision of a meaningless existence. Like the baroque too, in these images can be read a phenomenological text of the specific historical circumstances in which a melancholy text is generated, a text riddled with clues into the truth behind these historical circumstances themselves. Kierkegaard's melancholy inwardness thus becomes the truest expression of the phenomenology of the bourgeois *intérieur,* as well as the dialectical moment in which this phenomenology is referred to the idea of reconciliation:

> Kierkegaard's spiritualism is above all enmity toward nature. Spirit posits itself as free and autonomous in opposition to nature because it considers nature demonic as much in external reality as in itself. In that, however, autonomous spirit appears corporeally, nature takes possession of it where it occurs most historically: in objectless interiority. Spirit's natural content must be investigated if in Kierkegaard the being of subjectivity itself is to be explicated. The natural content of mere spirit, "historical" in itself, may be called mythical.[47]

Kierkegaard's spirituality, in its mournful fixity, thus renders the relation between subjective intention and nature into a productive dialectic. Not despite but through its dogged insistence on the lack of any real, concrete relationships with its objects, it places itself in an antagonistic relationship to them and thereby generates dialectical images of natural-historical objects themselves.

> For it is not as the continually living and present that nature prevails in the dialectic. Dialectic comes to a stop in the image and cites the mythical in the historically most recent as the distant past: nature as proto-history. For this reason the images, which like those of the *intérieur* bring dialectic and myth to the point of indifferentiation, are truly "antediluvian fossils."

This dialectic, too, is the fixed, petrified moment between absolute subjective inwardness and nature: "In the captivity of total immanence mythical ambiguous nature is divided since it does not endure inertly, but moves dialectically, and in its movement takes hold of nature in the depths from which it originates in order to pull it up to safety. . . . Kierkegaard's psychology of emotions portrays this movement as that of melancholy." In a manner virtually indistinguishable from the theory of baroque melancholy, Adorno depicts Kierkegaard's melancholy as the quintessential moment of dialectical possibility between subject and object. Dialectically pregnant, it points toward its own theology: "Just as in the *intérieur* the historical image presents itself as mythical, here mere nature—the melancholic temperament—presents itself as historical. Therefore it presents itself as dialectical and as the 'possibility' of reconciliation."[48]

The scare quotes that designate "possibility" as an ironic category should not conceal the genuine theological content in the melancholy dialectic, however. Indeed it is the theology of melancholy that is Adorno's chief concern, although he recognizes that this content cannot be "defined" or confronted directly. This content, rather, is to become perceptible only in the exploration of the historical nature of the idea of melancholy itself, through the strength of the construction alone.

For this construction, then, the historical relationship between baroque and Kierkegaardian modes of subjectivity is crucial. Not only by virtue of Adorno's theoretical adoption of the mode of reflection of the *Trauerspiel*, but also by virtue of objective, historically perceptible thematic regularities, there is a remarkable coincidence between baroque and Kierkegaardian melancholy. As Adorno points out, without any apparent knowledge of the *Trauerspiel* Kierkegaard seems to have intuitively recapitulated its central themes and concepts, as well as the allegorical thinking that generates it.[49]

The bourgeois *intérieur*, like the dramatic stage-court of the *Trauerspiel*, becomes the arena for the spectacle of allegorized nature. The baroque's fixation on the wealth of allegorical objects, generated by the mortification of the physical, which it understood and misunderstood as exercises in Christian virtues, is replicated in the profusion of reified articles that cram the *intérieur* to overflowing. In this sense, Kierkegaard constitutes another, related phenomenology, another set of origins generated by the same theology. The historical dimension of melancholia is thus precisely the index by which its allegorical products are referred back to the Ur-old text of alienation and redemption.

The correspondence between baroque and Kierkegaardian melancholy is thus no historical accident:

> If [Kierkegaard's] philosophy, unintentionally and without any substantial knowledge of the appropriate literature, produces not only allegorical forms of meaning but allegorical material contents right down to the choice of personal names, then this may demonstrate that fundamental connections between historically emerging philosophies are not established by "mental structures" and categories, but by pragmatic elements that serve prototypically as the fundament of the conceptual expressions and once again burst forth as soon as the objective constellation of the thought draws them near, whether or not the thought corresponds to the philosophical intention.[50]

While not a model of simplicity, this statement is central in identifying the basic theoretical agreement Adorno exhibits with Benjamin. It could be read, line for line, as an affirmation of the hermetic doctrine of the "motorial reaction" between empirical subjects and their a priori objects, the historical phenomenology of the *typus melancolicus*.

Melancholy philosophies or aesthetic expressions are ones whose historical specificities emerge in their fullness only when they are understood as phenomenologically distinct expressions of *Trauer;* that is, each historical instantiation wins its phenomenological concreteness, its specific set of originary images, by a dialectical collision of the archive of image contents made available by socioeconomic and cultural circumstances, (as content) with the motions of a "motorial reaction" of the subject, in which a certain finite set of "a priori objects"—meaningless nature—constitutes a form. Those particular concretions of form and content that yield "origins" will vary according to the historical register, and criticism of such texts consists in finding and representing such origins (the corpse, the *intérieur*).

According to this historiography, if melancholy is the "ailment of the age" for Kierkegaard just as much as for the baroque dramatists, then this is because "inwardness becomes melancholic through the specific struggle with historical *realien*." "In the reified world itself," Adorno writes,

> by its very history, mythical nature is driven back into the inwardness of the individual. Inwardness is the historical prison of

primordial human nature. The emotion of the trapped is melancholy. In melancholy truth presents itself, and the movement of
melancholy is one toward the deliverance of lost "meaning." A
truly dialectical notion. For if truth presents itself in melancholy, it indeed presents itself to pure inwardness exclusively as
semblance. . . .

Thus truth subordinates itself to melancholic semblance
through semblance's own dialectic. In its semblance melancholy
is, dialectically, the image of an other. Precisely this is the origin
of the allegorical of Kierkegaard's melancholy. In the face of
melancholy, nature becomes allegorical. . . . Melancholy itself,
however, is the historical spirit in its natural depth and therefore,
in the images of its corporeity, it is the central allegory.[51]

In this way Adorno recapitulates Benjamin's insight concerning the
peculiar vicious circle set in motion by the antinomy of the allegorical.
The "truth," or the messianic image of redemption encoded within the
fragment, is delivered to melancholy subjectivity, but only in its alienated form, only through the medium of concepts, which turn truth into
hieroglyph and transpose the moment of divinity dwelling within fallen
nature as a "hidden meaning" awaiting decipherment by the brooding
subject. For Adorno, this is the central paradox of melancholy: it
discloses truth only in the form of semblance (*Schein*). But this fact also
points to the moment where melancholia is shattered. "Through melancholy inwardness conjures up the semblance of truth to the point that
melancholy itself becomes transparent as semblance; to the point, that
is, that melancholy is wiped out and at the same time rescued." This
links the historically specific motions in which the baroque and Kierkegaard descend into the depths of melancholy inwardness to reveal,
beyond its last illusion, a paradoxical faith. As with the baroque,
Kierkegaard's melancholia liquidates itself in sacrifice. And faith,
rather than vaulting cleanly over melancholy inwardness, dwells within
its shattered fragments. Kierkegaard's either/or, the insistence on
decisiveness above all, is a faith haunted by the melancholia that
sacrificed itself.[52]

As the "mediating element" in Kierkegaard's thought from beginning to end, melancholia is dialectically aimed toward its own moment
of crisis. And it is in the image of the utterly personal, the "inward"
crisis, at the furthest remove from any philosophical idealism (and

in the last place that Kierkegaard himself would have looked), that Adorno finds the messianic content of Kierkegaard's melancholy philosophy. Kierkegaard's melancholia, like all melancholia, begins and remains at heart the loss of hope, the inability to remain in life. The loss of a sense of the potentiality of existence, of the notion of possibility, is Kierkegaard's truest definition of his melancholy. Adorno sees that this loss "is not so much a mirage of what has been lost as an unfulfilled, thin, prophetic but nevertheless exact schema of what is to be."[53]

As messianic expectation, melancholia gives voice to the theological promise of the redemption of the world; as the most subtle form of this hope, melancholia finds its proper home in the esoteric, since theological truths properly exist only in enciphered and distorted form, a riddled text to which melancholia dedicates itself. For Adorno's reading of Kierkegaard, as for Benjamin's reading of the baroque, script is the proper image for the transformation of melancholia into a model of hope. This truth, hidden from Kierkegaard himself, marks for Adorno the extreme expression of the melancholy crisis, one where melancholy slides into hope—not by the sterile abstractness of idealism, but in the human heart:

> No truer image of hope can be imagined than that of ciphers, readable as traces, dissolving in history, disappearing in front of overflowing eyes, indeed confirmed in lamentation. In these tears of despair the ciphers appear as incandescent figures, dialectically, as compassion, comfort, and hope. Dialectical melancholy does not mourn vanished happiness. It knows that it is unreachable.[54]

But melancholy also knows that there is a messianic promise bound up in the very unreachableness of this happiness, that, just as the sheer absence of the messiah is the sign of his quietest approach, there is in misery, in a happiness which never has been, a whispered promise. The philosophical representation of this promise marks the final dialectical moment in Adorno's book, and thus complements the corresponding moment at the end of the *Ursprung des deutschen Trauerspiels:*

> Such hope rejects all mythical deception, all claims to having once existed, by this *never:* it is promised as unattainable; whereas, if it were directly asserted as reality, it would regress to

the mythological and phantasmagorical, surrendering itself to the lost and the past. For the true desire of melancholy is nourished on the idea of an eternal happiness without sacrifice, which it still could never adequately indicate as its object. Although the wish that follows this aim is unfulfillable and yet full of hope, it originates in its aim, and just as it circles around happiness, the wish circles, fulfilled, in happiness itself.

In this image of the hope that is discernible only in the vision blurred by tears, Adorno has already moved beyond the "reading" of Kierkegaard. It marks the point where it is Benjamin, not Kierkegaard, whose melancholy becomes the object of critical writing. Indeed the image recalls his later recollection of his friend and mentor, for whom "all creation becomes . . . a script that must be deciphered through the code is unknown," for whom script, dimly illuminated, transforms itself into rebus images, which themselves originate, as we have already seen, in "his melancholy gaze, under which the historical is transformed into nature by the strength of its own fragility and every thing natural is transformed into a fragment of the history of creation." Adorno never doubted the complex of messianism and melancholy underlying this imagistic drive and understood that "the form of [Benjamin's] mind and the melancholy with which his nature conceived of the idea of the supernatural, of reconciliation, had to give everything he apprehended the shimmer of death." In this sense, the very "dialectics at a standstill" that constitutes Benjamin's most fragile intellectual achievement was "a name that he hit upon without knowing that Kierkegaard's melancholy had long since conjured it up."[55]

Comments such as these bring us closer to the true relation between the close of the *Trauerspiel* study and Adorno's study of Kierkegaard's melancholy. Adorno's creative adoption of Benjamin's thought in this case did not extend so thoroughly that Adorno was unable to perceive the extent to which Benjamin's own analysis, and not just its object, was constituted as a melancholy dialectics. Benjamin is not just the intellectual mentor of Adorno's analysis, but becomes its indirect object as well. Adorno sees the extent to which Benjamin's dialectic of melancholy subjectivity, played out in the *Trauerspiel* book not only between historically situated subjectivity and its objects, but between critical subjectivity and object of criticism as well, threatens at every moment to take back the treasures that Benjamin's critical vision produced, because melancholy subjectivity, as the basis of allegorical criticism, betrays its own interest in the redemption of its objects. Just as Kierkegaard's "overcoming" of his melancholia represented the sacrifice of the only moment in his thinking where a truly redemptive encounter was really possible, so, conversely, Adorno recognizes that Benjamin's own need to overcome melancholia, to formulate a meta-subjective doctrine of nonintentional truth that would replace "the notion of a subjective dimension itself," constitutes the central philo-sophical problem for Benjamin. Behind Adorno's constant concern with Benjamin's unmediated, atheoretical doctrine of the dialectical image—a concern that I will take up in greater detail presently—we can read its dialectical counterpart as well: his concern that, lurking under Benjamin's objectivism, indeed justifying its presence, melan-choly subjectivity itself remained.

For Adorno's Kierkegaard study—and this is perhaps its greatest divergence from the *Trauerspiel* work—the construction of constella-tions of recovered texts never occludes the manifest presence and ultimately practical interests of the critical author, and the dialectical image of the *intérieur* is not to merely "flash up" at the site of its construction, but is to be observed, explored, dialectically elaborated, until its usefulness in the critical dismantling of the illusions of bourgeois ideology becomes not just graphically but theoretically evi-dent. "Interpretation," as Adorno argued in "The Actuality of Philoso-phy," is not so much concerned with the recovery of meaning as with the construction of fragments powerful enough to negate violently the very puzzle-like character of the real itself.[56] Adorno is therefore able to grasp with far less ambiguity the extent to which the final leap into faith of both the baroque playwrights and Kierkegaard is "idealist" insofar as the "overcoming" of subjectivity, the "discovery" that sub-jectivity is merely the illusion of evil, the momentary absence of God's grace, is itself an illusion, is itself a fall back into myth. But to read Benjamin's own conclusion to the *Ursprung des deutschen Trauerspiels* as an unequivocal rejection of the "idealist" encounter with God beyond the vale of melancholy objects is to oversimplify a terrifically complex process, one that Adorno himself is, with extraordinary tact, attempting to register in his own Benjaminian critique of the melan-choly Kierkegaard.

The conclusion of the *Trauerspiel* book, while certainly not embracing the final spiritual moment of baroque melancholy—while recognizing that allegory thereby betrays its own objects and goes away empty-handed—is not unambiguously critical of it either. The final, postmelancholic image of faith that Benjamin summons at the close of the *Trauerspiel* study is remarkably free of irony, and Benjamin does not see it as constituting an objective mendacity, an illusion. It is rather the moment of Calderon's *ponderacíon misteriosa*, in which subjectivity, rather than remaining in mythic deception concerning its real mediation with its objects, reaches a moment of inwardness so profound that, "like an angel falling into the depths," subjectivity itself "is brought back by allegories, and is held fast in heaven, in God."[57] In light of this, Adorno's final invocation of the messianic but infinitely painful melancholia, which Kierkegaard himself cannot come to understand, marks not so much a final farewell to Kierkegaard as the greatest incarnation of the philosophy of the landlord, and far more: if not precisely a "critique" of his friend and mentor, then the textual testimony to Adorno's own perception that melancholy is not, for Benjamin, merely the object of criticism; that melancholy must be "sacrificed," taken to the extreme of its dialectical concentration, if it is to transform itself into the heartbreaking image of ever-withheld hope that Adorno perceives in it; that this transformation truly does bear with it the constant danger of a remythologization, of the subtle persistence of the brooding subject in a different guise. The critique of Kierkegaardian "idealism" is also a prayer for Benjamin—and a description of the very sort of heroic melancholia that Adorno perceived to shape the physiognomy of Benjamin's criticism.

Adorno saw all too clearly the terrific personal costs that were levied upon the thinker who attempted to employ melancholy against itself, to direct the productive force of the allegorical way of seeing upon the very material of reified nature, and understood that the inherent link between melancholy and semblance (*Schein*), that is, the ineffaceable dimension of the mythic in melancholia, could not but occlude its genuinely messianic dimension from the melancholy writer. Adorno's implicit appeal here is that melancholy can yield up its critical cargo, can remain as a source of critical energy, only insofar as it becomes the material for the critic who himself has mastered it, to whom it has "sacrificed" itself, for whom it has lost its mythic content and become theory. He therefore understood the terrific fragility of the dialectical images, which were born in pain, and of the price paid for the kind of heroic melancholy that Benjamin was subjecting himself to.

For the messianic criticism mandated by the *Ursprung des deutschen Trauerspiels*, melancholy must be both overcome and preserved. Its ability to impose a withering optic of natural history upon the mythic world, its cognitive absorption in the liberated fragment, its redemptive encounter with the messianic dimension of hope that arises at the heart of the allegorical intention—all these must subsist at the same time that the hyperintellectualism, the hypersubjectivity, and the paralytic depression and morbidity of the melancholy disposition are overcome, turned against themselves, mastered, and diverted into a fragile, productive critical subjectivity.

For Benjamin, the specific historical experience of the baroque indicates one highly unsatisfactory manner in which the dialectic of melancholy plays itself out. But it is not to be criticized for its manifest embrace of the experience of divinity. Rather, the idealism of the baroque consists in the failure to find a way to take the objects along with the subject. Heroic melancholy, under these historical specificities, fails due to the particular set of theological doctrines with which the baroque was confronted. But the image of paradoxical messianic hope that fills the center of this heroic melancholy, which Adorno alludes to in the image of the reader or the puzzle solver whose own bitter tears provide the optic to see the text of the world illuminated into ciphers of redemption, point toward another kind of resolution, another historical appearance of heroic melancholy. The great transformations of Benjamin's thought in the mid-1920s can be regarded as the effort to transpose a problematic of melancholia, subjectivity, critique, and redemption from its baroque to its modern form. Following this problematic, then, we can turn from seventeenth- to nineteenth-century melancholy writing in order to explore the relation of melancholia and modernity.

4 Melancholia and Modernity

I have found a definition of the beautiful. It is something intense and sad, something a bit vague . . . a contradictory impression of an ardor . . . and a desire for life together with a bitterness which flows back upon them as if from a sense of deprivation and hopelessness. I do not pretend that joy cannot associate with Beauty, but I will maintain that joy is one of her most vulgar adornments, while Melancholy may be called her illustrious spouse, so much so that I can scarcely conceive a type of beauty which has nothing to do with sorrow.
—Baudelaire, "Squibs"

Benjamin never wrote his analysis of modern allegory. The work on Baudelaire, which in part by deep predilection and in part by circumstance took on such a predominant role in the *Passagenwerk*, contains, it is true, a wealth of material on the specifically modern, capitalist form of melancholy allegory. But the exposition itself, which was to have formed the first section on a book on Baudelaire, never came into being.

The notes and documents discovered in the Bibliothèque Nationale ten years ago reveal the structure of the never-composed book on Baudelaire. The work, which was to have satisfied the wishes of the Institute for Social Research, would have been composed of three sections: "Baudelaire as Allegorist" would have presented Baudelaire as a point of access into the secret structure of the opening of the capitalist era; "The Paris of the Second Empire in Baudelaire" would constitute a storehouse of materials for the analysis of nineteenth-century Paris; "The Commodity as Poetic Object" would provide the construction itself.[1] The second section is the only one Benjamin wrote; submitted to the institute in 1938, it was harshly criticized by Adorno and resulted in a revision, "On Some Motifs in Baudelaire," in effect a version of the middle section of "The Paris of the Second Empire in Baudelaire." This essay was the one that was finally published in the *Zeitschrift für Sozialforschuung;* Michael Jennings argues that this last essay, which has become the "canonical" Benjaminian interpretation of Baudelaire, "is canonical for many of the wrong reasons," insofar as its lucid and continuous argumentative structure, and its willingness to offer theoretical explanations of textual constructions, is not representative of the montage and juxtaposition of discrete textual fragments that Benjamin clearly intended as his most significant methodological innovation, which are so admirably displayed in the "Paris of the Second Empire in Baudelaire." For Jennings, "On Some Motifs in Baudelaire" therefore constitutes in essence a submission to the will of Adorno, who insisted consistently on the leavening of Benjamin's montages with theory.[2]

The discovery of plans for the projected Baudelaire book strongly supports the contention that the book itself, and therefore to a limited extent its completed middle section, are intimately related to the Baudelaire *Konvolut* of the *Passagenwerk* notes, to the extent that the Baudelaire book was clearly considered to represent a "miniature model" of the *Passengwerk* as a whole.[3] Nevertheless, the heart of these controversies consists of the argument, by Michel Espagne and Michael Werner, that the Baudelaire book was conceived not as an offshoot of the *Passagenwerk,* that is, as a development of the Baudelaire *Konvolut,* partly in the interest of thematic progress and partly to appease the Institute for Social Research, but rather that the Baudelaire book constituted the attempt to save the Baudelaire material from the *Passagenwerk* itself, which Benjamin had begun to consider a failed project.[4] It is true that the existing Baudelaire essays, and more significantly the outlines for the Baudelaire book, consist entirely of notes from the Baudelaire *Konvolut,* giving the occasional impression that Benjamin was, Crusoe-like, carrying off all the serviceable material from a sinking ship. Still, as Buck-Morss argues, Espagne and Werner cannot explain why Benjamin continued to add material to all the *Konvoluten* of the *Passagenwerk* after the Baudelaire essay was completed. Nor, argues Buck-Morss, do they offer any compelling explanation as to why Benjamin would have abandoned the project that he had worked on since 1927. (One explanation, a central problem in the articulation and use of the dialectical image, will be discussed in the concluding chapter.)

On the evidence, it appears that the Baudelaire book and the *Passagenwerk* are two different forms expressing the same intent: the illumination through the montage of juxtaposed fragments of the nineteenth century, that is, the reconstruction of the process in which capitalist modernity in general, and the commodity form in particular, came to exert a mythic domination over European culture. In this sense—in keeping with our narrower interest in the idea of melancholia—this exegetical claim becomes significant. The planned structure of the never-written Baudelaire book can be taken as a highly significant insight into the structure and guiding interests of the *Passagenwerk* project as a whole. And the first section of this never-written book, "Baudelaire as Allegorist," clearly expresses the centrality of melancholia for Benjamin's treatment of Baudelaire. The first section was to have been composed of five divisions arranged, implicitly, according to a thematic development: "Critical Reception," "Sensory Makeup," "Aesthetic Passion," "Allegory," and "Melancholy."[5] Even a cursory glance at this plan reveals an important fact: the ordering of sections here demonstrates not so much the shocking juxtaposition of apparently heterogenous themes, but, on the contrary, a powerful thematic organization, an investigative path.

The montage structure of "The Paris of the Second Empire in Baudelaire," which Jennings praises for its juxtapositions of apparently discontinuous images, its disruption of theoretically sustained narrative, and its immediate depictions of Baudelaire's embeddedness within the structure of the emergent commodity economy, provides, according to Jennings's own observation, an archive of relevant material. But the *question* of Baudelaire and the nineteenth century, which this material was to answer,[6] is contained in the image of Baudelaire as allegorist, an image that is striking by its absence in "The Paris of the Second Empire in Baudelaire."

Indeed the ordering of themes in the plan for "Baudelaire as Allegorist" indicates, at least roughly, how this question was to have been posed. The history of reception—analogous to the historical "commentary" of Benjamin's earlier literary criticism—leads to an analysis of the dialectic of subjectivity and its historically produced objects; that is, the analysis of Baudelaire's "sensory makeup." But such an analysis leads inexorably to an analysis of Baudelaire's premier poetic gift, allegory. And allegory, in turn, can be critically represented only by a confrontation with its source, melancholia. Melancholia, as the most "subjective" moment of Baudelaire's productivity, can then be shown to be itself a mode of intuition that, in the form of *spleen*, is intimately linked to—in a dialectic with—concrete socioeconomic conditions in the early decades of industrial capitalism. In this way, the structure of the exploration argues for an analysis connecting the interiority of melancholy allegory with the commodity structure, that is, a historically informed construction of the "motorial reaction" between a "concretely structured world" and an extraordinary set of feelings, attitudes, and productive faculties. Insofar, then, as the Baudelaire book was aiming for the construction of the objective constellation of (modern) melancholy and modern capitalism, it is highly significant how Benjamin intended to present this material; that is, how the methodology of allegory and the methodology of the critique *of* allegory was to have articulated itself.

This question becomes all the more prominent in light of the dialectic between critical object and critical act—between allegorical subjectivity and its overcoming in (theological) illumination whose immense and paradoxical complexity we have explored in the structure of the *Ursprung des deutschen Trauerspiels*. Benjamin's treatment of Baudelaire stands in a situation highly comparable to his analysis of baroque allegory. In both cases, the critical analysis of the technique of allegorical production generates a tension, since the object of criticism is identified as a melancholy and hence ultimately failed moment of subjective intention, whereas Benjamin's critical act itself, in its claim to have transcended this dimension, nevertheless essentially replicates the method of allegorical construction itself.

The montage technique of "The Paris of the Second Empire in Baudelaire" is, as Jennings (and others) argue, a striking methodological innovation. Moreover, its disruptive-constructive strategy, which seeks to blast out the image of Baudelaire as a moment of resistance to the phantasmagoric power of capitalism, is for all its power nevertheless "allegorical" insofar as it consists of the willful wresting of fragmentary images and textual elements from their place in the history of literary reception and the construction of montages or constellations from these fragments, montages that are intended to illuminate the objective truth of contemporary social reality. We once again face the question of how Benjamin's constructions, unlike those of the baroque or nineteenth-century allegorists, can win this shocking, illuminatory power without themselves being subject to the same analysis of melancholy *Grübelei* that he applies to them.

He has an ox-blood red tie and pink gloves. Yes, we're in the year 1840 . . . in *some years, it was green gloves. Color did not disappear from clothing without* *regret. Now, Baudelaire wasn't the only one to wear these neckties of purple or* *brick. Not the only one with pink gloves. His mark is the combination of these* *two effects against the black of his suit.*[7]

Baudelaire was, Benjamin claims, anxious to be understood. He assumed, as it turned out quite correctly, that this would not be the case. But the various forms of misunderstanding of Baudelaire are, for Benjamin, as instructive as his poetry itself, for they provide the register of effects of Baudelaire's poetry in the nineteenth century, and it is the relation of the poetry to this century that is Benjamin's critical concern. "Baudelaire wrote a book which from the very beginning had little prospect of becoming an immediate popular success"; nevertheless *Les Fleurs du mal*, rejected and even condemned at its appearance in the mid-nineteenth century, represents the last European example of a lyric poetry "successful on a mass scale."[8] Baudelaire was, as a lyric poet, a straggler, a *Nachzügler* as much as a harbinger of later aesthetic tastes.[9] The appearance of his poetry brought about the strange state of affairs in which the growing success of his work runs parallel with—indeed is explained by—the very conditions that also explain why the lyric is increasingly incomprehensible.

This state of affairs is the condition for the later effect (*Nachwirkung*) of Baudelaire's poetry.[10] "The uninterrupted resonance which the *Fleurs du mal* has found up to the present day is profoundly related to the specific aspect acquired by the metropolis where it entered poetry for the first time."[11]

"Baudelaire's poetic genius consisted of an allegorical form of expression and, like other historical moments of allegory, found its characteristic voice in the assignation of moral captions to concrete images. The concern with morality was, of course, a central feature of *Les Fleurs du mal,* and the book's popular reception thus consisted of scandal—the scandalous depiction of outrageous violations of bourgeois morality, explicit sexuality and violence. The popular misunderstanding of *Les Fleurs du mal* consisted in the mistaken belief that Baudelaire was merely rejecting bourgeois morality. The critical reception of the work, on the other hand, consisted in a double error: the interpretation of Baudelaire's allegories in aesthetic terms (the perpetual misinterpretation of allegory, for Benjamin) and the tendency to see Baudelaire's moral sentiments as a renewed moral allegoresis inspired from premodern Catholicism, in particular that of Dante.[12] "One can easily distinguish the poet's reception of Baudelaire from that of the theoreticians. The latter keep themselves to the comparison with Dante and the concept of *decadence,* the former to the vocabulary of *l'art pour l'art* and the theory of *correspondances.*"[13]

The aestheticization of Baudelaire's lyric, its general dissolution into the "question of art" as it was posed in the mid-nineteenth century, could not help but overlook the enormous violence and productivity of Baudelaire's allegory and its peculiar relationship to the concrete social reality it addressed. Aestheticians focused instead on the foggy, mythicized doctrine of the *correspondances,* which must have been far more comforting and familiar than the allegory and which was therefore smoothly integrated into progressive schemata of aesthetic development: "Art theory has above all sought to take over Baudelaire's own doctrine of the *correspondances,* but has never decoded it."[14] It preferred instead to regard the sudden exposure of the wealth of supernatural analogies, the revelations of transcendent paradises, and the loss of the tortured self as a poetic fait accompli, as if the relation between the *correspondances* and the allegorical vision were, because undeveloped in Baudelaire, therefore of little importance.[15]

> Catalogue of Baudelairean subjects according to Jaloux: "irritable nervousness of the individual sworn to solitude . . . ; horror at the human condition and the necessity of granting oneself dignity by religion or *by art* . . . ; fondness for debauchery as a means of self-forgetting or self-punishment . . . ; passion for voyages, of the unknown, of the novel; . . . predeliction for that which makes one mindful of death (twilight, autumn, funerary spectacles) . . . adoration of the artificial; complacency in spleen. . . ."[16]

To this catalog (which reminds one of the list of themes of the *Trauerspiel*, but internalized) of "Baudelairean subjects" Benjamin appends the note: "Here is where it becomes clear that the exclusive consideration of psychological circumstances frustrates any insight into Baudelaire's true originality."[17] Not that there is anything inaccurate or out of place in this list. The problem, for Benjamin, is that such psychological-causal explanations do nothing to represent the true sources of Baudelaire's genius. The process must, instead, consist of a dialectic. The sources of Baudelaire's "sensory makeup," his poetic vision, lie only mediately and in a derivative sense in psychological factors. They are to be found in the relation between poetic vision and its objects, that is, at the point where Baudelaire's lyric intersects with, reflects, reacts to, and ultimately is consumed by the modern physiognomy of urban capitalism. This thesis, however, is far from reductionistic. Here as elsewhere, what concerns Benjamin is not so much the ability of social conditions to relate causally to aesthetic works, but rather the expressive relationship that obtains between them;[18] the capacity of objects to record and absorb the dreams, interests, and ambitions imposed upon them by a past historical epoch, and conversely, the capacity for literature, rescued from its consignment to literary theory, to demonstrate the imprints that a concrete economic physiognomy has left upon it.

Baudelaire's work, like the *Trauerspiel*, is in this sense always read as a palimpsest; it is "stroked against the grain" to reveal the moments of fissure, of discontinuity, unintentional moments where the reality of concrete social conditions records itself in the most inconspicuous fragments of poetic style. It is to do a violence against the work, but no greater violence than the incessant efforts of literary tradition to incorporate Baudelaire into its fold. Efforts to "capture" Baudelaire's poetic gift by reference to the manifest, deliberate accomplishments of the poet invariably take the form of apology, especially in light of the overwhelming and chilling power of the work itself. To render Baudelaire's poetic expression as a moment in the history of art, like the attempt to reduce it to psychological factors, is a mode of aesthetic "appreciation." A complicity with the forces of mythic domination is concealed in these tactics.

> The "appreciation," or apology strives to cover over the revolutionary moments in the course of history. For it, what matters is

the reconstruction of continuity. It lays stress only on those elements of the work which have already become part of its influence. What escapes it are the rough outcrops and jagged prongs which call a halt to those who wish to go beyond.[19]

"Rescue" (*Rettung*) on the other hand does not flinch from the "firm, apparently brutal grasp" of these discontinuities, no matter how sharp.[20]

The image of Baudelaire as the shocked poet, transformed by the commercial market at once into seller and commodity, parrying blows and jostled by the crowd, turned into mimic, monster, dandy, stroller, into a kaleidoscopic, constantly shifting mass of diffracted image fragments of the reality of the new, strange life in the big city—this vertiginous image produces the "poetic genius" and the "aesthetic passion" in Baudelaire's lyric. Benjamin wants to use this trope, "aesthetic passion," to investigate Baudelaire's singular ability to penetrate and record the physiognomy of capitalist experience in the nineteenth century, while at the same time remaining virtually oblivious of this very achievement. "Passion" unites in one image the secularization of Christian suffering that the poet inflicts upon himself and the moment where such an exercise produces passivity. The superficial "figure of Baudelaire" in his own time, on which Baudelaire himself was always working, is the figure of the libertine, the *decadent*; the scandalous criminal transforming his life into a continuous work of shocking art. "This image," Benjamin observes, "has been overlaid by another which, if its effect has been less widespread, has probably been more lasting. In it Baudelaire appears as the bearer of an aesthetic Passion, conceptualized at the same time (in *Either-Or*) by Kierkegaard."[21]

Passion, in this sense, is not so much characterized by the intensity of inner life, the moral-religious drive toward faith, as by the weightiness of objects that bear down on subjectivity like a soggy avalanche. Baudelaire and Kierkegaard, at opposite ends of the spectrum of the bourgeoisie, both experience this passion, which is very close to, indeed the first preliminary sign of melancholia. It is characterized in both cases by the imposition of memory by the objects. Secularized religious passion lodges within the space of the bourgeois *intérieur*. It finds in the reified articles of bourgeois life itself the contemplative objects that, as the ciphers of its own self-alienation, crowd around it, demanding attention, drawing the subject down to the level of the profane thing.[22] Passion, in this sense, is the subjective opening in which the "flood of memories" rushes in; both Kierkegaard and Baudelaire allegorize them, but in very different manners. Kierkegaard's privilege is connected to his attempt to spurn both memory and the object, rather than giving in to them. His passion, the moment of pseudopure decision, is the simple renunciation of any living, organic relation to the objects, and, as Adorno argued, it is the very impossibility of such a claim that makes his passionate inwardness so incomparably allegorical.

Baudelaire, conversely, records the process by which he himself is transformed into a commodity, and his lyric, fittingly, describes the precise dialectical mirror image of Kierkegaard's passionate ascent: the passionate descent into the very realm of the thingly. Baudelaire's poetic sensibility thus bears the mark of an experience of dehumanization, of reification or the transformation of the self into a dead object:

> Sensibility is the true subject of poetry. Sensibility is by its nature suffering. If it experiences its highest degree of concretion, its richest determination, in eroticism, it finds its ultimate consummation—which coincides with its transfiguration—in Passion. . . . Flowers adorn the particular stations of this Mount Calvary. They are the flowers of evil.[23]

This is Baudelaire's *Passionsweg;* in it, on "the melancholic's Way to Calvary, the allegories are the Stations of the Cross."[24] The old favorite of allegorical concentration, that is, the dialectical ambiguity concentrated in the dead or dying body, receives in Baudelaire's poetry a new and modern dimension: a form of sexual perversion horribly drained of all sensuous eroticism, reduced to a mechanized and deadly ritual that echoes the absorption of the worker's body into the industrial machine.[25] "Limbs" was to have been the original title of the *Fleurs du mal*, which in essence depicts the reduction of the human body, above all the woman's body, to pieces.[26] The skeleton, Benjamin observes, has a central place in Baudelaire's "erotology."[27] It is the depiction not of the eroticism of death, but of the devastating deathliness dwelling in things themselves, a morbidity that is not "timeless" or ancient but rather arises precisely before the eyes of the poet who is himself transformed into a thing. The reification of the woman's body, its transformation into isolated objects of frustrated and repetitive attempts at erotic satisfaction, is the register of the sinking of the erotic into another mode of oppression under the imperatives of capitalism.

The eroticism of Baudelaire is, in this sense, the historical transfiguration of the wooden piety of the baroque allegorists; the seventeenth century insists on the forced recovery of a gravity of religious intention, the transformation of the corpse into an allegory for life, however hollow and unlived it might have been, and however strongly the experiences of death might have spoken against it. For Baudelaire, the female body, "the most precious spoils in the Triumph of Allegory" is "Life, which means Death. This quality is most unqualifiedly characterized by the whore. It is the only thing which one may not bargain for and for Baudelaire, it is what it all comes down to."[28] Thingly eroticism, as aesthetic passion, finds its phenomenology in the "*Femmes damnées*" and in images of impotence and sterility.[29] The process whereby the body's "damned" eroticism is released as it is transformed into pieces by the "bloody apparatus of destruction" is the same process that releases Baudelaire's "passion."[30]

But "passion" also refers to the poet's self-relation, that is, the "prostitution" of the poet who enters the commodity economy to offer poems for sale. Aesthetic passion thus constitutes the historically specific moment wherein the poet, as object, confronts a market from which the bourgeoisie was just beginning to withdraw the "social commission" securing the poet the right of place. The pressures of the market drove Baudelaire's productivity, but also brought about his buffoonery. "In Baudelaire the poet for the first time makes known his claim to be an exhibition value. Baudelaire was his own impressario. The *perte d'auréole* affects the poet first and foremost. Hence his mythomania."[31] And indeed in the juxtaposition of these two motions—the "loss of aura" recorded by the self-commodifying lyric poet and the enormous weight of memories visited upon the melancholy mind, crystallizing into the infinitely repeated and diffracted image of the corpse—Benjamin finds the elements for a presentation of Baudelaire's specifically modern allegory.

Baudelaire's allegorical form of intuition was understood by none of his contemporaries, and for this reason was, ultimately, never remarked upon.[32]

In notes relating to the composition of the Baudelaire book, Benjamin recorded the following intention:

> The kernel of the first part [of the Baudelaire book, i.e., "Baudelaire as Allegorist"] develops the allegorical mode of perception in Baudelaire. This is to be investigated in its peculiar, so to speak its three-dimensional structure. Baudelaire's poetic sensitivity, which until now was virtually the only aspect that received attention, is only one of these dimensions. It is significant in itself by virtue of its polarity. In point of fact, Baudelaire's sensibility bifurcates into a spiritual, one could say a seraphic pole on the one side, and on the other side, an idiosyncratic one. The one pole represents the seraphic, the other the fetish. Baudelaire's poetic genius, however, cannot be grasped through this [sensitive] side. The melancholy genius enters into it. Here too, a meaningful polarization takes place. Baudelaire is no philosopher; he represents, in an uncommonly penetrating way, the temperament of the *Grübler*. His melancholy is of the sort that the Renaissance characterized as "heroic."[33]

Much of the interpretive task here is to examine this "kernel" a bit more closely. The insight, Baudelaire as *Grübler*, also appears in "Central Park": "Baudelaire was a poor philosopher, a good theoretician, but he was incomparable only as a *Grübler*. . . . As a historically specific type of thought, the *Grübler* is one at home among allegories."[34] We should accordingly begin by asking what specific relation exists between the image of the melancholy *Grübler* in its seventeenth- and its nineteenth-century forms of appearance.

In Benjamin's analysis of the baroque, as we have seen, *Grübelei*, though appearing only twice in the text of the *Ursprung des deutschen Trauerspiels*, does so at central theoretical points in the presentation of baroque melancholy and serves as a transitional figure in the depiction of the movement from the melancholy mood of the "great minds" of the baroque age to the specific allegorical talents of the authors of the *Trauerspielen*. Melancholia drains the world of meaning and plunges the subject into not only a descent of despair, but of contemplation as well; the moment when melancholy gives way to *Grübelei* marks the moment when the specific cognitive features of the melancholy disposition emerge. Brooding is oriented toward a world that melancholia perceives as fragmentary or ruined. Brooding thereby consists in the search for objective meaning within such fragments themselves and, more specifically, in the activity of juxtaposing or comparing word and image, of constructing corresponding sets of cognitive and visual elements, which thereby take the form of captioned pictures, imposing a claim to significance upon the fragmentary. Thus brooding marks the definitive emergence of melancholy in the form of the subject. For Baudelaire, as for the baroque *Grübler*, this activity of connection of word and image distinguishes brooding from mere depression. Baudelaire possessed "a preparedness to always place the image in the service of thought";[35] his melancholy therefore takes the form of a brooding that "polarizes itself according to word and image. This means that the image for him is never a reflex of sensibility alone, and the idea is never a mere relict of thought. Both play amongst each other, which is characteristic of the *Grübler*."[36]

This means that before even moving to the discussion of allegory, the melancholy brooding of two different historical epochs, with two different objective phenomenologies, is in essence united, not only by the form of the activity itself, but also by its characteristic context. Melancholia is both the hypertrophy of inwardness or private subjectivity and the simultaneous hypertrophy of the anamnestic concentration on the fragmentary thing. The latter marks the moment in which brooding reveals its messianic side; the former the moment in which the messianic necessarily fails to find adequate objective expression. In the Baudelaire *Konvolut*, Benjamin concentrates upon this state of affairs with far greater detail than in the baroque book:

> What essentially distinguishes the *Grübler* from the thinker is that the *Grübler* ponders over not just the thing itself but over his own pondering over it. The case of the *Grübler* is that of the man who once had the solution to the Great Problem, but then forgot it. And now he broods, not so much over the matter as over his past pondering of it. The thought of the *Grübler* thus stands in the sign of memory.[37]

In this way we are taken back to the puzzle motif discussed in the treatment of the *Trauerspiel* study. This relation between the fragment and memory—and memory and forgetting—is the central theme of Benjamin's presentation of Baudelaire's melancholy allegory. The image of *Grübler* as the ever-frustrated puzzle solver forms the chief thematic for the presentation of both baroque and Baudelairean allegory precisely because, for both, allegory is conceived as the result of the activity of brooding. "The *Grübler* and the allegorist are cut from *one* wood," Benjamin insists.[38] The brooder who grubs and shifts through the memory-laden fragments engages in a path of thinking with its own inner dialectic. The absolute absence of objective meaning in the fragments, and the assumption of absolute despotic control over them by the allegorist, brings about not just the paradoxical "redemption" of the objects from their fate, but also releases the originary anamnestic fragments from them, which glisten forth from the rescued fragments with a literary puzzling force. "The *Grübler* whose startled gaze falls upon the fragment in his hand becomes an allegorist."[39]

> The remembrance of the *Grübler* reigns over the unordered mass of dead knowledge. For this memory, human knowledge has become piecework [*Stückwerk*] in a peculiarly pregnant sense, that is, the heap of deliberately cut-up pieces out of which one constructs a puzzle. . . . The allegorist grabs now here, now there, out of the chaotic depths that his knowledge has presented him, pulls out a piece, holds it next to another and sees whether the two fit together; this meaning to that image, this image to that meaning. The result can never be predicted, since there is no natural mediation between the two.[40]

The "natural mediation" is lacking on theological and not on literary grounds, of course. Nature—as natural history—is the condition of the absence of any natural mediation between things. The image of Dürer's winged Melancholy, surrounded by objects to which it bears no natural, active relation, remains the image not only of baroque *Trauer,* but also—although as we will see in a uniquely modern form—of Baudelaire's brooding allegory. "Immediacy" implies the subjective imposition of a connection that, in the fragments, could exist "objectively" only in reconciled nature, and that therefore appears to the investigator negatively, under the sign of remembrance; that is, as absence, as forgetting. But forgetting, unlike ignorance, always implies a deprivation of a knowledge once possessed. The very perception of the fragmentary as fragmentary is memory tormented by the withdrawal of its true object and is the source of brooding. Dim memory traces lodge within the cut-up pieces.

Baudelaire thus opens himself up to the dizzying, weighty flood of memories that rush out of the puzzle-like fragments. "J'ai plus de souvenirs que si j'avais mille ans."[41] Here, as in Proust, memories emerge not just as the mass of fragments, threads, and rags from which the melancholy writer weaves the tapestry of remembering; they appear also as the dead, suffocating mass of inert material, under which thought is crushed—memory in the form that Nietzsche saw it, as hostile to life.[42] To live historically is to live in melancholy for Nietzsche, who, like Kierkegaard, argued for the importance of a liberating forgetting, a purging of the mass of memory-laden objects from the system.[43] For Nietzsche, the "dark invisible burden" of the past can only be relieved by the mobilization of the power of this complete, expansive forgetfulness. "Cheerfulness, a good conscience, belief in the future, the joyful deed—all depend, in the individual as well as the nation, on there being a line that divides the visible and clear from the vague and shadowy; we must know the right time to forget as well as the right time to remember."[44] This assertion captures perfectly the spirit of Nietzsche that entered in a formative way into the politics of the deed (die Tat) for the political sensibilities of Benjamin's own youth. It is the common legacy of all mid-nineteenth-century, post-Hegelian philosophical critics who articulate their political or ethical theories under the condition of mass commodification. Marx also insists, in the 18th Brumaire, that the dead bury the dead lest the weight of the past bear down like a nightmare on the brains of the living;[45] Kierkegaard argues, in the opening lines of Either/Or, that the only cure for the demonic power of boredom is the cultivation of "the art of forgetting."[46]

But the melancholic is not capable, or even especially interested, in establishing such a line between remembering and forgetting. What draws Benjamin's attention in Baudelaire—and in Proust and the surrealists—is the paradoxical comportment in which the rejection and embrace of the weight of the past results in a creative tension, a productivity in which the elements of the past surge forth. Memory, for all its invitation to subjective contemplation, does not itself appear as a matter of subjective decision. Under the weight of memory, the subject is pulled into the tide in which each fragment, overladen with memory, appears as a potential correlate to every other; every word with every image, every image with every word. The pull of "meaning" into this sea of memory is too strong for the mere organic will to triumph over it.[47] Meaning opens up the "abyss of knowledge."[48] Knowledge may be dead; it may, as Nietzsche warns, clog up and weigh down the mind; it might even be the very foundation of *ressentiment*.[49] But for the melancholic it is infinitely preferable to the celebration of the void that its deprivation would leave behind, the thin atmosphere that Nietzsche wishes to learn to breathe.

It was this cluttered abyss from which Baudelaire conjured up his images of beauty and evil, of the moment of hushed transcendence dwelling in rot and decay, or the lush, literal contours of sin and grace, of eroticism and monstrosity contained in the form of the human body, of the endless compaction of emotions contained in the glance, or the sound of a footfall, or the motion of fog in the abandoned city. Baudelaire's allegory is, like that of the baroque, most striking when it ruthlessly combines the most insistently graphic images of the tormented, isolated, or dismembered body with the description of evil. It is a connection whose result, the allegorical image, renders the appearance of the new urban landscape into its Ur-old form. The myth of the modern as infinite progress slides into its true appearance, the repetition of the horrors of existence, in all their "beauty."

Seventeenth-century allegory allegorizes in the face of a world that was already ruined as a result of general social and political chaos. This provides its historical index. The image of concrete historical suffering—the ruined structure, and above all the dead body—is the dialectical image around which the baroque allegory circles. The dreary moral pedagogy that was often invested in them is broken, however, by the form in which the allegories are produced; that is, in the recovery and juxtaposition of the imageworld of antiquity, the pantheon of classical gods and heroes, laden with multiple and often contradictory meaning by their migration through the Middle Ages and the Renaissance. The central question that arises for Benjamin thus becomes how—or better, why—Baudelaire is able to reactivate the allegorical voice if his world, quite unlike that of the baroque, is, far from being "ruined" by decades of grisly war, teeming with the material abundance of the first triumphant decades of industrial capitalism.[50]

The question, posed in this way, essentially answers itself. Allegory proceeds from *Trauer*. *Trauer* is a feeling that finds its proper phenomenology in the matrix of a priori objects to which it responds according to a motorial reaction. It is therefore neither "subjective" nor "objective," neither arbitrary nor messianic, but rather is produced at the dialectical crossroads where, in the fallen world, the realm of the subject and the object meet. In this sense, if Baudelaire marks the reemergence of the allegorical intuition in European literature for the first time since the seventeenth-century baroque, then we are naturally led to ask what is the specific form in which *Trauer* is reactivated. What are its a priori objects, what is the given matrix of historical objectivity to which Baudelaire's allegory responds?

Benjamin's answer is at once both extremely simple and compelling: "The allegorical mode of apprehension always arises from a devalued appearance-world. The specific devaluation of the appearance-world represented by the commodity is the foundation of the allegorical intention for Baudelaire."[51] The appearance of allegory, once again, is explicated not by aesthetic considerations, far less by any appreciation of artistic genius as a (mythical) originality, but rather refers to the concrete world into which the allegorical subject enters and to which it dialectically reacts. "The devaluation of the world of objects within allegory is outdone within the world of objects itself by the commodity." The modern allegorist thus brings an allegorical intuition to bear on a world already far more powerfully devalued and fragmented than any "aesthetic" attitude could accomplish. And yet the distinctive element of specifically modern allegory for Benjamin rests in the state of affairs in which this economic allegorization itself takes on a mythic character; that is, it assumes the illusory appearance of stasis. Allegory's "motorial reaction" against such mythic appearances underlies the relation between modern allegory and the mythic appearance of (allegorized) commodities:

> Ever more callously the object world of man assumes the expression of the commodity. At the same time advertising seeks to veil the commodity character of things. In the allegorical the deceptive transfiguration of the world of the commodity resists its distortion. The commodity attempts to look itself in the face. It celebrates itself becoming human in the whore.[52]

"As embodiment of the commodity, the prostitute achieves a central role in Baudelaire's poetry. The prostitute is the other side of the allegory-turned-human."[53] Modern allegory confronts a world of a priori objects that themselves have already been allegorized by the advent of the commodity. Exchange value, in which the object is hollowed out, to be rendered "meaningful" only by the arbitrary assignation of price, is a "devaluing" force far more powerful than the *Trauer* with which the baroque playwrights contemplated their world. As commodities, objects receive exchange value only according to the fluctuating rhythms of the market. Just as the *Grübler*'s arbitrary assignations of meaning correspond to the absence of any organic, real relation between objects in fallen reality, so the relation between commodity and exchange value is necessarily arbitrary:

> How the commodity receives its price can never really be foreseen, either in the course of its manufacture or later when it finds its way to the market. This is precisely what happens to the object in its allegorical existence. No nursery song tells it which meaning the *Tiefsinn* of the allegorist is going to ship it off to. And once the object attains this meaning, the meaning can be replaced for another one at any time. The fashions of meaning change nearly as fast as the price of the commodity. In point of fact, the meaning of the commodity is: price. As commodity it has no other. Thus, in the commodity, the allegorist is in his element. As flâneur, he had reached the soul of the commodity through empathy; as allegorist, he re-encounters, in the "pricetag" with which the commodity enters the market, the object of his *Grübelei*—meaning. The world in which this newest meaning has made him feel so at home is not a friendly one. In the soul of the commodity, which gives the illusion of having made its peace in its price, a hell rages.[54]

"The refunctioning of allegory in the commodity economy must be presented" if one is to understand how this economic allegorization informs Baudelaire's lyric. "It was Baudelaire's endeavor to make the aura which is peculiar to the commodity appear. In a heroic way he sought to humanize the commodity."[55] Of course, this project is only the counterpart to the process by which the poet himself is dehumanized into a commodity. The ascent of the commodity into a human form, like the descent of the poet or prostitute into a thing, is the synthesis of Benjamin's theory of baroque allegory and Lukács's reading of Marx's commodity fetishism as "reification" that Adorno had already described in his 1932 essay "The Idea of Natural History."[56] Commodities are elements of objective nature frozen into a mythic, hence illusory stasis. Their mythic appearance is linked to their status as concealed allegorical objects, and this explains how they can, as can all allegorical objects, become hollowed-out vessels for the assumption of arbitrary meanings while nevertheless retaining the ability to appear as elements of an image of eternal totality and harmony, in the phantasmagoria of capitalist "eternal progress."

The world of commodities is an enchanted world. This understanding of mythic capitalism underlies Benjamin's attempt to identify in Baudelaire the same feature that he found in the baroque allegorists: allegory as antidote to myth.[57] Allegory may be, in its brooding and subjective assignation of meaning, an essentially arbitrary process insofar as the "arbitrary" is understood as characterizing any "meaning" other than that which is truly objective, transcendent. However, the arbitrariness that lodges in the heart of the allegorical process is always mitigated by the state of affairs according to which the *exercise* of allegory bears a critical-redemptive force. In its insistence on the destruction of the pretension to unchanging and harmonious nature and its fragmentation of this nature into ciphers of transience, allegory corresponds, unwittingly, with the true character of historical time. Allegory dissolves myth by depicting the nakedness and degradation of the object for what it is and for exposing, however momentarily, the soul of the commodity as hell. The false light of totality goes out, and the image of the *cosmos* that contained it shrivels up and blows away. In the modern allegory this process is the source of the true "*Nachwirkung*" of Baudelaire's "ruthless" lyric: elements of a critique of capitalist modernity lodged in the form of poetic expression itself.

The following point is clearly a central one for Benjamin's analysis:

> Relation of commodity and allegory: "value" as natural magnifying glass outdoes "meaning." Its illusory image [*Schein*] is more difficult to disperse. Also, it's the newest. The fetish-character of the commodity was still relatively undeveloped in the baroque. Moreover, the commodity had not yet stamped its stigma—the proletarianization of the producers—so deeply into the production process. Thus the allegorical mode of intuition was, for the baroque, stylistically formative; for the nineteenth century no longer. As allegorist, Baudelaire was isolated. He attempted to

trace the experience of the commodity back to the allegorical. This was bound to fail, and in doing so showed that the ruthlessness of his charge was outdone by the ruthlessness of reality.

As with the baroque, the critical representation of the allegorical intention is not complete without the depiction of the allegory's moment of failure. Baroque allegory "goes away empty-handed" at the moment when the descent into brooding subjectivity reaches a point where the wealth of allegorical, memory-laden objects of *Grübelei* transmute themselves into arrows pointing mutely to God; the puzzle character of objective reality simply vanishes, leaving the subject supposedly alone before the Absolute. By a prodigious act of self-deception Kierkegaard was still able to summon up this illusion of objectless subjectivity in the nineteenth century. Baudelaire's allegory, deprived of this privilege, is for this reason able to exert its corrosive force on the commodities themselves. But the "heroic" destruction of the aura of the commodity fails. Baudelaire's allegory "missed reality, and just by a hair."[58]

Isolated and pitted against a world for which he was no match—not even truly understanding the nature of his poetic gift—Baudelaire comes to "appear as a comic figure: as the chicken whose triumphant crowing marks the Hour of Betrayal" against capitalist dream time; a figure who "unites the poverty of the ragpicker, the scorn of the *Schnorrer*, and the desperation of the parasite."[59] The poet whose halo has literally been shocked off his head can appear in no other way. But these images—and the fact that, without halo, the poet can now travel incognito—also imply that we see the poet as secret agent, gathering classified information against capitalism. The failure of Baudelaire's allegory is that this information itself is a source for brooding.

Baudelaire himself does not attain the moment of recognition, the shock of awakening, in which the allegories appear as explosive insights into actual, concrete socioeconomic conditions. They appear instead as tantalizing clues, dredged up by the temporal force of the modern, to the reconstruction of the image of eternal beauty. By pointing out the relation between Baudelaire's allegorical way of seeing and the advent of the commodity and the rise of commodified consciousness, Benjamin has answered questions concerning the nature and sources of Baudelaire's poetic genius; that is, why Baudelaire's allegory appears when and as it does. But substantial questions still must be posed: What is it about this allegorical vision that frustrates the moment where it can recognize the true nature of its objects? Why does Baudelaire's allegory "miss reality, and just by a hair"? The questions provide an implicit bridge from the treatment of allegory to the culminating division in Benjamin's proposed "Baudelaire as Allegorist": melancholia.

"Spleen is the feeling that corresponds to the permanent catastrophe."[60] "Spleen" refers specifically to the mode of melancholia in which the subject can no longer mournfully "observe" the permanent catastrophe of natural history, but rather, in a quite literal sense, *is* this catastrophe. Baudelaire's heroism and his specifically modern form of melancholia are explained by this fact: the commodification of the social world, unlike the allegorization of the natural world, leaves no sanctuary for subjectivity. Baudelaire has no choice but to subject himself, full-force, to the hell of the commodity form. "As rich in information as the poet is in his art, he is clumsy [*unbeholfen*] in finding evasions in the face of his times." This makes a central (and once again dialectical) distinction between baroque *Trauer* and *spleen*, its specifically modern form. The concentration of selfhood specific to modernity is also self-alienation. "Baroque allegory sees the corpse only from the outside. Baudelaire sees it also from the inside." Seeing the allegory from the fractured lens of the allegorical object constitutes not only the characteristic concentration or magnification of melancholy subjectivity but also a diffraction of selfhood through the fragmented and devalued allegorical object. "Self-alienation" implies here not primarily a gap that opens between concrete social existence and some essential being, but rather the mirror-upon-mirror multiplication of selfhood through the infinity of its objects. "The decisive ferment which, entering the *taedium vitae*, transforms it into *spleen*, is that of self-estrangement. Of the infinite regress of reflection, which in Romanticism simultaneously expanded living space in ever-expanding circles and reduced it within ever more narrowly defined boundaries, all that remains in the *Trauer* of Baudelaire is the *tête-à-tête sombre et limpide* of the subject with itself."[61] It is as if each fragment of the allegorical rubble, turning into a puzzle piece, also is transformed, horrifyingly, into a fractured mirror, an image of the subject itself.

For this reason, spleen differs from baroque *Trauer* in the power and complexity of its emotional response to devaluation, or better, the tenacity with which emotional and cognitive responses tangle and intersect within the allegorical temperament. The "sadness" of baroque melancholy is, in modernity, replaced by an emotional complex consisting of various permutations composed of the two simple elements of profound fear and rage: primal emotions, in keeping with the power of the commodity to awaken prehistoric, savage modes of existence. Spleen is characterized in the first instance as "naked horror";[62] that is, the primitive, infantile fear of being swallowed up by the mass of objects, the fear of flying to pieces, disappearance in the diffraction and multiplication of selfhood. In this way self-alienation, the dispersion of the self through its objects—the reified "overcoming" of the polarity between subject and object in the fetishization of the commodity and the commodification of the poet—takes the form of an antagonism of the self with itself.

In the "Short Poems of Prose" Baudelaire remarked that "the study of Beauty is a duel, in which the artist cries out with fear before he is defeated";[63] the depiction in "Le Soleil" of the solitary poet, stumbling through the deserted city:

> Practicing my fantastic fencing all alone, / Scenting at every corner the chances of a rhyme, / Tripping upon words as upon paving stones, / Striking, sometimes, long dreamed-of verses.[64]

It is a duel with but one duelist, a never-ending series of "tiny improvisations."[65] ("It would perhaps be pleasant," writes Baudelaire in a related context, "to be alternately victim and executioner."[66])

The second element of this "primal" emotive dimension of spleen is rage, and this, for Benjamin, is decisive. Rage is the destructive moment in Baudelaire's allegory; it occupies precisely the same position in the phenomenology of melancholia as does fragmentation or *Verstückelung* for the baroque. Baroque *Trauer* freezes and dries up the false image of totality. In sharp distinction, however, Baudelaire's allegory wields the "bloody implement of destruction"[67] that turns in rage upon the world of the commodity.

The image of baroque melancholia remains Dürer's winged Melancholia; sunk in brooding, tools—saw, blockplane, nails, whetstone— lie discarded at her feet. They are implements of construction. Their use presupposes the creative, sensuous, and dynamic relation between subject and object—physical, productive labor. Winged Melancholy has no use for them, since this dynamic dialectic between subject and nature has withdrawn, become frozen in melancholic fixity.

These implements are sharp. "Construction" is not their only possible use. In "La Destruction," the first poem in the section entitled "Les Fleurs du mal," the poet is tormented by a demon who, knowing his great love of art, takes the form of a beautiful woman, and in this form the demon

> addicts my lip to infamous potions. / Thus he leads me, far from God's view, / Panting, broken with weariness, / To the vast deserted plains of boredom, / And hurls into my confused eyes / soiled clothing, open wounds, / and the bloody implement of destruction!"[68]

For Benjamin this poem "contains of all Baudelaire's poetry the most forceful summoning forth of the genie of allegory. The bloody implement of destruction that this genie wields is the tool with which allegory itself reduces the world of things to ruined and debased fragments, over whose meaning she [allegory] is mistress."[69] For Benjamin, as intimately familiar as he was with the imagistic history of the melancholy disposition, the interpretation of the poem turns naturally to the observation of the historical transformation of images of melancholia: Dürer's Dame Melancholy is now the prostitute, the human-turned-commodity; the "bloody apparatus of destruction" are "the scattered household implements which—in the innermost chamber of Baudelaire's poetry—lie at the feet of the whore; she who has inherited the powers of the baroque allegory."[70] Again the characteristic feature of Baudelaire's allegory consists in the blurring and doubling of the self. Just as the self is engaged in a duel with itself—seeking, as Baudelaire once put it, to be simultaneously scalpel and wound—knife-wielding Melancholy throws the bloody implements of destruction into the poet's eye (reminiscent of a well-known aphorism of Adorno). Sharpness of insight, the allegorical vision, is at once granted to and inflicted upon the commodified poet.

Allegory as knife-wielding prostitute: not only the historically specific form in which Dürer's winged Melancholy reappears in the world of the commodity,[71] but also the operative image underlying the urge of spleen toward destruction. "Baudelaire's allegory bears, in contradistinction to that of the baroque, traces of a wrath which was at such a pitch as to break into this world and to leave its harmonious structures in ruins."[72] Allegory slices the mythic appearance of the commodity to pieces; it is in this way a genuinely critical response to the already chopped-up "real" world of the commodity. The dialectic of memory and forgetting, self-recognition and alienation, fear and rage, all end here, in spleen as the will toward absolute destruction: "To interrupt the course of the world—that is Baudelaire's deepest wish. The wish of Joshua. From this wish sprang his violence, his impatience, and his anger."[73]

Destruction as the ever-frustrated wish to interrupt the course of world history: this insight takes us deeper into the character of Baudelaire's modern spleen. The infinite destructiveness of spleen is only one of its aspects; the other consists in a specific form of time consciousness, which again bears significant affinities with baroque melancholy, but differs from it as the transience of natural creation differs from the repetitive endlessness of the commodity.

"Baudelaire's ire is part of his destructive bent. One approaches the matter more closely when one recognizes in these attacks an "*étrange sectionnement du temps*" (strange sectioning of time).[74] The phrase, according to Benjamin, is Proust's and marks a point where Proust's own melancholy time consciousness enabled him to understand Baudelaire's completely.[7] Benjamin, for his part, finds its expression most clearly in "L'Horloge" (The clock). Here the clock appears as a sinister, impassible deity; its message, repeated with every tick of its hands, is the ultimate melancholic repetition: "Three thousand six hundred times per hour, the Second mutters 'Souviens-toi!' "[76] The repetition itself is a kind of devouring of human meaning: "Each passing instant snatches from you the cake-crumb of happiness / meant to last the year." Memory as condemnation: even the postlapsarian multiplicity of human languages makes no difference: the clock's "metal throat" knows them all, and the injunction to remember is universally translated.

The image of time as an oppressive force or malignant demon is a common one in Baudelaire's poetry and prose. "We are all weighted down, every second, by the conception and sensation of time."[77] An expression of *taedium vitae*, to be sure: Baudelaire's reflections on the antipathy between implacable time and the human struggle for happiness and meaning is in one dimension a reenactment of one of the oldest of poetic sentiments. The image of the clock, like the sickle of Chronos or Shakespeare's "antique pen" is an emblem, albeit for Benjamin one that "bears a particularly high rank" insofar as it "groups together desire, the present, time, decay, virtue and remorse. . . . The consciousness of time running empty [*der leer verrinnenden Zeit*] and the *taedium vitae* are the two weights which keep the mechanism of melancholia running."[78]

And yet, clearly, the imagery of "the clock" conveys something more than just this neoantique sentiment: evoked in the mid-nineteenth century, it also calls forth the dim insight into the changed nature of time consciousness and of experience in general that arises with the advent of modern forms of industrial labor and commodity consumption. Spleen in Baudelaire is the attempt to interpret specifically modern temporal structures in terms of supposedly timeless insights into the repetitive and meaningless nature of human time. If it remains obtuse to itself about this specific nature—that is, if Baudelaire's spleen itself does not recognize that it is in essence a critique of capitalism—then this missing of reality "by a hair" is complemented by the fact that spleen nevertheless constitutes "nothing less than the quintessence of historical experience."[79]

The image of time running empty appears as the Nietzschean doctrine of eternal recurrence, Blanqui's last theories of the "eternity of the stars," and forms the heart of Baudelaire's criticisms of the idea of progress. All are linked as reactions to the advent of commodity capitalism that mistake themselves as reflections upon the nature of time "as such." This insight underlies the ambition of the *Passagenwerk* to demonstrate "with every possible emphasis that the idea of eternal recurrence intrudes into the world of Baudelaire, Blanqui and Nietzsche at approximately the same moment."[80] The reaction to the modern form of *taedium vitae* in these three figures marks the range of possible responses to the devaluation of the world of things under capitalism: Nietzsche's heroism consists in the "heroic composure" with which Zarathustra masters the eternal recurrence understood as the ultimate test of values; Blanqui, for his part, approaches Nietzsche's heroism, but with a far greater emphasis on stoic resignation.[81]

With Baudelaire it is different. Baudelaire's modern heroism consists in submitting himself precisely to the forces that he perceives are the most hostile to the achievement of poetic beauty. Baudelaire's melancholy bears, all along the line, the mark of the willful imposition of a self-discipline, a kind of moral-aesthetic hygiene through which he could wrest the timeless experience of beauty from within the very heart of the present. Modernity is the ultimate poetic object for Baudelaire, and this means that his heroic melancholy is of a particularly modern kind. Heroism is the strength of the subject to withstand the forces of allegorization, diffraction, and fragmentation imposed upon it, to conjure up "the new" from out of the ever-the-same. The effort to do so by the already-antiquated implement of the lyric is for Benjamin the clearest example of Baudelaire's heroism.[82]

The modern artist as hero: this is of course the central theme in the last division of "The Paris of the Second Empire in Baudelaire." In that context, the image of heroism is a synthesis of mythic and antimythic insights. The poet as hero sacrifices his *physis* for the sake of his poetry. This is myth. The insight that this mythic sacrifice is in fact an encoded script of the productive relations in which the poetical imagination is transformed into a mass article is the antimythical pole of the heroic image. In "Central Park," however, this conception of heroism receives another, one is tempted to say truer expression—heroic melancholy:

> Melanchthon's term *melancolia illa heroica* (this heroic melancholy) characterizes Baudelaire's gift most perfectly. Melancholy bears in the 19th century a different character, however, to that which it bore in the 17th. The key figure of the early allegory is the corpse. The key figure of the later allegory is the "souvenir" (*Andenken*). The "souvenir" is the schema of the transformation of the commodity into a collector's object. The *correspondances* are the endlessly multiple resonances of each *souvenir* with all the others.[83]

Baudelaire's modern melancholy is "heroic" for precisely the same reasons that the Renaissance melancholy of Ficino or Melanchthon was heroic. The melancholic realizes that the sentence of melancholia is, if inescapable, also endowed with a dialectical force. The same powers that torment the subject with sadness, despair, and the *taedium vitae* can, through the self's submission to a discipline, be transformed into the powers of a higher insight into the occult secrets of nature. Ficino, for these reasons, understood the dialectic of Saturn to promise the elevation of the soul into the transcendent realm of mystical correspondences even as the soul remained tormented by the symptoms of melancholy sadness. The Ficinian correspondences were the elements of a system of astral connections and relationships extending from the most lofty celestial bodies to the most minute and fragmentary natural objects. There is a genealogy that runs from this most esoteric expression of Renaissance Neoplatonism through Swedenborg to Baudelaire's doctrine of natural correspondences. As one interpreter has argued, the doctrine of correspondence plays such a powerful and complex role in the Renaissance "episteme" because the role of the "sorrowful investigator" must maintain a sort of structural ambiguity as both discoverer of the infinite network of divine-astral correspondences and as the medium in which the natural sign system articulates itself within nature.[84]

For Benjamin, however, the distinguishing factor in Baudelaire's appropriation of this older mystical doctrine is the centrality of the category of time. Mandating both an attitude of radical isolation and a structural blurring of the role of the contemplative mind as it operates at the dialectical crossroads of self and world, the doctrine of correspondences maintains that such a mind can render itself capable of summoning forth, from the mass of images and memories presented to it, moments in which the tedious course of chronological time—the time of allegory—is momentarily suspended. At these times, the correspondences come fleetingly into view. They are the timeless, eternal moments of natural unity, of objective meaning, which provide the poet with a glimpse of nature in its reconciled past, from "*la vie antérieure*."

In the last Baudelaire essay, "On Some Motifs in Baudelaire," Benjamin cites Proust in order to show that the role of the correspondences for Baudelaire is, in essence, one of temporal arrest. The allegorical voice is interrupted with evocations of time as *kairos*, as fulfilled or completed time, which stand out from the chronological time of "The Clock." "They are days of recollection, not marked by any experience," Benjamin claims. "They are not connected with the other days, but stand out from time." For Benjamin, then, their relation with melancholy spleen, as mournful time consciousness, is clear from the start: the correspondences can only be intuited under the schema of something irretrievably lost.[85]

In the often-cited sonnet "Correspondances," nature appears as the mystic temple in which the "forest of symbols" observes the passing subject with "familiar regards." It is a realm of shadow and stillness; the work of light, of contour and color, of sound, is still blended as the reflection of "one deep and shadowy unity," is still in correspondence with each other. Moments in which timelessness encapsulates itself are moments in which time stands still. Such moments are embedded within a temporal continuum that spleen reveals as evil. "What Baudelaire meant by *correspondance* may be described as an experience which seeks to establish itself in crisis-proof form."[86] This is a melancholy realization, and the hopeless demand to preserve and muster the moments of correspondence against the time in which they must appear is the poetic heart of Baudelaire's heroic melancholy. The correspondences, as moments of divine meaning, are to stand outside of the range of the contemplative—brooding—subject. They are, in this way, presented as theologically distinct from the allegorical images. Accordingly, Benjamin observes that whereas the allegorical intention is characterized by "a highly concentrated contemplation" in Baudelaire, the poetic receptivity to the fragile appearance of correspondences arises from "a highly intensified sensitivity." Indeed Benjamin recognizes that the tension between these two poetic faculties constitutes "the decisive basis of Baudelaire's production."[87]

There is one place where Baudelaire does develop, with a great deal of self-consciousness, the relationship between the correspondences and spleen as two contradictory modes of time consciousness. This occurs in the *Spleen de Paris*, specifically in one of the *Petits Poèmes en prose*, entitled "La Chambre double." The prose poem begins by establishing precisely the kind of temporally charged atmosphere—of boredom, fixity, dim light, overcast skies—that draws Benjamin's attention. It is a room in whose "stagnant atmosphere" the soul "bathes in languor, scented with regret and desire." The strangely liquefying atmosphere of this room is erotically charged to the bursting point. Every detail of the room, every piece of furniture, the diffuse evening light playing on the bare walls, bears the faint perfume of another world. The voluptuous goddess stretched upon the bed swims into focus: Beauty. In this realm, time stands still—"No! there are no more minutes, no more seconds! Time has disappeared, it is eternity that reigns, an eternity of delight!" At the moment when this prehistoric vision of eternal-erotic beauty appears, however, a terrible noise, like a blow, announces the entrance of a Specter. Its mission is swift and merciless: "Yes! Yes! Time has returned; now time reigns as sovereign; and with this hideous beast returns the whole demonic cortege of souvenirs, regrets, spasms, fears, anxieties, nightmares, fevers and neuroses. . . . Yes! Time rules; he has reassumed his brutal dictatorship."[88] The enchanted appearance of the double room now shows itself in another light: what once was "crepuscular" is now dim and dreary; the magic flicker of light and shadow was all along the cold and cheerless rain that etched the filth of the windowpane. The purity of the bare wall now looks stark and desolate. The furniture is moth-eaten and pathetic. The perfume of other planets is nothing more than the fetid odor of old tobacco, a trace of the desperate, lonely, nauseating smell of old hotel rooms.

The "brutal dictatorship" of chronological time wins a complete victory here, and one might easily win the impression that the relation between the time of the correspondences and allegorical time is a static opposition: ideal, confronted with spleen, loses every time. In fact, the situation is far from static. No ideal without spleen; no spleen without ideal. Benjamin's analysis of Baudelairean allegory would not be complete without an analysis of this dialectic and why it could not reveal its true nature to Baudelaire himself.

As Benjamin carefully notes, Baudelaire never develops the relationship between the correspondences and allegory. "Baudelaire never made the slightest attempt to construct any connection between these speculations, each so central to his concerns. His poetry arises from the interplay of these two tendencies invested in him."[89] Why Baudelaire was so reluctant to establish such a relationship can be explained on a number of Benjamin's own grounds: first, of course, is the claim that Baudelaire, unsurpassed as a *Grübler*, was nevertheless a poor philosopher and had no interest in the theoretical depiction of poetic-theological tensions. Second, one could mention the very Benjaminian sensibility mentioned earlier; that is, a certain inveterate unwillingness to reveal rashly or betray the tiny set of extraordinary experiences that form the heart of poetic or philosophical production. Esoteric doctrine is based on esoteric experiences. To mediate such experiences in theory is to make them something other than esoteric.

Third and far more significant is the consideration that the relationship between the allegory and the correspondences, whose tension is the motor of Baudelaire's poetic production, cannot be articulated because of the fundamental paradox lying at its heart, one that Baudelaire himself could not have grasped. Benjamin indicates that the relationship between allegory and correspondence—or between allegorical and symbolic art forms as reflections of a basic theological situation—is one in which a finite set of themes articulates itself within the richness of a historically specific range of concrete elements. The reconstruction of the truth content of the themes themselves, visible by a reconstruction of these elements, is the responsibility and the privilege of the critic, not the artist.

In the case of the correspondences, Baudelaire himself could not grasp the rootedness of their relationship to his own allegory in terms of the emergent socioeconomic physiognomy of high capitalism. The correspondences are wishes for the persistence of a precognitive dimension of transcendent meaning subsisting not only among elements of "first" nature with each other, but also between nature and the spontaneous prerational poetic subject. They are anamnestic, insofar as they arise from memory mobilized to record the dim traces of unalienated nature. In the context of Baudelaire's lyric, these wishes for meaning take on their own distinctive meaning when understood as a creative response to the commodification of inner and outer nature. The correspondences, mythic though they may be, bear a messianic content: they mobilize hope for the survival of nature beyond its allegorized, devalued existence. But this messianic content is mythicized in the conviction that the gulf between real and allegorical nature, between the objective-divine and the allegorical-arbitrary set of natural signs, can itself be bridged by the poetic subject. Baudelaire wishes to capture the correspondences in poetry; his melancholy spleen arises from the realization of both the necessity and the impossibility of this task.

In this way, Benjamin perceives that Baudelaire's melancholy essentially reenacts the same dialectical paradox of baroque melancholy. Subjective brooding, in its allegorizing power, willfully assigns meaning upon the fragmented world; as it does so, however, elements of transcendent meaning that appear to the melancholy subjectivity as metaintentional and as transcendent glimmer forth. These are clues to the recovery of that picture of wholeness which drives the process of allegorization itself. The paradox consists precisely in the moment where the melancholy subject becomes capable of "capturing" or representing these fragile moments of transcendence within the medium of (poetic) language. Insofar as the poet succeeds in doing so, the correspondences must necessarily lose their status as preconceptual, prelinguistic, prelapsarian moments of divine meaning and become meaning *for* the poetic subject.

In allegory, this moment of self-contradiction becomes graphic, crystallizes into images that remain available to the critic. In the baroque, this contradictory moment of allegory emerges in the originary image of the corpse. As image, the corpse concentrates into a dialectical unity the subjection of the human spirit to the creaturely, to the consignment of all things to ruin. The corpse is the most graphic representation of subject turned object. But at the extreme limit of allegorical reflection, the corpse is also the hope for redemption encoded into the most physical and most profane of all possible images. Baroque allegory proved itself incapable of containing this dialectical image and remaining true to its own redemptive mission. The power of the image of the corpse expels the baroque allegory from the realm of things altogether, into the "treacherous" realm of objectless faith.

For Baudelaire, a similar process occurs. His melancholy, unlike that of the baroque, is heroic. He will therefore resist the pull of the "absolute spirit" toward the false light of pure transcendence. Like his Renaissance predecessors, Baudelaire will attempt to master the force of melancholy and remain in the realm of things. But as he does so, the attempt to "grasp" the moments of transcendent meaning from within the continuum of natural history leads to the impossible task of an expression of the timeless beauty of the correspondences from within the fallen language of allegory. For Baudelaire's poetic work, bringing the correspondences into the realm of allegory and allegorical time consciousness means that moments of temporal transcendence are to be poetically constructed as a part of the temporal continuum itself. Transcendent time within the temporal continuum crystallizes in the image of the souvenir. The souvenir is the product of messianic time consciousness that undergoes commodification: this is *Erlebnis*; time as strangely segmented, as a series of discrete moments that bear no organic continuity with one another, that do not flow. Correspondences become souvenirs as they are brought into the reified realm of modern allegory. They are saved, but saved as dead: "The souvenir is the complement of the *Erlebnis*. In it the increasing self-alienation of the person who inventories his past as dead possession is distilled. In the 19th century allegory moved out of the surrounding world, in order to settle in the inner world."[90]

The souvenir is the correspondence that dies in the hands of the poet who attempts to carry it into the realm of allegory.[91] Like the corpse, the souvenir as dead body contains both a positive and a negative pole: it is the graphic depiction of the death of experience, of life reduced to the null point of significance, as static object or hollow fragment. At the same time, however, as souvenir it marks the moment where the commodity is, by the effort of the subject, removed and hence rescued from the process of the endless circulation of commodities in the market. The transformation of the commodity into souvenir is, it is true, a sort of double death; even the hollow life of the thing as a commodity is now denied. On the other hand, the transformation of commodity to souvenir bears a dim messianic echo in the deliverance of the thing from its status as commodity. A logic of redemption is visible in this process. According to the same logic, however, to save the thing from its status as commodity can only be accomplished *by the brooder* as the act of assertion of subjective intention over the redeemed object, in the appropriation where the redeemed thing only emerges as the hollow vessel awaiting subjective meaning.

The antinomies of the allegorical here emerge in the medium of the commodity economy. The allegoresis of allegorized nature, which directs its violence against the world in order to save the thing, seeks to save the thing as correspondence, but what it gets is souvenir. The thing is now "saved" from its fate as a commodity, but only insofar as the allegorist embraces it as a souvenir; that is, as the reflection of intention, as the crystallization of lifeless memory. "The relic derives from the corpse; the souvenir from deceased experience [*Erfahrung*] which calls itself euphemistically *Erlebnis*."[92]

This is the result of Baudelaire's melancholy allegory and the reason why Baudelaire could not grasp the relationship between allegory and correspondence. From the point of view of the melancholic, this relationship could only be grasped by resolving or overcoming its dialectical tension; that is, by developing a vision of poetic expression whereby the correspondences could be given voice without sacrificing the things themselves to the intention of the subject. But this is precisely what the allegorist can under no circumstances do. Transcending allegoresis, as in the baroque, betrays the objects. Mastering allegoresis heroically, as in the Renaissance or Baudelaire, betrays the objects as well—and betrays the redemptive will at the heart of allegoresis.

Heroic melancholy in the age of the commodity redeems the object, but only as souvenir. The transformation of the experience of divine remembrance into the souvenir is a source of Baudelaire's allegorical rage. Rage is, at bottom, the response to loss. The correspondence— as *ideal*—is the resonance of blessedness that still lingers like a faint fragrance amongst the assembled souvenirs. "The *Ideal* supplies the powers of remembrance; spleen musters the multitude of seconds against it." Nostalgia is unknown to Baudelaire, who is overcome by the feeling of bottomless desolation at the loss of experience itself.[93] Rage against the real is, in the end, the rage of impotence, and Baudelaire's poetic gift lies in the expression of this rage throughout the lyric, the unlikeliest and therefore the most poetically moving alternative. But the explosive, redemptive force that lodges in the heart of the commodity still remains untapped in Baudelaire's lyric. For the materialist critic, his poetry thus does not bear just the status of an encoded text of the emergence of capitalism upon the imagination of the nineteenth century. In his project of heroic melancholia, the critic can read how modern allegory "appropriates" this messianic force, and by so doing fails by translating this power back into the language of the commodity, as dead commodity or souvenir.

This is the manner in which Baudelaire "missed reality, and just by a hair." As much as the critic thus reads Baudelaire's lyric as a secret register of the dominion of the commodity, and as much as this text bears within it an encoded critique of the ideology of progress, Baudelaire's lyric is even more pregnant with significance for the materialist critic insofar as it crystallizes the challenge that allegory presents to criticism itself, in a manner far clearer and more pressing than it could in its baroque form. How does one formulate a critical practice that could tap into the enormous critical-redemptive, destructive-constructive powers of the allegorical way of seeing, while at the same time avoiding the paradigm of the melancholy subject under whose weight the critical-redemptive encounter with the thing is necessarily translated into its other? How can the critic harness the flood of memories without translating the memories into souvenirs?

Heroic melancholy is, like all melancholy, "about" death. Memory is both the medium of the correspondences and the source of the bitterness that kills them. This is the field of rubble that is the habitat of the *Grübler*. As Benjamin recorded in notes for the section "Baudelaire as Allegorist," melancholy is always to be analyzed from the schema whereby death emerges at the "nullpoint in the co-ordinate axes of passion." At the center of the melancholy dialectic stands the corpse, both in its modern and in its baroque variants. This is apparently the guiding motive for the movement from "sensory makeup" through "passion" to "allegory" and thence ultimately to "melancholy" in Benjamin's planned treatment of Baudelairean melancholy. "The center of the intersection of axes for the schematisms of the first section ["Baudelaire as Allegorist"] will form [*bilden*] death or the corpse. In the corresponding place in the third part ["The Commodity as Poetic Object"], the commodity will stand as the social reality which underlies the dominion of the death principle in this poetry."[94]

The theory of Baudelairean allegory, in developing these schematisms, itself must confront the critical challenge of redemption through representation without killing what it wants to redeem. Not death but revolution—life—must stand at the moment where materialist criticism grasps its objects, pulls them from their mythic fate, and stands them upright once again. In metatheoretical terms, then, a reconstruction of Benjamin's analysis of Baudelaire's melancholy allegory actually serves to sharpen the critical challenge posed by melancholy itself. What Benjamin needs is a means for a postmelancholy criticism; allegory without the *Grübler*. The answer, Benjamin already saw, lay not in theory but in method. The paradigm of this answer—and its problematical development—is illustrated by surrealism.

5 On the Road to the Object: Surrealism as Postmelancholy Criticism

The obscurity of our utterances is constant.
The riddle of meaning should remain in the hands
of children.—André Breton, "For Dada"

In a central, early passage in Aragon's *Paysan de Paris*, the strolling interlocutor, wading through the landscape of Paris's back streets, pauses while descending a short flight of stairs from an arcade to street level. The lulling, subaquatic calm of the arcade suddenly gives way to the choppy, bright surface of street life. Standing at the intersection of the languid dreamworld of the arcade and the waking bustle of the avenue, the flaneur finds himself straddling "the two views which oppose exterior reality against the subjectivism of the arcade like a man teetering on the brink of his abysses, tempted equally by the rushing current of objects and by the whirlpool of self."[1] The vertiginous feeling produced by this spot arises from its status as a dialectical crossroads, a confluence where "the two great cross-currents of the mind" come together: the inner depths of subjectivity and the intoxicating, selfless fascination with the objects. In this synergy, the objects take on the hue of subjective intentions; the self begins to break down, to diffract itself infinitely through its objects. The arcade-self balances, for a moment, with the tumult of discontinuous, absurdly juxtaposed images that scatter and rush headlong in all directions from the "real" world.

Life at the frozen dialectical crossroads of subjectivity and its objects: by now we can recognize this as not just a spot of dialectical tension, but as the originary locus of melancholy. No stranger to melancholy dialectics, Aragon is fully aware of this. This crossroads of subject and object is also the moment where, for Aragon, the melancholy way of seeing takes over:

> From this sentimental crossroads, as I regard alternately this land of disorder and the great arcade illuminated by my instincts, at one or another of these *trompe-l'oeil*, I perceive not even the tiniest moment of hope. I feel the ground tremble, and I find myself suddenly like a sailor on board of a ruined château. Everything signifies devastation. Under my contemplative gaze, everything falls into ruin.[2]

The allegorical vision once again arises with the inevitability and precision of a motorial reaction to a concretely structured world. Aragon is not content, however, to allow the phenomenology of *Trauer* to stop here. It is not a matter merely of conjuring up the world as the translation of spleen; rather, the melancholy provoked by the experience of the crossroads of subjectivity and objects is to be negated, so that the rich field of surreal experiences will become, for the first time, accessible without the baggage of the mournful, hyperconscious rational subject. Aragon thus repeats the ancient strategy of endowing melancholia with a human form; not only out of mythical fear, but also in order to render the fear visible, and thereby to harness it and bring it into control: "The feeling of futility crouches next to me on the lowest step. It is dressed like me, but more nobly. It carries no handkerchief. Its face bears an expression of the infinite; in its hands it holds an unfolded blue accordion, which it never plays. On the accordion we read: PESSIMISM."[3] A remarkable surrealist image: the most modern anthropic image of melancholia. Dürer's winged Melancholia appears, now, mingled with the figure of the riddling, mocking dwarf who squats upon Zarathustra's shoulders as he struggles up his mountain path: the former is the controlled image of the infinity of contemplation; the latter is the horrible challenge of time, of infinite gravity.

For Aragon, however, the figure has become not so much comic as laughable. This figure carries neither the sickle of Saturn-Chronos nor Dürer's occult compass, nor Baudelaire's "bloody implement of destruction." It holds a blue accordion. The folded bellows of the accordion, on which "PESSIMISM" is written, can be pushed together, in and out, folding and unfolding, thus effacing and recovering letter after letter of the inscribed word. Playing the instrument, it wails in infinite permutations of the dance of consonants and vowels of the inscribed "pessimism"; searching, in the last incarnation of Aboulafian Kabbalism, for the meaning of meanings in the repeated act of signification. Everything, for the urban stroller, signifies devastation; but for surrealism, the petrifying melancholy vision becomes a little tune, a dance of letters. Ultimately, tiring of the game, the melancholy figure tosses the accordion into the Seine; sinking, it disappears one letter at a time and is gone. The melancholy companion now appears in his true form: "There he is, balancing with one foot in his hand, a bit theatrical, a bit vulgar, his pipe in the ground and his cap over one ear, singing, I believe, 'Ah, if you knew the life of the snails of Burgundy . . .', at the top of the steps, in the grit and the trash, the charming boy: the sentiment of futility."[4]

The dominion of melancholy is broken, not by a Nietzschean act of assertion of will so much as a magical transmutation of melancholia itself—driving into the heart of the act of signifying, revealing the inner connection between signification and hopelessness, between meaning and ruin, Aragon turns this very realization into the image material for a new vision: melancholy stands at the crossroads between subject and object, but as a jester, not a guardian. Mournfulness is transformed into (black) humor. But in this unmasking, something else is acquired: the outer edge of reality, where the force field between subject and its objects is most intense, now becomes accessible to the subjective inquirer in an incomparable manner. Surreal objects, dredged from their immersion in "reality," can now be recovered without "futility" imposing itself upon them. The critical motion of allegorical redemption, for the surrealist construction, need no longer fear the image of melancholia. Indeed the pessimism inscribed upon the accordion's bellows is not precisely transcended but is overcome, sacrificing itself to the new model of subjective inquiry, turning the formerly mournful play of subjective signification into a new play, a truly postidealist "unfolding" of the surreal object.

The paradigmatic role of surrealism for Benjamin's methodological ambitions is difficult to underestimate. Benjamin's own virtually ecstatic experience upon his initial contact with Aragon's work attests not only to an essential, perhaps inexpressible affinity of intellectual temperaments and habits, but also to the potential he perceived within surrealist texts to provide him with methodological models. As Tiedemann reports, these first contacts were as early as 1925, a year after the appearance of the first *Manifesto*.[5] Benjamin's first published text concerning surrealism, "Traumkitsch," signals clearly enough the central role of the dream and of the relation between dream and history: "Dreaming has a share in history." "The history of dreams has yet to be written," he observes, adding that such a history would constitute a "historical illumination" that could "strike a decisive blow against the superstition of the subjection to nature."[6] The power of a critical examination of the history of dreams—its awakening effect—consists, as the surrealists had already perceived, in the ability of dreams to dredge up, recover, and present to consciousness the "grey dusty region of the things," that is, the range of ruined, outmoded, and discarded objects that, excluded from the mythic rhythms of technical production and capitalist consumption, take their leave of phantasmagoric "reality": their moment of farewell from capitalist reality is their motion up the gangplank on the freighter bound for the surreal. This leave-taking marks them as kitsch, as surrealist objects. The moment of kitsch in the object, for Benjamin the "most worn-down place" (*abgegriffensten Stelle*) of its physiognomy, is where the dreamer seizes it.

In this evocation of the messianic power dwelling in the outmoded, Benjamin is already moving toward a point where the ability to grasp and redeem these imperiled objects can be underwritten no longer by a manifest theology, in which the role of the conscious, contemplative subject reaches such fantastic complexity, but rather in a depiction of a range of extraordinary precognitive experiences that are opened up to the subject only insofar as conscious subjectivity is, by dream or intoxication, overcome. "The fantasy images of the things as pages of a Leporello Picturebook 'The Dream' clatter to the floor. Explanatory captions [*Sinnsprüche*] stand beneath every page."[7] The older allegorical motion here is turned upside down. The *Sinnsprüche* that are assigned to dream images are themselves nonsensical; the brooding moment of intensity that insists on the "correct" assignation between moral caption and age-old, overused image is overcome by a defiant abandonment of the very paradigm of the subject itself, and the concomitant abandonment of any interest in "meaning" in favor of an exhilarated game of substitution, assignation, and repetition, whose goal is not the recovery of originary meaning but rather the destruction of the very "real" in whose terms the world takes on its puzzle-like appearance. This inherent relation between a "metasubjective" allegoresis and *praxis*—the destruction of the puzzle, rather than its solution—is what Benjamin perceives at work in the formulation of surrealist practice and what constitutes the key to Benjamin's reception of surrealism. The surrealists—so Benjamin's clear intention—are drawn to the production of emblem books according to motives that bear a hidden, productive relationship to those of the baroque. The critical appropriation and reworking of these motives provides a clue for the project of "historical illumination" beyond the paradigm of melancholy subjectivity.

Before turning to Benjamin's appropriation of surrealism, it is important to recall a few of the developed motifs in surrealist practice. This practice arises from the need to transcend the confines of the bourgeois subject. Intoxication and automatism, dream and montage, constitute practical means for the critical destruction of the paradigm of the subject. The model of the organic unity of the bourgeois artwork is abolished at the same time as the model of the solitary aesthetic genius is abandoned. For this reason, the ideological imperatives of capitalist modernity lose their validity. As surrealist practice shakes off the bonds of the bourgeois "real" these bonds themselves are debunked and appear as objects of humor, scorn, and ridicule. Thus Breton's attempts to link surrealist and communist practices is based on the critical dimension of the former, its ability, through the mobilization of dream, to transform the landscape of reified capitalist modernity into a new mythology. Dream landscape is the intended result, one where the most solid elements of bourgeois rationality melt into air, and where the debris that capitalism leaves in its wake becomes charged with a special significance as vessels of an anamnestic resistance to ideology and as tools for surrealist constructions.[8]

The "power of intoxication" that surrealism was "to make useful for the revolution," as Benjamin had already observed in notes written well before his larger essay on surrealism, was in essence a strategy for the "revelation of an experience. The stage of this revelation is memory." Surrealist practice for Benjamin thus achieves a blurring in the

dialectical concentration of subjectivity and its objects—as it dissolves the structures of fixed subjectivity in intoxication, it thereby
unleashes the incomparable anamnestic-revolutionary power locked
into the most reviled, scorned, and ridiculed thoughts and creations of
the present. "Overcoming of rational individuality in intoxication—of
the motorial and affective individuality, however, in collective action: this characterizes the whole situation." Thus a central surrealist
achievement for Benjamin was "the overcoming of the private. This is
in point of fact a revolutionary virtue."[9]

In the essay of 1929 ("Surrealism: The Last Snapshot of the European Intelligentsia"), this theme of the overcoming of subjective individuality through intoxication takes on a central role. There, the
"dialectical kernel" that later grew into surrealism, the "dream-wave"
of Rimbaud, grew into a torrent of unleashed memories and enchanted
visions that swept the movement in its path:

> Everything with which it came into contact was integrated. Life
> only seemed worth living where the threshold between waking and
> sleeping was worn away in everyone as by the steps of multi-
> tudinous images flooding back and forth, language only seemed
> itself where sound and image, image and sound interpenetrated
> with automatic precision and such felicity that no chink was left
> for the penny-in-the-slot called "meaning." Image and language
> take precedence.[10]

This sentiment itself represents admirably the moment in the formation of surrealist practice that, for Benjamin, was decisive. One might
call it the moment at which *Grübelei* is definitively negated and transcended. "Language takes precedence," not only before "meaning,"
which now appears in a trivial, indeed laughable form, but before the
subject itself. "In the world's structure dream loosens individuality
like a bad tooth. This loosening of the self by intoxication is, at the
same time, precisely the fruitful, living experience (*Erfahrung*) that
allowed these people to step outside the domain of intoxication."[11]

This brings us a bit closer to the matter: surrealism represents, for
Benjamin, a methodological alternative to melancholy allegorical construction. More, it represents the only alternative that offered the
possibility of relating the act of critical construction immediately to
the prospect of revolutionary practice. The recovery of *Erfahrung*, of

the wholeness of experience, is itself a political act, insofar as it marks a moment where the hegemony of capitalist dream time is broken. The flood of memories that emerges from this rupture marks a "profane illumination," the "historical illumination" that Benjamin had sought in his first review of surrealist techniques.

Surrealist writings are "concerned with experiences." Esoteric theory is to have no place in them. The intoxication of drug, of dream, of automatic writing (to which, curiously, Benjamin pays no attention whatsoever) mark not so much the material of surrealist writings as the technical means for the achievement of a mode of genuinely revolutionary experience, which itself is to be attained independent of narcotics: "the true, creative overcoming of religious illumination certainly does not lie in narcotics. It resides in a *profane illumination*, a materialistic, anthropological inspiration, to which hashish, opium, or whatever else can give an introductory lesson."[12]

The precise relation between the moment of profane illumination and the dialectical image cannot be developed at this point. The significance of the profane illumination as a mode of genuine revolutionary historical experience, however, resides in its quality of spontaneity, its shocking force, that is, its total indifference to the realm of subjective intention and private contemplation.

Breton emphasized this quality of surrealist inspiration constantly. He insisted that surrealism was "based on the belief in the superior reality of certain forms of previously neglected associations" and came back time and again to his own ecstatic moment of inspiration, wherein the unbidden appearance of a discrete linguistic element—a phrase—was accompanied by "a vague visual image." Rather than the brooding subject assigning the meaning that unites linguistic element and graphic image, the two—and the organic immediacy of their connection—appear "gratuitously," unbidden, unmediated by subjective intention. This establishes the surrealist production of "illuminating" images within the medium of language. ("Language has been given to man so that he may make Surrealist use of it.")[13] Breton explains:

> It is true of Surrealist images as it is of opium images that man does not evoke them; rather they "come to him spontaneously, despotically. He cannot chase them away; for the will is powerless now and no longer controls the faculties." It remains to be seen whether images have ever been "evoked." If one accepts, as I do,

Reverdy's definition it does not seem possible to bring together, voluntarily, what he calls "two distant realities." The juxtaposition is made or not made, and that is the long and short of it. . . . In my opinion, it is erroneous to claim that "the mind has grasped the relationship" of two realities in the presence of each other. . . . It is, as it were, from the fortuitous juxtaposition of the two terms that a particular light has sprung, *the light of the image*, to which we are infinitely sensitive. [14]

For Benjamin, the enormous expansion of the scope of possible experience effected by these techniques not only suppresses subjectivity, not only provides access to the enormous explosive power contained in the mnemonic traces locked into fragments of modernity, but also points toward that overcoming of the distinction between theory and practice where the subject itself is revealed as a moment of bourgeois ideology—or in older language, that subjectivity itself, and the restrictive model of rationally transparent experience of objects that it mandates, is the oldest and most durable legacy of the mythic. The revolutionary virtues of metasubjectivity, of experience occurring "in a glass house" is most evident for Benjamin in Aragon's *Paysan de Paris*. The enchanted stroll through a mythologized Paris reveals an infinite network of dream images, correspondences, and connections, unwilled juxtapositions. The physiognomy of the city becomes a maze of "crossroads where ghostly signals flash from the traffic, and inconceivable analogies and connections between events are the order of the day." [15] But these crossroads are of incomparable value for their critical potential. The newest forms of technology appear in the forms of ancient monsters and gods. The most recent, now enchanted with the appearance of the Ur-old, gives up its ideological grip on the reified consciousness, and technological novelty itself appears as the acting-out of age-old mythological compulsions: the fascination with the labyrinth, the thrall of mythic demons and astral forces, nature as an infinite network of secret powers and influences. [16]

In the same way, the "mythologization" of the rational modern landscape of technological implements finds its dialectical counterpart, as Buck-Morss observes, [17] in the same moment in which surrealism attaches itself to the fragmentary and the outmoded. For Benjamin, "the trick by which the world is mastered . . . consists in the substitution of a political for a historical view of the past." The dreamlike appearance of the newest as Ur-old, like the sudden, shocklike access to the contemporary relevance of the out-of-fashion, is the foundation of a revolutionary criticism. Breton was

> the first to perceive the revolutionary energies that appear in the "outmoded," in the first iron constructions, the first factory build-ings, the earliest photos, the objects that have begun to be extinct, grand pianos, the dresses of five years ago, fashionable restaurants when the vogue has begun to ebb from them. The relation of these things to revolution—no one can have a more exact concept of it than these authors. No one before these visionaries and augurs perceived how destitution—not only so-cial but architectonic, the poverty of interiors, enslaved and enslaving objects—can be suddenly transformed into revolution-ary nihilism. [18]

The "profane illumination" whereby such marginalized objects sud-denly flash up in juxtapositions that encapsulate the entire historical process within them is related to revolutionary *praxis* precisely insofar as it *ceases* to conform to the model of the mournful search for meaning of the private allegorist and instead gives up the search for "meaning" altogether by giving up subjectivity. But it is only by giving up the search for objective meaning that the very objectivity of the profane illuminations establishes itself. The content of *memory* that character-izes the profane illuminations as truly remarkable forms of experience, and that allows the surrealists to "master the world of things," differs from the hypertrophied memory of the melancholy allegorist only insofar as, in surrealism, memory is released from the model of the self-reflecting subject and dispersed into the energized field of objects. Melancholy subjectivity is the axis upon which either the revolutionary or the regressive potential of the anamnestic interrogation of the objec-tive is actualized.

This idea is supported by what Benjamin himself understood as the dialectical "counterpole" of the surrealism essay, that is, the essay on Proust. A brief look at this essay not only illuminates the central issues involved in Benjamin's appropriation of the surrealists, but also sup-plements and enriches the reconstruction of Benjamin's critical en-counters with melancholy writers as well. [19]

Proust, as melancholic, exhibits hallmark symptoms: hypertrophied memory, fixation on the arrangement of experiential fragments, obsession with time, depression, contradictory behavior, self-absorption. The production of melancholy texts by Proust therefore exhibits the same set of productive paradoxes. The project of the recovery of past experience leads Proust ever deeper into the infinite web of memory. Remembrance is infinite for the melancholic. It becomes not just the material for the work, but dictates the form of the work itself. The text (Benjamin reminds us that the Latin *textum*, "web," carries within it the image of weaving) is the infinite woven tapestry of memory. The intention of the author—the application of literary traditions such as narrative seriality, plot, character development—is merely the obverse, the pattern that appears upon the back of the fabric. Like the surrealists, Proust set out consciously to reclaim the regions of experience lost and embedded in sleep. Unlike them, however, he plunged into a life-or-death struggle with sleep, rather than giving himself over to it (e.g., Apollinaire). It was a project that produced another profoundly melancholic feature: Proust's loquacity, his irresistible urge to dedicate fresh batches of words to fill up with remembrance the holes that life kept introducing into his text. The vertiginousness of textual infinity that permeates Proust's writing, with its affinities with the ostentatious verbiage of the baroque, is thus produced from memory: "For an experience is finite—at any rate, confined to one sphere of experience; a remembered event is infinite, because it is only a key to everything that happened before and after it."[20]

Yet, for Benjamin, Proust's struggle against sleep and night, his struggle to wrest from forgetting the hour, the *kairos* of fulfilled, complete time, also underlies the extent to which Proust mastered the laws of the sleeper, of the enchantment of forgetting, what Cocteau called the laws of "night and honey." "By submitting to these laws," Benjamin writes, Proust "conquered the hopeless sadness [*hoffnungslose Trauer*] within him (what he once called 'l'imperfection incurable dans l'essence même du présent'"). Cocteau—and now Benjamin—recognized Proust's immense *Trauer* for what it was: "Proust's blind, senseless, frenzied quest for happiness." Indeed the image of Proust that Benjamin offers up bears striking parallels to the messianic intensity—the always-frustrated, nevertheless always-renewed wish for happiness—that Adorno, in his Kierkegaard study, identified as the last and deepest invocation of the tear-blurred, hopeless-hopeful optic of melancholy. The demand for happiness "shone from [Proust's] eyes. They were not happy. But in them lay happiness as it does *in* play or *in* love." It is a will that Proust carefully concealed from his own readers, driven by a sort of moral hygiene not to spoil them with the sweet image of hope that permeated his most disappointed and *grüblerish* siftings and weavings through piles of memories. Proust's work evokes an "elegaic happiness" in the depths of its melancholy: "the eternal repetition, the eternal restoration of the original, the first happiness."[21]

This implies a revisioning of the perception of time. Proustian time loses all linearity and becomes convoluted and tangled like yarn, in which moments in an experiential continuum that lie chronologically distant can touch one another. The present and a distant lived moment of childhood intersect, are brought together to form a simultaneity and instantaneous unity. Time is depicted in "its most real—that is, space-bound—form." Each moment upon it draws magically near its counterpart; the flashes of temporal *correspondances* thus acquire in Proust's work a special force as the materiality of life, its touches, smells, and tastes, deliver up shocking moments of temporal concentration, sudden and unwilled contemporaneity from the depths of the personal archaic. The "painful shock of rejuvenation" of the *mémoire involontaire* causes the contraction of the entire span of lived time; such pain—akin, in fact, to Ficino's—awakens, "charges an entire lifetime with utmost awareness,"[22] and fills the consciousness with a spiritual acuity and sharpness of insight so intimately bound up with sadness that the two become indistinguishable.

Such agendas require all the subtlety of a melancholic frame of mind. Proust's technique consists of disciplined boredom, turning the experience of melancholia against itself. Boredom leads to dream; Proust's "pointless stories" enchant the fields of memories—our memories as well as Proust's—in preparation for their recovery. Like the surrealists too, Proust's "cult of similarity" has its origins here, in the need to summon forth the archaic networks of materialistic correspondences from memory itself. In the childlike world of dream correspondences, which Proust conjured up while struggling all the while against the dream *form* in which they were contained, memory's dialectic unfolds: as for Kierkegaard, the relation with things intrudes deep into the heart of subjective inwardness. As for Kierkegaard, too, writing summons the unnameable thing whose presence alone could assuage homesickness. Proust "lay on his bed racked with homesickness, homesick for the world distorted in the state of similarity [*Änlichkeit*], a world in which the true surrealistic face of existence breaks through."[23] The image is the "fragile, precious reality" that is distilled from Proust's mournful, hopeful writing. The image is the moment of quiet, the suspended breath in which the mournfulness and homesickness of one addicted to memory comes closest to its messianic fulfillment in happiness. It emerges from dust and detail and transfigures them into the hour of redemption.

Proust takes his rightful place in the halls of nineteenth-century melancholy writing. Like Kierkegaard and Baudelaire, his melancholy gaze falls upon and transforms the object-realm specific to the reality of a historical epoch. In this sense Proust's melancholia directs itself toward commodities. Proust, the "young snob" and playboy (as Kierkegaard) becomes the site for the self-expression of the archaism of the commodity world of the nineteenth century with a clarity and graphicness unknown to reformist authors such as Zola. Melancholy *Handlungshemmung* intrudes in the one by the voluntary idleness of the salon; in the other in the self-obscure occlusion from relations of production. Proust is an aristocratic parasite; Kierkegaard is a bourgeois landlord. Proust's depiction of the salon thus bears notable affinities to Kierkegaard's *intérieur*. In both cases—in Proust's representation of *Geschwätz* as the inner structure of society, as in Kierkegaard's—the aloofness from society and the inscription of social pathologies into suffocating spaces provide the form in which a desperate insight into transience and the evaporation of meaning finds expression. But whereas Kierkegaard withdraws ever deeper into inwardness, Proust attempts to smash the realm of bourgeois ethics with laughter. His aristocracy makes him incapable of moral indignation.

This underlies Proust's allegories. They are fed by his desire to disappear into the elite, the "polished professionals of consumption."[24] In this way Proust's characteristic allegory arises from the vision of a chasm separating meaning from physical existence and the consignment of the latter into transience; into the endless rhythm of consumption.[25] This is the moment of social actuality in Proust's weaving: "the attitude of the snob is nothing but the consistent, organized, steely view of life from the chemically pure standpoint of the consumer." By (unwittingly) revealing the economic physiognomy of this class, Proust's texts direct a shocking power of recognition, of waking, toward it. "And much of the greatness of this work will remain inaccessible or undiscovered until this class has revealed its most pronounced features in the final struggle."[26]

The "final struggle" whose negative image is perceptible in Proust is, for Benjamin, proclaimed in surrealism in bright, even gaudy colors. The subtle social indictment of the economic elite in Proust is matched by the surrealists' manifest ability to summon forth, exoterically and free of all spiritual hocus-pocus, images that not only demand revolution, but also assist it.

Proust's images, powerful as they are, are delivered by a lonely aristocrat. Proust is as isolated as Baudelaire; his work "has as its center a loneliness which pulls the world down into its vortex with the force of a maelstrom."[27] The immense isolation and concentration of selfhood in Proust determines the yield of memories and defines the boundaries of the images as well. His images can shock, but they cannot touch, they cannot move.[28] The images dredged up by the *mémoire involontaire* remain embedded in the endless fabric of Proustian prose, where *praxis*, the occasion for equally endless reflection, fades into another occasion for the solitary work of memory. No one illustrates better than Proust the dialectic fixity in which inspiration and illness are contained in one productive whole. Each image in Proust is colored by resignation, by the ebbing of the force of life. Each line is, for Proust almost literally, marked by the fragrance of death.[29]

Surrealist images retain the possibility of avoiding this condition precisely in their capacity to issue from exoteric, indeed automatic practices in which the paradigm of sorrowful selfhood is definitively overcome. Without loneliness, without pain and disease, without the whole depressed gray-upon-gray spectrum of melancholy thinking to which they had been prisoner, the images of profane illumination spring forth from memory in order to shock, but also to mobilize, to urge revolutionary *praxis*. Only in this way could surrealism effect a link between its image production and the real world of concrete social conditions. The politicization of the surrealists was itself a dialectical process; the movement from sarcasm to political action was only possible with the help—through hostility—of the bourgeois themselves. "In the transformation of a highly contemplative attitude into revolutionary opposition," surrealism was finally given an impetus from the outside world that solitary bourgeois writers were denied: hatred.[30]

This insight—surrealism as the distilled imagistic power of allegory, liberated from its confinement within the model of the isolated melancholy subject—becomes one of Benjamin's premier models for the ideal of the decisive political engagement of the left-wing writer, one that is formative for his criticisms of his own Weimar colleagues. We have seen that the period in which the "surrealism" essay was written coincided with Benjamin's most vituperative attacks upon leftist writers whose programs for the politicization of literary production in many senses closely resembled his own. ("Linke Melancholie" and "Surrealism," for example, were written less than a year apart.)

Along with Brecht's political lyric, surrealism provides one of the few helpful examples for the decisive politicization of the bourgeois writer, and it is highly significant that this transformation from contemplation to action takes the form of the deliberate loss—or concealment—of the paradigm of the contemplative (reified) artistic subject, together with the apparatus of theories of art spun from it. In this sense surrealism's insistence on exoteric practice, unleavened by theoretical speculation, is comparable with Brecht's "crude thinking." Both recognize a situation quite similar to the one that Benjamin described in "Linke Melancholie"; that is, the subversion of the genuine interests of a political movement at the hands of mournful intellectuals by their very support of it. In the essay on Kästner, Benjamin had described not a false but a genuine, historically specific emergence of melancholia, whose particularly pernicious effects were explained by the situation in which melancholic poets deliberately attempted to align themselves with movements that demanded not contemplation but practical intervention.

The nineteenth-century melancholia of a Proust or a Baudelaire was a "motorial reaction" to the emergent world of commodity capitalism and gained its critical potential not through Baudelaire's or Proust's "politics," but by the ability of their writing, independent and often in contradiction to their conscious intentions, to record the imagistic impressions of the mythic physiognomy of the commodity itself. This seismic sensitivity of capitalist allegories had very much to do with the luster of newness of the capitalist world, whose hidden mythic, Ur-old dimension revealed itself in the allegorical way of seeing. Fifty years later, however, the "most recent" melancholics have themselves been so thoroughly incorporated into the rhythms of the commodity that even their melancholia is nothing more than a moment in the production and dissemination of articles for consumption; their melancholia has turned into one of the most far-flung and most effective outposts of the culture industry.

Melancholy subjectivity stands as a dividing line between the historically distinct appearances of the image production of Proust and surrealism and, even more sharply, as the contemporary political opposition between competing forms of the aesthetic avant-garde. Expressionism, activism, and above all *Neue Sachlichkeit* in Germany were, according to Benjamin's analysis, all the modes of "the so-called well-meaning left-wing bourgeois intelligentsia" just as much as their French counterparts. Both must therefore be "considered a potential source of sabotage."[31] Left-wing intellectuals, both French and German, that is, remained tied to a febrile, reified conception of morality, itself a mask for the world-weariness and resignation characteristic of melancholia in its specifically modern, "stupid" form. "Irremediably" coupled with any conception of political practice, such reified moral glosses invariably diluted and undermined a *praxis* that must proceed ruthlessly and radically. Moral qualms thereby transform *praxis* from a moment of sheer decisiveness to a callow aesthetical reflection, to irony and satire, which, as Benjamin observes in reference both to Kästner and to his French counterparts, bourgeois society is more than able to handle.

For surrealism, the "cult of evil" had an admirably practical application; it actually emerges as "a political device, however romantic, to disinfect and isolate against all moralizing dilettantism."[32] In this way, the inherent relation of surrealist practice to revolution consists in finally clearing the air of the "sclerotic liberal-moral-humanistic ideal of freedom," to insist in its place upon a conception of freedom that does not shy away from vileness, violence, destruction. One might say that not only this nineteenth-century ideal, but also the melancholia that is so closely associated with it, is transformed, and that the surrealists achieve the admirable feat of winning the powers of allegorical insight while at the same time replacing the isolated *Grübler* with the "destructive character" (Benjamin's model was the aptly named Gustav Glück,[33] while the premier surrealist example of this type would surely be Vaché). In contrast to the claustrophobic inwardness of the melancholic, the destructive character "knows only one watchword: make room; only one activity, clearing away. His need for fresh air and open space is stronger than any hatred." "Young and cheerful," the destroyer demands human company to the same measure as the creative character requires solitude; the frenzy of destruction, the Nietzschean aptitude for forgetting is always presenting new possibilities. Indeed, while the melancholic sees in the world of things ciphers of universal transience, the destructive character observes only more things to destroy: "Because he sees ways everywhere, he always positions himself at the crossroads. . . . What exists he reduces to rubble [*Trümmer*], not for the sake of the rubble, but for that of the way leading through it."[34]

The surrealist clears away the overgrown, depressed world of objects that crowd around him yammering for meaning and, rejecting the puzzle-like character of the real as much as the inward self, celebrates the arbitrary, constructs montages of violently rescued trash, and enjoys the fantastic images that flash up. Presumably, then, the surrealist overcomes melancholia, but does not thereby go away empty-handed. The images that the surrealist retains become implements in revolutionary struggle; rescued from their puzzle-like existence as from their previous oblivion in the "harmonious" world of capitalist myth, these images become practical implements and in this way, true to Marx, capitalism produces, dialectically and by strict adherence to its own inner logic, the implements of its own undoing.

According to Benjamin's own logic of destruction, construction, and redemption, an out-of-date fashion circular, a souvenir on its way to meet its fate in the dustbin, could have a more direct relation to revolutionary practice than a "politically motivated" novel, to an evening of harangues, or to a demonstration. The "decisive" moment consists far more in the identification of the interruptive, shocking moments lodged in the anamnestic recovery of the everyday, by which the everyday itself is revealed as strange, mythic, and artificial. Modern melancholics, for Benjamin, despite their posturing, nevertheless retain at bottom a sort of fatuous optimism.

In contrast, the "organized pessimism" of surrealist practice takes as its first goal the violent, laughing expulsion of all "moral metaphors" from politics; indeed "to discover in political action a sphere reserved one hundred percent for images. This image-sphere, however, can no longer be measured out by contemplation." Benjamin's conclusion, his dogged position of the 1930s, is clear enough: "proletarian artists" will, as Trotsky argued, have to wait for a successful revolution to come into being. The bourgeois artist who wants to assist the advent of such a revolution will not do so by the (contemplative) adoption of attitudes; it is collaboration, not support that is needed. "In reality it is far less a matter of making the artist of bourgeois origin into a master of 'proletarian art' than of deploying him, even at the expense of his artistic activity, at important points in this sphere of imagery. Indeed, might not perhaps the interruption of his 'artistic career' be an essential part of his new function?"[35]

The enormous importance of surrealism for Benjamin thus emerges in its *methodological* innovation, in its mobilization of decontextualization, montage, shock, and provocation. It consists primarily in the capacity for methodological achievements to retain the inherently critical-redemptive force of allegory while abandoning the paradigm of *grüblerishe* subjectivity in which this force loses both its redemptive encounter with the objects and its political efficacy. The paradigmatic role of surrealism extends to the heart of the *Passagenwerk* as the subsumption of esoteric theory in the name of an exoteric practice capable of recovering and summoning up the trash of nineteenth-century history into configurations so explosive that the dream time of capitalist modernity will be jolted awake.

The status of the *Passagenwerk* as a construction out of salvaged and juxtaposed fragments of the nineteenth century is of course its most prominent methodological feature. Buck-Morss's study has so thoroughly and completely documented the *Passagenwerk* as an "interpretation through the details," as a transposition of the method of montage from art into historiography,[36] that there is no need, at least at this point, to add anything substantial to this analysis. What matters more here is the extent to which the appropriation of surrealist montage as so to speak an antidote to *Grübelei* succeeds or fails, and the extent to which this appropriation introduces intractable problems in Benjamin's own critical constructions.

Benjamin's later substantial critiques of surrealism are fairly well known and consist in essence of his realization that the surrealists were not capable of transposing the "shock" of the profane illumination from the model of dream to that of waking:

Setting off the slant of this work against Aragon: Aragon persistently remains in the realm of dreams, but we want here to find the constellation of waking. While an impressionistic element lingers on in Aragon ("mythology")—and this impressionism should be held responsible for the many nebulous philosophemes of the book—what matters here is the dissolution of "mythology" into the space of history. Of course, that can only happen through the awakening of a knowledge of the past that is not yet conscious.[37]

In this way Benjamin reiterates the insight of his first text on surrealism (*"Traumkitsch"*) where, it will be recalled, the task for an appropriation of surrealist practices is the formulation of a "historical" illumination forthcoming from a history of dreams. The surrealists, especially Aragon, are not able to overcome the production of images determined by the mythical "subjection to nature"; Aragon's enchanted peasant enchants Paris, and this enchantment, it is true, has a critically powerful alienating effect upon an already mythological capitalist reality. Benjamin recognizes that this critical potential remains largely untapped in surrealist texts; the power of the slightly out of date has been identified and constructed, and the explosive force of such constructions has been detonated, but not at the points where the structure of capitalist dream time is most fragile.

This chink in the armor of capitalist modernity is the specific myth of eternal progress, read onto the phantasmagoric endless appearance of commodities. Thus capitalist modernity is weakest at the moment where its commitment to an ideology of eternalized temporal progress breaks down, and the image of transience, of natural history (the commodity as dialectical image) winks through this mask. The transition from dream to waking, that is, the transition from the mythologized consciousness of the surrealists to the mobilization of materialistic illuminations Benjamin reserved for his own critical constructions, implied not the abandonment of the methodology of montage, far less the perceived transcendence of the paradigm of melancholy subjectivity, but rather the elimination of mythological "philosophemes" by their exposure to the "space of history"; that is, the temporal index of historical catastrophe in which the truly redemptive encounter with the objects alone becomes possible. The "constellation of waking" is thus a dialectic that incorporates at once the redemption of the object and, if no longer the "representation of the idea" as in the *Erkenntniskrit-*

ische Vorrede, the explosive shock of recognition by which the mythic character of historical happening becomes visible, loses its stranglehold on collective consciousness, and reveals itself as only one possible historical alternative.

It is indeed precisely in the space between sleep and waking that the essays on Proust and surrealism constitute themselves as "counterpoles." Proust the lonely aristocrat was able to conjure from the somnolent web of text and memory the experience of waking from the dream of the nineteenth century; the surrealists tapped into the powerful vein of postmelancholic, postallegorical recognition of the structure of commodified reality, but could only do so insofar as they conceived of this recognition as dream consciousness. Benjamin's own recognition of this opposition and its vital importance for his own criticism is crystal-clear; in the notes to the *Passagenwerk* he wondered,

> Should awakening be the synthesis out of the thesis of dream-consciousness and the antithesis of waking consciousness? If so, the moment of awakening would be identical with the "Now of recognizability," in which the things take on their true—surrealistic—expression. Thus the importance, in Proust, of wagering one's whole life upon that ultimate, most intense dialectical breaking point, waking. Proust sets out with a representation of the space of the one waking up. [38]

The question that emerges in this context is this: does the dissolution of the "mythological" philosophemes of surrealism suffice in order to make surrealist practices and methodologies adequate to serve as the definitive model for Benjamin's historical criticism? An answer to such a question must begin by the realization that, for all its professed exotericism surrealism remained to the end a profoundly esoteric doctrine, so much so that we are obliged to wonder whether the mere elimination or suppression of the sorrowful theoretical dimension relevant to the act of decontextualizing and recombining cultural fragments could ever be adequate to make the activity of construction itself something other than melancholy. Such theory, which the surrealists were so intent on leaving behind them, seems to return forcefully as soon as any surrealist practice is interrogated closely.

The "profane illumination," which Benjamin was so eager to see as an entirely secular and materialistic phenomenon, increasingly bore for the surrealists themselves—above all Breton—the mark of mystery, of ecstatic transport, and Breton's descriptions of it partook of increasingly unabashed occult language in order to describe it. The illumination that the surrealists had in mind had, to be sure, a close relation to the *constructive* act of the juxtaposition of rescued, out-of-date objects, one in which the shock value was to arise not just from the most modern trash suddenly appearing as prehistoric, but also from an irreducibly *objective* element, for which the dreaming surrealist subject was nothing more than the stage. What appeared on this stage was the image of reconciliation beyond the confines of a conceptually dirempted reality. As Breton wrote:

> Everything tends to make us believe that there exists a certain point of the mind at which life and death, the real and the imagined, past and future, the communicable and the incommunicable, high and low, cease to be perceived as contradictions. Now, search as one may one will never find any other motivating force in the activities of the Surrealists than the hope of finding and fixing this point. [39]

The magic moment of transcendence encoded within profane language and the timeless image of absolute reconciliation, of the intimate connectedness of all things beyond dirempted, conceptually shattered "reality," was first made possible, it is true, by technical rather than theoretical means, by the elimination of consciousness and subjectivity in chance. But insofar as chance came to be regarded as "objective" (*l'hasard objectif*), the arbitrary itself, which Breton welcomed, was arbitrary neither in the sense of an imposition of subjective meaning upon liberated fragments, nor in the sense of an accidental or fortuitous (thus in essence meaningless) arrangement.

In the first manifesto Breton had insisted that the dissolution of the puzzle-like character of thought lay in the celebration of the arbitrary and the concomitant abandonment of the brooding search for meaning; indeed the "greatest virtue" of the surrealist image consisted in its status as "arbitrary to the highest degree."[40] By the time of Breton's 1935 essay, "The Surrealist Situation of the Object," objective chance had rendered the entire understanding of the arbitrary highly problematic. Breton himself admitted that "certain overwhelming coincidences" in different surrealist works introduced objective chance as a mysterious necessitation forming the very production of the image itself, for which the constructive act became a sort of invitation or beckoning.[41]

Peter Bürger has described the doctrine of objective chance as the moment where surrealist practice reveals its relation to ideology. The increasing significance of objective chance belies the surrealists' conviction that a dimension of objective meaning exists, despite their claims to have done away with the search for meaning. Bürger rightly understands that the moment where the surrealists fall into the arms of such a commitment to the possibility of a *recovery* of objective meaning is the moment where their status as (resigned) bourgeois individuals becomes visible. But such a recovery, Bürger argues, could only succeed insofar as it transpired within the network of mean-ends rationality, by which it would lose its character as protest. Bürger thus identifies an essentially epistemological paradox concerning the necessity and impossibility of the recovery and expression of remarkable sets of "meaningful" experiences within the context of a fallen or dominative medium of expression, an insight that points all the more strongly to the essential continuity between allegorical and surrealist construction, rather than the latter's supposed decisive overcoming of the former.[42]

It is specifically the tendency toward occult speculation, and presumably the relation of such speculation to myth, however, rather than the (more visible) relation between objective chance and passivity, that seems to have been Benjamin's most immediate concern in his appraisal of surrealist practice. Benjamin was untroubled by the "ghostly signals" and "inconceivable analogies" of surrealist images, and the insistence, even in 1929, to interpret them by reference to language, that is, "as magical experiments with words." It is in this sense that we may interpret his support in the context of his own magical theory of language, whose influence was still strong and whose transformation into materialist terms Benjamin would shortly attempt in his essays on the mimetic faculty.

Nor is the dabbling into Satanism objectionable, as we have seen, provided that the "romantic dummy" of satanic occultism is emptied in the name of the definitive overcoming of the last vestiges of bourgeois ethics. But the surrealists'—particularly Breton's—tendency to lapse into citations of parapsychology in the context of the presentation of the profane illuminations were, for Benjamin, "disturbing symptoms of deficiency":

Now I concede that the breakneck career of Surrealism over rooftops, lightning conductors, gutters, verandas, weathercocks, stucco work—all ornaments are grist to the cat burglar's mill—may have taken it also into the humid backroom of spiritualism. But I am not pleased to hear it cautiously tapping on the windowpanes to inquire about its future.[43]

The humid back room of occultism, like the "too temperate climate" of the *Ursprung* study, stifles not just thought but action. Benjamin's mistake, in the case of the surrealists, may have been the overhasty assumption that one can exit this chamber by choice.

By the second manifesto Breton was calling for the end of the present, "preparatory," and therefore merely artistic period of surrealist development, prone to all sorts of popularizations and profanations. "The approval of the public is to be avoided like the plague," Breton wrote. "It is absolutely essential to keep the public from *entering* if one wishes to avoid confusion." The future of surrealism was, in this sense, anything but "exoteric" practice; indeed it was one in which the inherently esoteric dimension of surrealist experience could come into its own.

Breton, thinking of the future, demanded the "profound, the veritable occultation of Surrealism." He suggested an exploration of astrology and "metapsychics" as media for the exploration of objective chance. The overcoming of subjectivity and the inauguration of a genuinely inter- or multisubjective conception of aesthetic-political practice was now conceived as the "pooling" of isolated intuitive minds, in which several surrealist writers produce, without interaction, coherent texts, pictures, or "the forecasting of events." And it was not entirely in the spirit of jest when Breton observed that he, Eluard, and Aragon were all born at the conjunction of Uranus and Saturn, thereby justifying the intense investigation (Saturn) of the most distant and mysterious matters (Uranus).[44]

Looking back on the development of surrealist practice decades later, in 1953, Breton's conception of the essence of surrealism becomes totally clear:

It is a matter of common knowledge today that Surrealism, as an organized movement, was born of a far-reaching operation having to do with language. In this regard it cannot be repeated too often that in the minds of their authors the products of free association or automatic writing that Surrealism brought forth in the beginning had nothing to do with any aesthetic criterion. . . . What was it all about then? Nothing less than the rediscovery of the secret of a language whose elements would then cease to float like jetsam on the surface of a dead sea. To do this it was essential to wrest these elements away from their increasingly narrow utilitarian usage, this being the only way to emancipate them and restore all their power. . . .

The spirit that makes such an operation possible is none other than that which has always moved occult philosophy; according to this spirit, from the fact that expression is at the origin of everything, it follows that "the name must *germinate*, so to speak, or otherwise it is false."[45]

It appears that Benjamin's attempt to find in surrealism a model for the conversion of his esoteric and theological theories of language into an exoteric and materialist form found a movement in which esotericism was not so much overcome as temporarily concealed for expediency. The surrealist image, for Breton in 1953, constituted

the means of obtaining, most often under conditions of complete relaxation of the mind rather than complete concentration, certain incandescent flashes linking two elements of reality belonging to categories that are so far removed from each other that reason would fail to connect them and that require a momentary suspension of the critical attitude in order for them to be brought together.

The *Grübler* may have relaxed, even dozed off in surrealist construction. But in the intention for the intentionless sudden event of correspondence, and in the implicit hope in an objective necessitation that would transport the tormented subject with it out of a reified and painful reality, surrealism disclosed its true status: the brooding subject and the puzzle world that is its natural counterpart remain. For the surrealist way of seeing, writes Breton, "the world seems to be like a cryptogram which remains indecipherable only so long as one is not thoroughly familiar with the gymnastics that permit one to pass at will from one piece of apparatus to another."[46]

On the weight of evidence, Adorno concluded that the overcoming of melancholy subjectivity in surrealism, like its overcoming of the search for "meaning" and the puzzle character of objective reality, was itself an objective illusion. The harshness of his judgment belies, I suspect, the despairing insight that Benjamin's adoption of surrealist practices was as unsuccessful a heuristic experiment as his adoption of Marxism, and that a heavy cost—the elimination of theory—was levied upon Benjamin's thinking for these errors. In his essay, "Looking Back on Surrealism," Adorno insisted that dream images do not really succeed in overcoming the puzzle character of objective reality. "There is a shattering and a regrouping, but no dissolution." The dream images, which pin their hopes on the definitive recovery of a nondominative, anamnestic relation with the objects, fail by the naive insistence on the adequacy of dream and intoxication to overcome and transcend the subject's embeddedness in a reified social totality. The surrealist's attempted "self-annihilation" of subjectivity was designed, on the one hand, to bypass the structures of reified subjectivity applied by concrete social conditions, and on the other, to open a region of disclosure in which the objectively present dream images of reified social reality could emerge as elements in a program of critical political *praxis*. But insofar as the surrealists merely replaced the conscious bourgeois subject with the dreaming one, the dialectics whereby subjectivity itself is constituted merely installs the subject more firmly by a false sublation of its relation to its objects, and the so-called immediacy of the surrealist experience is in essence nothing more than an unwitting record of the history of life among fetishes, rather than the explosion of this life.[47]

The montages, Adorno argues, may have tapped into the realm of images of bourgeois life embedded in childhood memories, the archive of illustrations of the parents' generation. But the attempt to bypass subjectivity in the interest of a reawakened realm of childhood memories is in fact the accomplishment of a subject thrown back upon itself by total reification. As absolute, the surrealist subject appears not as dreaming but as dead, and it is here that Adorno observes the essential continuity, rather than decisive rupture, between allegorical and surrealist practices. "The dialectical images of Surrealism," like those of Kierkegaard, "are images of a dialectic of subjective freedom in a situation of objective unfreedom."[48] The surrealist montages may "rescue" elements of the realm of trash where the forces of commodification have receded from the object, but only do so by recording them as literally "*nature morte,*" as a frozen image of dead bodies, a precise replication of the baroque antinomy of the allegorical.

The images of dead bodies—newspaper clippings, ticket stubs—are themselves fetishes, abandoned erotic objects. "Surrealism's booty is images, to be sure, but not the invariant, ahistorical images or the unconscious images of the unconscious subject to which the conventional view would like to neutralize them; rather, they are historical images in which the subject's innermost core becomes aware that it is something external, an imitation of something social and historical."[49] In this sense—and this is Adorno's unkindest cut not only toward surrealism but toward Benjamin's appropriation of it—the surrealist movement ought to be seen as nothing other than a sort of ideological twin to *Neue Sachlichkeit*. Both of them direct themselves "critically" against the superfluous object. Both, for Adorno, provide not so much critical alternatives to the melancholy subjectivity of late capitalism as examples of its most insidious forms of cultural domination. They are modern forms of betrayal of the objects, modern forms of withdrawal from action.

Not only does the moment of critical insight and revolutionary *praxis* dissolve; but even the melancholia itself may have been merely transformed, rather than overcome. Writing on Benjamin's own saturnine temperament, Susan Sontag has observed that the quintessential contribution of the surrealists was the triumph over melancholia, which liberated melancholia's prodigious talent for objective insight and made this critical talent serviceable for politics. "The melancholic always feels threatened by the dominion of the thing-like, but Surrealist taste mocks these terrors. Surrealism's great gift to sensibility was to make melancholia cheerful."[50]

Under the impetus of a Benjaminian (and Nietzschean) hope for the appearance of a "destructive character" whose malicious cheerfulness would prove strong enough to purge the melancholic body of the weight of memories and attachments, it is tempting to read the surrealists in this way. But the "cheerfulness" of surrealism is of a highly unusual sort, having more to do with an infinite sadness and fragile hope, a spiritual tropism toward the fragment and the detail, conjoined with a powerful rejection of all conformity to bankrupt forms of enforced reality. What once appeared as melancholic in the search for meaning is transmuted into a scorn and rage toward reality that, it is true, changes the appearance of melancholia. But "cheerfulness," lightness of spirit, is not the surrealist's gift. Humor, above all the "objective" or "black" humor that emerges as the *pendant* to the doctrine of objective chance, is an attitude of perfect rebellion, a metaphysical refusal to participate in reality and to find sources of meaning from it.

The total revolt against the real is the basic attitude against which Benjamin's political sensibilities and those of surrealism developed. Total revolt conditions, in both cases, the prodigiously creative, critical energy with which Benjamin and the surrealists turned to the refuse of the real in order to fashion revolutionary implements from it. At the same time, however, this attitude of total revolt also underlies the essentially aporetic, or at best ambiguous conceptions of critical-revolutionary agency and of the meaning of radical *praxis* that plagues both. Total revolt is by no means compatible with decisive action. On the contrary, as Bürger points out, "the regression to a passive attitude of expectation . . . must be understood as stemming from the total opposition to society as it is."[51]

Black humor—is the term's conjunction with the melancholy syndrome another uncanny surrealist coincidence?—mocks the melancholy that it replaces as pitilessly as anything else. The capacity to mock melancholia implies, it is true, a moment of self-recognition that is the hallmark of a dialectical relationship. But mocking a nightmare is something quite different from overcoming it. If surrealism perceived the thingly world not just as mournful but also as ridiculous, then the laughter of black humor breaks the spell of the world of objects that weighs so heavily upon the melancholic. This shattering effect of black humor, as Breton wrote, is that by being shattered, "the insignificant, or presumed to be so, suddenly takes on an incredible set of meanings; this is where objective chance comes in."[52] It is also the precise point where surrealism reveals itself to be a form of *spleen*, of *Trauer*, and of the allegorical puzzling of the *Grübler*. Montage, automatism, and dream image are the modes in which melancholy allegory appears in the guise of the avant-garde.[53]

But if the power of avant-garde montage is in this manner reabsorbed into the discourse of melancholia, if it thereby loses everything that was most peculiar to it and goes away empty-handed once again, the question must inevitably arise as to precisely how Benjamin's criticism, which insists resolutely on the access to moments of dia-lectically frozen objective truth embedded within the continuum of profane history, is to claim coherently its difference from melan-choly allegory, either in its seventeenth-, or nineteenth-, or twentieth-century variants. The question of Benjamin's own attempt to reconcile his critical sensibility with melancholia has, in other words, led the discussion to a point where we must ask how Benjamin seeks to justify the distinction between the allegorical and the dialectical images; that is, why the former are arbitrary, subjective, politically poisonous, and melancholy, whereas the latter are to be taken as objective, historically necessary, and charged with a historical-messianic power capable of blasting the phantasmagoria of capitalist modernity to smithereens.

6 The Trash of History

Pourtant, sous la tutelle invisible d'un Ange,
L'Enfant déshérité s'enivre de soleil,
Et dans tout ce qu'il boit et dans tout ce qu'il mange
Retrouve l'ambroisie et le nectar vermeil.
—Baudelaire, "Bénédiction"

"If a man has character," says Nietzsche, "he will
have the same experiences over and over again."
—Walter Benjamin, "A Berlin Chronicle"

The dialectical image is the central methodological and theoretical undertaking of Benjamin's mature criticism. An exploration of the nature of the dialectical image can thereby justifiably be said to be the most important issue facing contemporary interpretations of Benjamin.

The exploration of melancholy is an example of this challenge. The question concerning the status of the dialectical image is the sharpest form in which the role of melancholia for the development of Benjamin's conception of criticism can be posed. This assertion is justified by the reconstruction of melancholia. The results of this reconstruction, complex though they may be, indicate that the development of categories such as critical versus melancholy subjectivity, allegory, and catastrophic history in Benjamin's thought emphasize from different perspectives the persistent need to distinguish clearly between allegorical image, which is melancholic, and dialectical image, which *cannot be*. The former consists in the arbitrary assignation of meaning. Especially in the context of a commodified cultural landscape, such practice invariably will lose the moment of critical-messianic insight proper to it and will decay into hypersubjective brooding, self-commodification, *acedia*, political passivity. The latter, the dialectical image, must be defined in explicit contrast to this.

The centrality of the dialectical image for resolving these questions is itself certain. Even the most cursory look into Benjamin's various formulations of the status and role of the dialectical image reveal, however, that the significance of this doctrine for understanding Benjamin's thought is matched by the great difficulty that faces any unified or consistent "theory" of the dialectical image. No such theory is, it appears, to be found in Benjamin's own work.

This is due not to the lack but rather to the sheer contradictory richness of Benjamin's attempt to determine the status of the dialectical image. Susan Buck-Morss has rightly observed that the dialectical image is "overdetermined" in Benjamin's work;[1] Rolf Tiedemann comments that the concept "never achieved any terminological consistency."[2] And indeed Benjamin's formulations concerning the dialectical image, from the earliest sketches of the *Passagenwerk* from the late 1920s to the last theses on history, can be likened not so much to a steady drawing near to a theoretical objective as to a constructed constellation of often theoretically disparate moments or perspectives. The parts add up not to the image of a unified coherent whole but rather to a surfeit, an entire family of possible meanings of "dialectical image."

The concluding question here, then, will rest not so much on a thorough, theoretical reconstruction of the dialectical image, but rather will concentrate specifically on Benjamin's efforts to develop, self-consciously, a doctrine of the dialectical image that would definitively distinguish his own critical enterprise from the subjectivity and arbitrariness of melancholy allegory. In this context, the question of the *nonarbitrariness* of the dialectical image is of principal interest.

On the basic doctrines of historical materialism: (1) The object of history is that which is rescued by knowledge. (2) History disintegrates into images, not stories. (3) Where a dialectical process takes place, we deal with a monad. (4) The materialist presentation of history carries with an immanent critique of the concept of progress. (5) Historical materialism bases its procedure on experience, on common sense, on presence of mind [Geistesgegenwart] *and on dialectics.*

The richest textual field for the analysis of the dialectical image is the first half of the "N" *Konvolut* of the notes for the *Passagenwerk;* other significant sources are the 1935 Baudelaire essay "Paris: Capital of the Nineteenth Century" and the final theses on the concept of history. Regarding this first source, Tiedemann has demonstrated that, like most of the *Konvoluten,* "N" bridges all three chronological stages of the compilation of notes for the *Passagenwerk;* according to his analysis, the first thirty-seven entries in "N" correspond to the earliest stage of development, roughly simultaneous with the essays on surrealism and Proust; the middle forty-eight entries correspond with the second stage, running from 1936 to 1938 (that is, from the composition of the "Work of Art" essay to the second Baudelaire essay, "The Paris of the Second Empire in Baudelaire"); finally, the last ninety entries correspond with the final stage of development, that is, 1939 and the first months of 1940, from the last Baudelaire essay ("On Some Motifs in Baudelaire") to the theses.[3]

This chronological *sectionnement du temps* is useful for reminding us that the original impetus for articulating a notion of dialectical image distinct from the earlier occult "origin" is as old as the inspiration of the *Passagenwerk* itself, and can be read in the doctrine of "profane illumination" in the surrealism essay as well as in the concept of dream time and, at least implicitly, in the lush physiognomy of cultural objects, above all of the outdated industrial object both in that essay and in the first sketch of the "passages" from 1927. In the very first notes for the *Passagenwerk,* from mid-1927 (many of which later appear in the first and the second stages of the "N" *Konvolut*), Benjamin had already understood the "dialectic at a standstill" as the "quintessence of method."[4] Moreover, even though this original formulation, like the entire first section of the "N" *Konvolut,* shows little or no influence of a quasi-Marxist interpretation of the "expressive" relation between cultural physiognomy and productive forces and relations, what is striking about the various entries in "N" is that, amidst all the permutations and variations that Benjamin attempted in formulating the dialectical image, there is indeed a remarkable degree of consistency. This consistency can be understood to revolve around a very small number of key terms: dream and waking, myth and critical

insight, historical continuum and shocking interruption, phantasmagoria and image, fetish and historical object.

Susan Buck-Morss has presented a thorough and theoretically mas-
terful account of the genesis of the dialectical image in the notes to the
Passagenwerk. For Buck-Morss the dialectical image, as the historical
object (commodity), is an image generated at the intersection of essentially philosophical axes; that is, at the moment where the axes of
dream and waking (consciousness) and petrified and transitory nature
(reality) meet to form the tense, fleeting, historically concrete "crystallization" of "antithetical elements in one graphic visual moment."
Buck-Morss introduces Benjamin's thought according to a schematism
of these axes and its spatial dispersion into fields of representation
according to the mythic or critical generation of images out of petrified
or transitory nature, in order to understand the specific characteristics
of the production of images in general for Benjamin. ("Each field of the
coordinates can . . . be said to describe one aspect of the physiognomic
appearance of the commodity, showing its contradictory 'faces': fetish
and fossil, wish image and ruin."[5]

The imposition of this schematism on the material of the *Passagenwerk* allows Buck-Morss to impart a strong organizational structure to
the admittedly abyssal plenitude of the material itself, which without
such a structure threatens "epistemological despair." The argument is
that the dialectical image occupies none of the fields of images, but
rather situates itself precisely at the moment of greatest dialectical
tension, occurring at "the null point where the coordinates intersect."[6]
This dialectical compaction, for Buck-Morss, would tend to explain
the premier characteristics of the image itself: First, its monadic
structure, that is, the ability of the dialectical image to contain within
itself the entire pre- and posthistory of the fate of the commodity in its
consignment to capitalism, not despite but because of its graphicness
and its fragility. Related to this monadic structure is the dialectical
image's property as a disturbance in the "smooth" transmission of
historical happening under capitalist dream time. The image encapsulates not a "present" but a "now," "loaded to the bursting point with
time." Second, there is the suddenness—the shock—with which the
dialectical image "flashes up."[7] This metasubjective emergence is
related intimately with the political efficacy of the image. Rather than
the mere propagandistic dissemination of images of capitalism as

oppression, the dialectical image is a tool for the dissolution of myth, for the waking from the dream time of capitalism. Unlike propaganda, the image has an intentionless explosive power that, presumably, *forces* the beholder to see the true face of mythic capitalism in a way that no propagandistic creations or constructions could.[8]

Irrespective of the success or failure of this argument to schematize the production and dissemination of images in the *Passagenwerk* according to these axes and fields, Buck-Morss's strategy raises a number of (by now familiar) questions concerning the manner in which the subjectivity of the critic/materialist historian enters into the sudden emergence of the dialectical image. And an immediate problem is that, while the properties that Benjamin most urgently wants to attribute to these images clearly entail the virtual eradication of the active, constitutive critical subject, this very disappearance of the subject renders the shocking political effects that these images are to have highly problematic.

The dialectical image is characterized from very early on as the sudden, shocking crystallization of an imagistic experience or an experiential image, which, in absolute graphicness, springs forward from the mythic repetition of (capitalist) dream time. Its premier characteristics, irrespective of its particular visual content, thus consist of a combination of two formal determinants: first, its destructive relation to historical time, its character as a "now," its shocking, sudden quality; second, intimately related with this first, is its character as a crystallized image from within the field of historical objects and historical experience itself, its quality as metasubjective, an experience undergone by the critical subject, to be sure, but nevertheless demonstrating a concreteness and an explosiveness lying beyond subjective intention. It is on the basis of these qualities that Benjamin extends various claims for the monadic character of the dialectical image; its ability to contain the entire fated history of the image-object within itself as monad.

This double character of explosive immediacy and what one might refer to as "meta-intentionality" (since "objectivity" is too theologically laden a term to be of much further use) emerges as a precise negation of the two hallmark characteristics of the allegorical image; hypersubjectivity and the repetitive infinity and slowness of the allegorical activity itself. The "lightning flash of intuition" is essentially foreign to the allegorical vision, both baroque and modern.[9] *Tiefsinn*'s "intimacy" with the historical object, such as it is, is one of contemplative intensification; in this way the concentration on the object is parallel with the infinite refraction and magnification of the subject, for whom the object becomes the hollowed-out cipher of potential intentional "meaning." In contrast, the *dialectical* image is precisely "like lightning," in which the "past must be held like an image flashing in the now of its recognizability."[10]

This comes out clearly in a long, early entry in "N": Benjamin contrasts the dialectical image to phenomenological essences, arguing that the distinction between them consists in the former's "historic index."[11] This implies that phenomenological essences lack historical reality insofar as they are conjured up by a falsely inflated subject. They partake of the historicist illusion of an autonomous subject who "wills" a certain appropriative relation with elements of inner or past experience. Such an attitude, which treats the field of historical objects as a mere reservoir for instrumental use, is duplicitous with the forces of barbarism, as Benjamin would argue in the theses, and as Adorno would demonstrate at length in his critique of Husserl.[12] The abandonment of the entire paradigm of the appropriating, intentional subject, however "careful" such a subject may be, is for Benjamin the key to a historical insight:

> The historical index says not only that they belong to a specific historical time; it says above all that they come to legibility only at a specific time. That is, this "to legibility" attains a determinate critical point of motion within them. Every present is determined through the images that are synchronic with it; each now is the now of a specific recognizability [*Erkennbarkeit*].[13]

Dialectical images mark in the first instance a peculiar, nonreproducible structure in the movement of history. To the critical vision, this structure takes the form of a disturbance. Thus while the *Vorrede* of the *Trauerspiel* study had insisted that truth, existing only in the mosaic representation out of assembled fragments, thereby constitutes "the death of intention," here too the image (which now counts as historical truth) is the moment where truth "is loaded to the bursting point with time. (This bursting, and nothing else, is the death of *intentio*, which thereby corresponds with the birth of genuine historical time, the time of truth.)"[14]

This "time of truth" marks a momentary rupture in the continuum of "profane" time: "It is not that the past casts its light on the present, or the present on the past; rather, image is that in which that which has been enters, like lightning, into a constellation with the Now."[15] The statement, and many others like it, mark Benjamin's final declaration of independence from the ideology of hermeneutic interpretation.[16] The juxtapositions of the traditional jargon of bourgeois historiography (past and present, *das Vergangene* and *das Gegenwart*) with the transfigured terms in Benjamin's new, pyrotechnic understanding of history (that which has been and the now, *das Gewesene* and *das Jetzt*) signals the extent to which Benjamin recognizes the gulf separating the dialectical image from all previous attempts to "understand" or "interpret" the past.[17] The appropriative moment of interpretation ends when the entire continuum of historical happening is blasted apart, exploded by the sudden "telescoping of the past through the present."[18]

The rescue that is achieved in this manner can be achieved only for that which becomes "lost forever at the next instant."[19] The continuum of history gives up its images and loses its grip upon them; in the process it loses its grip upon collective consciousness as well. The sudden appearance of the commodity, no longer as archaic wish image, but as startling dialectical image, is the moment where the object as image is rescued from its consignment to the "continuity" of repetition, and also the moment when this continuity itself is revealed as mythic. That which has been no longer maintains its chronological, tamed distance from the present, in which both are integrated into a seamless and harmonious vision of eternal progress.[20] Rather, the comforting illusion of linear distance itself is collapsed or exploded, and the image of the commodity springs forth as a moment of awakening. ("In the dialectical image, the past [*das Gewesene*] of a particular epoch is also the 'always has been' [*das 'Von-jeher-Gewesene'*]. As such, however, it appears only to a very specific historical epoch; that is, the one in which humanity, rubbing its eyes, recognizes this dream-image for what it is."[21]

In this way the dialectical image declares its status as a direct descendent of the doctrine of origin. The "eddy in the stream of becoming" that Benjamin found concentrated in the baroque image of the corpse in the *Trauerspiel* book constituted a specific moment of "legibility," occasioned not so much by the imagination of the critic as by the objective correspondence between the concrete structures of historical experience for the baroque and the present. Moreover, Benjamin recognized that both origin and dialectical image are descendants of the Goethean *Urphänomen*, perhaps more than he had been able to perceive ten years earlier. In the notes to the *Passagenwerk*, Benjamin had "realized quite clearly that my concept of origins in the book on tragedy is a strict and compelling transfer of this first principle of Goethe's from the realm of nature to that of history. Origins—the concept of the primal event, carried over from the pagan context of nature into the Jewish concept of history. In the arcades project, I am dealing with an exploration of origins too."[22]

"The dialectical image is that form of the historical object, which meets Goethe's demand on the object of analysis: it exhibits a true synthesis. It is the primal phenomenon of history."[23]

In the recovery of this primal phenomenon, the activity of critical historiography—what the historian actually does—appears in a characteristically convoluted manner. Surely the appearance of the historical object as dialectical image contains an irreducibly transcendent, theologically explicable moment, in which the field of historical images itself suddenly yields forth a rare, monadic visual image of its tormented, oppressed structure. In this sense, there is something *unbidden* about the dialectical image, and this character of the sudden appearance of the ineffable is so palpable in Benjamin's notes that it is tempting to regard the dialectical images as a truly theological event, and the critic as little more than a sort of region of disclosure in which this event transpires.

This temptation, however, must be resisted. First of all, this simplistic view of the dialectical image is not itself dialectical. It fails to grasp the complexity with which theological categories must, for Benjamin's purposes, find their proper expression in terms of the most subtle and fragmentary moments in the sphere of cultural objects. This understanding, in fact, precedes the *Passagenwerk* by at least a decade and is one of Benjamin's firmest theological convictions, to be broken only sparingly and with extreme caution. Truth exists only in the arrangement of the fragments whose very fragmentation generates the literal texts of the absence of truth; as palimpsest truth is always and only written, and this writing enters into a dialectical relation with truth by denying its essence. The image is the moment in which this tension becomes productive. The "image" is not truth, but an image of truth. The image, it is true, "springs forth" at the dialectical crossroads of past and present, or of consciousness and reality, but also at the intersection of messianic and profane. As image, it retains its materiality. As dialectical, this very materiality contains the representation of its truth within it, and this truth fills out and expands to the bursting point the very materiality of the image itself.

In a parallel manner, the temptation to understand the role of the critic as entirely receptive must also be resisted. The apparent spontaneity of the dialectical image arises from the state of affairs in which the critic has, according to the principle of historical montage, constructed juxtaposed complexes of historical fragments. The critic must be in a position to understand the situation of historical emergency in which concrete elements of the historical past move into relationships of proximity with corresponding elements of the contemporary. The construction of montages of historical trash provides a portal or a medium for this proximity to find a form of concrete expression. This implies an irreducible subjective element into the dialectical images themselves.

The critic must be able to muster the force of a vision in which the mythic, "comforting" appearance of history as a smooth continuum of progress loses its validity; otherwise the critic is in no position to become receptive to the image. This is, in essence, a mode of *receptivity* for images that presupposes a particular attitude or disposition; a critical rejection of myth. This disposition is indispensable for the critic to be able to *recognize* that state of affairs in which, beyond the mythic veil of capitalist phantasmagoria, a concrete visual element of that which has been approaches the present in such a way that a "now," fully charged with time, becomes representable. Moreover, the critic must also be in a position to effect the representation of this moment through the juxtaposition of fragments culled from the "reject" heap of capitalist modernity. This implies the critic's own ability to understand the redemptive-anamnestic power that inheres in the fragment, as well as the critic's ability to master and bend to his own wishes the enormous mythic-alienating force of the "fragmenting" motion of the commodity economy in which he operates. For the critic, in other words, the world must transform itself into fragments as the provision of material. Finally, the critic must assume responsibility for the *correct construction* of fragments of the recovered archive of (textually expressed) historical objects in order for this "now" to achieve existence as image.

The montage principle, translated from art to history, here supplements—and not without some paradoxes—the parallel translation of the Goethean *Urphänomen* from *nature* to history. This means that the image that is to spring forth from the montage of constructed fragments is, far from the sum total of the fragments themselves, an "originary" monadic, crystallized moment, beyond the intentionality of the critic. But at the same time, the image only exists insofar as it is represented within the construction itself. And this means that, while the image is clearly not arbitrary because it is beyond the arbitrary realm of subjective (artistic or naturalistic) intention, it also extends a claim to nonarbitrariness insofar as the critic constructs the fragments *in the right way*; that is, in such a way that the fragile, transient image does indeed spring forth as legible, as graspable, as politically useful. In a central quote, Benjamin reveals that it is not just the moment of frozen *history* that marks the site of the dialectical image:

> Both the motion and the standstill of thinking is a property of thought. When thought comes to a standstill in a constellation saturated with tension, the dialectical image appears. It is the caesura in the movement of thought. Its position is, of course, not arbitrary [*beliebig*]. In a word: it is to be sought where the tension between the dialectical contradictories is greatest. In this manner, the object constructed in the materialist representation of history is itself the dialectical image. It is identical with the historical object; it justifies its explosive removal from the continuum of historical happening.[24]

For all Benjamin's emphases on the property of the image as a monadic temporal rupture, and as a meta-intentional event, it also retains an irreducibly subjective dimension. The triple task of recognition, collection of material, and construction of the dialectical image constitutes a perhaps unacknowledged degree of subjective involvement in the image itself. Moreover—and more to the point of this analysis—a close parallel emerges between these activities and the activity of "petrification," "fragmentation," and "construction" of the baroque (and nineteenth-century) allegorists.

The allegorical intuition arises when a subject enters into a mutually determining, dialectical relationship with its objects, such that *Trauer* comes to impose a lawlike, perceptible structure on subjective productivity. The specific contents of this productivity will vary with the concrete historically and economically determined objects and conditions with which this subject is confronted, and indeed the subject's productivity will, invariably, produce melancholy writing that serves as a medium for the encoding of the true nature of these historical objects themselves. In this sense, the transformation of natural *Trauer* into melancholia consists of the formation of a historically variable but formally nonarbitrary "disposition" of melancholia, according to which the mythic appearance of harmony and totality—*Schein*—decays; this moment marks the petrification or the devaluation of the world of appearances. There is a parallel between this production of a disposition, composed of both subjective and objective determinants, and the generation of the critical awareness of the mythic character of capitalist modernity—this point seems indisputable enough not to warrant further pleading. For the melancholic, this "devaluation" of the world is always already critical insofar as the "world" that is devalued is the false image of totality. It deserves to be devalued.

For the critic, too, the devaluation of the world of capitalist wish images and collective dreams is, of course, "spleen"; it is not an occasion for happiness. It is the destruction of accepted cultural and social values, and promises the experience of exclusion. In both cases, the coinage of this devaluation of the falsely valuable is sadness.

But a far more relevant parallel occurs insofar as we understand the basic *productive* homology at work here; that is, the transformation of a devalued world into a world of fragments. This productivity of "fragmentation" is of course in principle an act of destruction. I have analyzed in detail the extent to which destruction lies at the heart of the baroque but above all the nineteenth-century allegorical production of images. For Benjamin's dialectical image as well, destruction is a necessary condition. The emergence of the field of cultural objects not merely as commodities, that is, not merely as satisfactions of collective wishes, but also as fragments to *another* text, to a construction that would blast the world open, is at the heart of Benjamin's productivity as well. For Benjamin's Baudelaire, allegory is the bloody implement of destruction, which chops up the world (and the reified self) but is also the only tool suitable for hacking through the overgrown, mythic structure of the commodity. Benjamin too wants to fashion a cutting tool in order "to clear access to fields in which until now only madness reigned. Forge ahead with the razor-sharp axe of reason, without looking left or right, so as not to succumb to the horror which beckons from the depths of the forest primeval. Reason must finally clear out all the underbrush of madness and myth. This is what will be achieved here for the nineteenth century."[25]

For Benjamin, who realizes far better than Baudelaire (or Aragon, or Kästner) the dangers of the remythologization of those very elements that the melancholy vision wrests from myth, destruction not only liberates material, but it also protects it from reenchantment: "The destructive moment in materialist historiography must be conceived as the reaction to a constellation of danger threatening both the content of transmission and those to whom this content is transmitted." In contrast to this governing metaphor for the allegorical intention, however, Benjamin distinguishes his own activity not only as cutting, but also—and primarily—as blasting:

> The destructive or critical moment in materialist historiography reveals its worth in the explosion of the historical continuity, an explosion in which the historical object constitutes itself. In fact, an object of history cannot be targeted [*visiert*] in the continual process of history. From the beginning, historiography has, accordingly, simply seized an object from out of this continuous process of history. But this occurred without any basic justification, as a necessary expedient, and this historiography thus always tended to reinsert this object back into a continuum that historiography had renewed through empathy. Materialist historiography does not choose its objects lightly. It does not seize; rather, it blasts them out of the historical process. Its precautions are more wide-ranging; its events are more essential.[26]

"If the historical object is to be blasted out of the continuum of the historical process," Benjamin concludes, "this is demanded by its monadological structure. This structure initially emerges in the blasted-out object." Insofar as this is the case, critical competence is the moment in which this monadology emerges, shockingly, as legible. This implies not only destruction and fragmentation, but also the critical construction of constellations of redeemed fragments, the (textual) medium of the appearance of the dialectical image as monad. And indeed one of the central *methodological* tensions running through the "N" *Konvolut* is that between the notion that critical vision "blasts" the dialectical image out of the continuum of mythic history on the one hand, and on the other hand, that this same critical talent "constructs" the dialectical image from the "trash of history." This tension does not dissipate, but is certainly rendered more clear by the realization that here "construction," as the transposition of the technique of the montage from art into historiography, is itself a violent, indeed a pyrotechnic operation. There is, to be sure, a specific destructive moment in materialist historiography that methodologically precedes construction: "For the materialist historian," Benjamin warns, "it is important to keep strictly separate the construction of a historical state of affairs, and what one customarily refers to as 'reconstruction.' 'Reconstruction,' through empathy, is one-dimensional. 'Construction' presupposes 'destruction.' "[27] Destruction not only removes the object from its embeddedness in the historical continuum, but also it demolishes this continuum. The wealth of fragments is the material for historical reconstruction. The dialectical image does not simply appear, fully formed, as the result of destruction. Destruction is the necessary but not sufficient condition for the appearance of the dialectical image. Only by the constructive act of materialist historiography does the dialectical image appear as monadological; that is, not as the archaic image, but represented through the details, fully concrete and historically determinate yet also monadically containing its entire pre- and post-history within it.

In this way "construction," montage, or the art of pyrotechnic quotation emerges as the central subjective element in the dialectical image. This in itself is not particularly surprising; it would have been far more odd, and far more at risk of remythologization, for Benjamin to have insisted that the dialectical image required the materialist historian merely as a passive stage or backdrop for its unbidden appearance. The moment of contact between a past epoch and the present, which underlies why certain kinds of historical insight are possible under certain determinate conditions (why dialectical images are possible only at specific times), is of course thoroughly beyond the creative control of the critic.[28]

The "commentary on reality" that Benjamin is attempting is obliged to operate by "erecting the largest constructions out of the smallest, sharpest, most cuttingly manufactured structural elements. Indeed, to discover the crystal of the total event in the analysis of the tiny single moment itself. Therefore, to break with historical vulgar naturalism. To grasp the construction of history itself. In the structure of commentary. 'Trash of History.'"[29] The subtle equivocation evident in this sentiment is significant. Given the structure of commentary it is not entirely certain whether the task is to grasp the structure of history itself from within the tiniest, most finely tailored fragments, or whether to use these fragments to construct larger, more imposing historiographic structures. The dialectical image, to be sure, is a moment of "messianic cessation of happening" that emerges within the oscillation between these two moments. But, between the critical *apprehension* of the universal within the particular or the critical *construction* of an image of the universal from carefully crafted particulars, there rests a dialectical opposition that, while not necessarily in need of resolution, does present our old question in a new form. What is it about the *constructive* moment of materialist historiography that assures the *correct* construction of the finely cut fragments?

This question is posed with the older, allegorical image of the jigsaw puzzle in mind. The construction that Benjamin is thinking of clearly bears close affinities to it. In both cases, image fragments, presented to the subject by the destructive moment, are refigured and are transformed from "mere" fragments into puzzle pieces. Benjamin's reference to the "trash of history" as "the most sharp, most cuttingly fashioned structural elements" of a construction signals this clearly. The puzzler seizes these pieces at random. The originary memory of the puzzle's solution is withheld; the brooder has forgotten the Great Solution. But this solution is visible through its absence. The brooder remembers that there is a *correct* construction of the pieces, but does not remember what it is. This is the theological ground of the ruthless imposition of subjective meaning upon the fragments, that is, their degradation into mere ciphers, empty vessels awaiting whatever meaning the brooder chooses to impose upon them.

Now, Benjamin clearly understands that the redemptive-critical moment of the allegorical intuition is lost precisely at that moment when the brooding subject, through the *imposition* of meaning, "betrays" the objects while rescuing them, and it is this imposition of subjectivity that ultimately underlies the various forms of failure that allegory exhibits in its different historical forms. His project for the reactivation of a kind of materialistic-collective memory, as we have seen, operates within the force field between the strategies of anamnestic liberation in the surrealists and in Proust and struggles to clarify a kind of recovery of concrete, graphic elements of the past that would not, in the process of this recovery, become ciphers of subjective intention. The attempt to describe this sort of redemptive encounter with the objects of the cultural past has, accordingly, continued Benjamin's far older epistemological project of grounding modes of extraordinary cognition by eliminating, or suppressing, the role of the intentional subject. But the doctrine of the dialectical image, the crowning achievement of this project, nevertheless raises, albeit in "materialist" terms, the question of the role of the subject in the act of construction. Does the materialist historian make the dialectical images or find them?

This is in effect nothing other than the vexing problem of philosophical representation that Benjamin had confronted in the *Vorrede* of the *Trauerspiel* study. Here, the "problem of construction" clearly emerges as the central methodological problem of the entire *Passagenwerk*. It is, moreover, the heart of the disagreement between Benjamin and Adorno over the development of Benjamin's work.

Adorno's critique of the 1935 précis of the *Passagenwerk*, "Paris: Capital of the Nineteenth Century," is instructive in this regard. The breadth and depth of the issues involved in this debate forbid any substantive analysis in this context; moreover, the basic issues and arguments of this disagreement are well documented and thoroughly discussed in the secondary literature.[30] However, focusing specifically on the twin problems of the task of construction and the role of the critical subject will clarify the theoretical problem that Benjamin's final conception of criticism confronts—or reconfronts.

Adorno's first response to the thoroughly montagelike construction of the 1935 exposé was swift and unambiguous: "You have left the concept of construction completely unilluminated; as both alienation *and* mastery of material, it is already eminently dialectical and should, in my opinion, forthwith be expounded dialectically."[31] The problem was, of course, the montage tactic itself; Adorno was convinced that the theoretically unmediated juxtaposition of sheer textual elements could just as easily be taken as mythical rather than evoking the explosive image that Benjamin had in mind. For Adorno, "construction" implied nothing more than the juxtaposition of historically contradictory elements (that is, archaic images and images of modern industrial objects). What was missing was the dialectical theory, supplied by the critical subject, that would illuminate that the juxtaposed contradictories in fact were contradictory. Only by such mediation, for Adorno, could the contradiction move from a mere static presentation of facts to a truly dialectical critique of the underlying social causes for the antinomy to exist.[32]

Benjamin's need to "demythologize" the dialectical image by making the image "appear" by virtue of exoteric, materialist construction alone—that is, without the mediation of the subject—results, ironically, in the very remythologization of the dialectical image that Benjamin most feared. Accordingly, Adorno urged the reintroduction of the theological dimension of the dialectical image that Benjamin had been so careful to conceal.[33] Two weeks later, Benjamin wrote to Greta Karplus: "This much is certain: the constructive moment for this book means that which the philosopher's stone means for alchemy."[34]

The move from the montage technique of the 1935 essay to the (famously rejected) first "Baudelaire" essay recapitulates the problem. It is still one of the disappearance of the subject in the act of construction. Adorno's rejection of "The Paris of the Second Empire in Baudelaire" is again based on method: "I am aware," wrote Adorno in 1938,

> of the ascetic discipline which you impose on yourself to omit everywhere the conclusive theoretical answers to questions, and even make the questions themselves apparent only to initiates. But I wonder whether such an asceticism can be sustained in the face of such a subject and in a context which makes such powerful inner demands. As a faithful reader of your writings I know very well that there is no lack of precedents for your procedure [of montage]. I remember, for example, your essays on Proust and on Surrealism which appeared in *Die literarische Welt*. But can this method be applied to the complex of the Arcades? Panorama and

"traces," flâneur and arcade, modernism and the unchanging, *without* a theoretical interpretation—is this a "material" which can patiently await interpretation without being consumed by its own aura?[35]

For Adorno, simple montage-juxtaposition of the cultural object as the sole principle of construction "conspire[s] in almost demonic fashion against its own interpretation." The "artificiality" of such an approach—that is, the willful *suppression* of the activity of the intentional, interpreting subject—not only remythologized the images, but also it thereby undermined the images' political efficacy. The shocking force of the images was lost by the introduction of "behavioristic overtones" to the images; that is, the act of "relating them immediately and even causally to corresponding features of the infrastructure. Materialist determination of cultural traits is only possible if it is mediated through the *total social process*."[36]

What Adorno wanted, on one level, was simply the return of theory. This alone, Benjamin's theological, "resolute, salutary, speculative theory" would force Benjamin away from "the wide-eyed presentation of mere facts"; that is, off "the crossroads between magic and positivism." "It is the claim of this theory alone that I am bringing against you."[37] Given the enormous project Benjamin undertook to develop a "construction out of facts" alone, indeed a "construction within the complete elimination of theory,"[38] it was a particularly devastating charge.

There is a strong tendency to read this exchange solely in the light of the series of catastrophes that was about to transpire. Adorno's patient condescension on the question of dialectics seems so frustrating because, in one relevant sense, he is calling for the theoretical dilution of precisely the talent for fascination, for the creative blurring of the distinction between subject and objects, that constituted Benjamin's special genius and that Adorno so clearly lacked. There is, as an astute critic has observed, a temptation to read Adorno's call for more theory as a call for Benjamin to bring his thought back down to the more "philosophical" level of Adorno; to see Adorno as a sort of Salieri, insisting that Benjamin's Mozartian, untheorizable gift for object-magic be translated, whatever the cost, to the dreary categories of Western philosophy.[39]

This tendency is, to be sure, valid to some extent. But more significant is the understanding that, even more than theory, it is the role of the critical subject that is the bone of contention here. Adorno sees more clearly than Benjamin that the total elimination of theory only comes at the cost of the total or near-total elimination of the subject; moreover, that this elimination is elusive and dangerous. We have seen how this attempt in the surrealist avant-garde in fact functioned to reintroduce subjectivity at an "occult" level, with the concomitant decay of the political relevance of the surrealist image. Adorno is correct in wondering whether Benjamin's dialectical images could, without any theoretical mediation, manage a politically relevant, subjectless "construction" without succumbing to myth.

The elimination of the subject is, to be sure, the elimination of the *Grübler*. This is how the construction of dialectical images was to distinguish itself from the construction of allegorical images; how the former was to escape the *arbitrariness* of imposed meaning of the latter. Adorno, to his credit, understood that the mere *assertion* of metasubjectivity, underwritten by an adherence to materialist principles and surrealist methods, would not guarantee the disappearance of the *Grübler* any more than the immediacy of juxtaposition would deprive Benjamin's constructions of their character as puzzles awaiting decipherment. Although Adorno embraced as invaluable the fragmentary nature of Benjamin's thought, and the prospects for a postidealist construction of constellations in the service of the representation of a fleeting, historically embedded truth, he was never without his doubts concerning the mythic dimension latent within Benjamin's epistemology, especially in the *Vorrede*.[40]

Adorno's own conception of the puzzle character of theoretically guided critique, though glanced at earlier, can be mentioned once again in this context. In his 1931 inaugural address, "The Actuality of Philosophy," Adorno expressed in encoded form an anxiety concerning Benjamin's method: in opposition to the undialectical conception of "objectivity" in the phenomenological tradition culminating in Heidegger's fundamental ontology, Adorno turns to the model of postsystematic, essayistic, negative philosophical representation, the image of the construction of constellations from his reading of the *Ursprung des deutschen Trauerspiels*, comes suddenly to a reformulation: philosophy as puzzle solving. But Adorno's conception of the jigsaw-puzzle nature of philosophy differs from Benjamin's in one apparently incon-

spicuous, nevertheless crucial aspect. The role of the puzzler is transformed from *Grübler*, who wants to solve the puzzle, into philosopher,
who wants to destroy it. To "solve" a puzzle, for Adorno, consists not in
reassembling its pieces but in the discovery or invention of the "key,"
which at once makes the puzzle spring open, but which also thereby
dissolves (*aufhebt*) its status as puzzle.[41]

The implication, though subtle, is clear. The philosophical conviction that insists on solutions that leave the puzzle intact are in themselves moments in which philosophical idealism finds another hiding
place. The "solution" that dissolves the puzzle in the process of
answering it is one in which philosophical interpretation can complete
itself only in the transition to political *praxis*. Anything else is *Grübelei*—could this be what Adorno feared in Benjamin's case?

Adorno came increasingly to suspect that the "elimination" of subjectivity in Benjamin's materialist criticism served not the interests of
the destruction of the puzzle-like character of the real but, on the
contrary, tended in fact to reinforce this very commitment to spontaneous and metasubjective "meaning" by the most subtle of routes. The
image of the world as laden with meanings, to be discovered in the
picture-puzzle, is antithetical to the moment where social criticism
moves to *praxis*. Adorno's insistence that Benjamin "reintroduce" the
subject is not merely the call to drag categories of bourgeois idealism
back into a philosophical thinking that had so laboriously done away
with them. The problem is that "doing away with the subject" cannot,
in philosophical thinking itself, determine of its own whether the
"subject" has been transcended dialectically or merely concealed.
Moreover, the activity whereby the subject is *falsely* transcended can
indeed, as in the case of surrealism, constitute a slip back into the
antinomies of bourgeois idealism by positing a realm of essential
ahistorical meanings lying beyond, and implicitly justifying, the realm
of actual social conditions. Camouflaging the autonomous subject
could constitute that gap in thought, in which the reified subject can
install itself all the more tenaciously. The vigor with which the thinker
rejects the model of subjectivity as brooding interiority, as the source of
wholly subjective, hence arbitrary meanings, can indeed lead to a
rejection not so much of melancholy subjectivity as of subjectivity in
toto, and this rejection may itself be an implicit adoption of the very
conviction of the real existence of metasocial "meaning" that underlies

the brooding subject itself. To reveal that the world does not in fact have a puzzle-like character—to reveal that this character itself is produced by economic imperatives, by the fetishism of the commodity—is quite different from the attempt to overcome the brooding subject in order that the puzzle be *truly* solved, that the "real meaning" spring forth over the place where the subject once stood, blocking its entrance.

In 1931 Adorno still seemed confident that the inroads into new strategies of philosophical representation that Benjamin had laid out in the *Trauerspiel* book could lead to a truly dialectical criticism, to the illumination and destruction, through the fragments themselves, of the very fragmentary, puzzle-like character of the real. Five years later, it seems that Adorno feared that Benjamin had begun to slip back into the ideology of real meaning. What Adorno feared happening in the Baudelaire essays and in the *Passagenwerk* is not too little subjectivity but, in a curious way, too much.

"Construction" as hiding the melancholy subject is a suspicion that goes hand in hand with another one: the notes to the *Passagenwerk* as the mounds of cut-up picture-puzzle pieces awaiting the patient, tireless reconstruction by the solitary historian. "I wonder," Adorno once wrote to Benjamin, "whether such ideas need to be immured behind impenetrable layers of material as your ascetic discipline demands." In another, more telling passage: "Gretel [Adorno] once said in jest that you are an inhabitant of the cave-like depths of your Arcades and that you shrink from finishing your study because you are afraid of having to leave what you have built."[42] An insensitive remark, given Benjamin's precarious refuge, burrowed deeply in the inhospitable cave of the Bibliothèque Nationale. Benjamin nevertheless seemed to have the same impression, which even rose on occasion to the level of a methodological postulate: "Something to say on the method of composition itself: how everything one is thinking must, at any cost, be incorporated into the work one is doing." For the vast, cross-indexed, labeled, sorted, filed, and annotated mass of notes that constitute the *Passagenwerk*, it is true that "knowledge is always lightning-like; the text is the thunder rolling long afterward."[43] But with the lightning gone and only its textual imprint continuing to roll on and on, the image of the *Passagenwerk* as a never-finished puzzle is a strong one.

What remains of the *Passagenwerk* is a series of juxtapositions.

Masses of images and snatches of text are culled from the archival cultural field of the "dreamtime" of the nineteenth century. They are provisionally sorted into piles. Some of them have been "fitted"; this image with that text, this text with that image. Many have been fitted together a number of times, with different partners. The *Konvoluten* record the process of this repeated shuffling and juxtaposition, as well as the process whereby the heap of fragments awaiting fixture in the construction mounted ever higher. The final construction cannot be guessed at, even with the help of the many outlines, plans, and hints left over.[44] What emerges is the mass of emblems. Ripped from their context, they begin to appear as runes. The distance between the allegorical and the dialectical image collapses as the ground for Benjamin's elimination of the melancholy subject begins to crumble.

Reflecting on the relation between allegorical and dialectical image in the *Passagenwerk*, Susan Buck-Morss has remarked:

> When Benjamin conceived of the Arcades project, there is no doubt that he was self-consciously reviving allegorical techniques. Dialectical images are a modern form of emblematics. But whereas the baroque dramas were melancholy reflections on the inevitability of decay and disintegration, in the *Passagenwerk* the devaluation of (new) nature and its status as ruin become instructive politically.

Accordingly, the sudden insight of the transiency of bourgeois monuments to eternal progress "does not cause sadness; it informs political practice."[45] It is also possible that it is not so much the political efficacy of the dialectical image that allows it to transcend melancholia (and thereby distinguish itself from allegory) but, on the contrary, that only by overcoming melancholy allegory first can the dialectical image acquire any political relevance. This is, of course, the question of the arbitrariness of the dialectical image once again.

In her discussion of the theoretics of the *Passagenwerk*, Buck-Morss takes this same question seriously and understands that the question of the suspected "arbitrariness" of the dialectical image involves the distinction between it and the allegorical image. The task for Benjamin was to show that "materialist historiography," as opposed to allegory, offered a genuinely redemptive model for the critical intervention into the realm of the object. This, in turn, devolves upon the theoretical explication of the role of the subject in the production of the allegorical and the dialectical image.

Buck-Morss understands the resultant paradox in this way: there are (apparently) contradictory requirements of the historical montage ("I have nothing to say. Only show"), with its concomitant suppression of theory, on the one hand, and on the other, the clear requirement for some—any—intrusion of subjective imagination into the production of the dialectical image. Buck-Morss asks, "Are the dialectical images too subjective in their formulation? Or not subjective enough?"[46]

By reconstructing the positions of Hans-Robert Jauss and Peter Bürger, Buck-Morss shows that both alternatives, developed to their extremes, become unacceptable. Jauss observes the "allegorical" character of Benjamin's own critique of Baudelairean allegory (as Witte observes in the allegorical criticism of the baroque) and ultimately celebrates the "disappearance of the object" and the exhilarating arbitrariness of the field of references in allegoresis; thus what Benjamin had objected to as the betrayal of the object by baroque and modern allegory, Jauss celebrates as a liberation from an antiquated commitment to "objectivity" and a thinly disguised, insupportable naturalism. Bürger, in his cautionary reading of the hidden commitment to a theology of meaning in the surrealists, warns of the "disappearance of the subject" in the automatic manipulation of meaning-laden, mysterious nature, with its concomitant concession to political resignation. If both the object and the subject disappear, argues Buck-Morss, "one is left only with language and its textual traces—in fact the epistemological ground of that contemporary position held by certain structuralists, deconstructionists, and postmodernists who have claimed Benjamin as their precursor."[47]

Buck-Morss is not willing to entertain the possibility of the disappearance of the subject or the object, let alone both. She acknowledges that "with the dialectical image, [Benjamin] had consciously placed himself in close proximity not only to the Surrealists, but to the Baroque emblematists as well."[48] The task, at this point, is to show how Benjamin managed to appropriate dimensions of the critical/pictorial conduct of both, in order to fashion a criticism that would satisfy a series of interlocked demands: the dialectical image must be nonarbitrary without being mysterious, politically explosive without being propagandistic, and true to the objects without sinking into subjective, melancholy inwardness.

Buck-Morss's answer to this question is highly illuminating, for what it does and does not resolve: she turns, as one must in the face of this question, to theology. Specifically, Buck-Morss argues that Kabbalism provided Benjamin with the theoretical and the methodological model for appropriating what he needed both from surrealist and allegorical image production. In Kabbalism, Buck-Morss observes, Benjamin found precisely what he was looking for: a contemplative attitude toward the fragments of reality that would both "read" them as textual elements, that is, as an encoded message of the promise of the destructive/redemptive return of the Messiah (and a nonpropagandistic critical indictment of the reality of social oppression and injustice), and also cherish these same fragments not as mere ciphers awaiting interpretation, but as valuable, divine elements of God's creativity, themselves in need of and deserving rescue. Kabbalism, according to Buck-Morss, thereby

> provided an alternative to the philosophical antinomies of not only Baroque Christian theology, but also of subjective idealism, its secular, enlightened form. Specifically, Kabbalism avoided the split between spirit and matter which had resulted in the Baroque dramatists' "treacherous" abandonment of nature, and it rejected the notion that redemption was an antimaterial, otherworldly concern.[49]

What follows in Buck-Morss's argument is a recapitulation of the historical and interpretive tenets of Kabbalistic practices, derived (as virtually all such recapitulations are) entirely from Scholem. The doctrine of the shattering of the *Sephiroth* as the metaphysical source and counterpart of the historical *Galut*, the mystical significance of words, the ability to read fallen nature as an encoded text of the promise of the Messiah's apocalyptic return, alienation as ignorance of, rather than separation from God—this provides, for Buck-Morss, the doctrinal ground on which to build her case for the mystical authority of the later dialectical image.

An obvious question here becomes why a transferral of the question of the arbitrariness of interpretive images from Benjamin to another intellectual model should solve the question. Why are the "images" of the Kabbalists not just as open to the charge of arbitrariness as

Benjamin's? Buck-Morss turns to Scholem's reading of the Kabbalistic image for the answer.

Scholem has a very conventional understanding of the distinction between allegorical and symbolic forms. The former is the infinite, repetitive, subjective assignation of meaning; it subsists in the profane gap between thing and meaning, and thereby tends to grow into an infinity of meanings in which anything can mean anything else. The latter is the divine, pellucid immediacy of image and meaning. Scholem compares the production of the Kabbalistic image to the *theological symbol:*

> For the Kabbalist too, every existing thing is endlessly correlated with the whole of creation; for him too, everything mirrors everything else. But beyond that he discovers something else which is not covered by the allegorical network: a reflection of the true transcendence. The symbol "signifies" nothing and communicates nothing, but makes something transparent which is beyond all expression. Where deeper insights into the structure of the allegory uncover fresh layers of meaning, the symbol is intuitively understood all at once—or not at all. . . . It is a "momentary totality" which is perceived intuitively in a mystical *Nu*—the dimension of time proper to the symbol.[50]

For Buck-Morss, this answers the question of the arbitrariness of the lightning image of Benjamin as well:

> The Kabbalist may start out like the allegorist, juxtaposing sacred texts and natural images; but when past text and present image come together in a way that suddenly both are illuminated in the Messianic light of redemption, so that the historical present becomes visible as pregnant with the potential for worldly utopia, then allegory's arbitrariness is transcended.

According to this appropriation, via Scholem, of the symbolic structure of Kabbalism, Buck-Morss is thus prepared to indicate the true, that is, the theological basis for the distinction between allegorical and dialectical images:

> Allegorical and dialectical image are distinct. The meaning of the former remains an expression of subjective intention, and is ultimately arbitrary. The meaning of the latter is objective, not

only in the Marxist sense, as an expression of sociohistoric truth, but also, simultaneously, in the mystico-theological sense, as "a reflection of the true transcendence," to use Scholem's phrase.[51]

Difficulties emerge from this argumentative strategy. There is, first, the risk of overemphasizing the role of Jewish theology, in particular its mystical, Kabbalist form, for the genesis of Benjamin's theory of the dialectical images. Sensitive to this problem, Buck-Morss argues that Kabbalism operates not as manifest theology but as a *Grundbestimmung*, a basic intellectual vision, a heuristic pattern for the development of a mystico-materialist, redemptive encounter with the fragments of the nineteenth century.[52] The centrality of the redemptive moment within the dialectical image, accordingly, can be traced, if not back to Kabbalism itself, then back to the sensitivities to the object, to the messianic intensity, and to the hermeneutics of care that Benjamin discovered in his creative appropriation of it.

But a deeper hermeneutic problem occurs when we consider the complexity of the process by which Benjamin himself "appropriated" this basic attitude of Kabbalist mysticism. It was, as Michael Löwy has argued, a process in which the reading of Jewish theology through the filter of German romanticism provided a set of aesthetic-theological problems that, while certainly germane for the theological tradition of Judaism, are nevertheless quite distinct from them.[53] In particular, it is this historically unique synthesis that underlies Benjamin's difficult understandings of subjectivity, of subject-object relations, of sadness, of the task of critical thinking. Indeed, insofar as Kabbalism here refers specifically to the (historically concrete) achievement of Scholem, who was fully as much a member of this group of "secular Jewish messianists" as was Benjamin, one must be sensitive to the possibility that an act of textual appropriation is simply not a sufficiently complex model to account for the ambiguity attending the doctrine of the dialectical image. Indeed, one could even argue that Scholem's own reconstruction of Jewish mysticism, inspired by his own earliest intellectual experiences, was itself a mark of the influence of Benjamin, a possibility that would certainly confuse the issue of *Benjamin's* appropriation of Kabbalism!

Moreover, following this line of thought, the argument that Kabbalism establishes the nonarbitrariness of the dialectical image based upon it relies, virtually entirely, upon Scholem's claim that the imagistic productivity of the Kabbalistic-dialectical mode of speculation is "symbolic"; that is, unlike the arbitrary allegory, it marks a moment of "true transcendence." Now, it is surely correct to observe that one central polarity between allegorical and dialectical image, according to Benjamin, is the temporal one; allegorical slowness and repetition versus dialectical shock and temporal rupture. And it is tempting to attribute this shocking moment directly to the ecstatic moment of intuitive illumination of the theological symbol. But to attribute this to the symbol at the expense of the allegory is to read things quite contrarily to Benjamin himself, who after all argued at length not only that there was a messianic, redemptive force lodged, however paradoxically, within the *allegorical*, but also that, conversely, it is the *symbolic* mode that hides a moment of myth.

Indeed, in citing Scholem, Buck-Morss observes that Scholem appeals, like Benjamin, to Creuzer for the distinction between symbol and allegory. But, as Menninghaus has argued, Benjamin actually deliberately *reverses* Creuzer's identification of myth with allegory, of redemption with symbol—the very traditional interpretation that Scholem embraces here. The mythology of the "wooded interior" of the symbol is in fact quite plain both in the *Goethe* essay and in the *Ursprung des deutschen Trauerspiels*. As we have seen, allegory, the "antidote to myth," is the optic in which the mythic image of symbolic totality, of a lawlike and static order of transcendent, eternal meaning, is dried up, chopped to bits. To identify the dialectical image with symbolic forms of intuition, in this context, makes no sense.

Finally, an even deeper hermeneutic problem presents itself. Even if reference to the theological grounds and sources of Benjamin's critical sensibility can cast a great deal of light upon the unique characteristics of the dialectical image itself, such reference can do no more than render more comprehensible the claim that the dialectical image differs from the allegorical image in its objectivity—but it cannot definitively answer this claim. Reference to Jewish theology in this context can help us understand better why and how Benjamin may have believed that the dialectical image is not arbitrary. But it only answers the question insofar as we are prepared to accept the thesis that the theological symbol, or something like it, enables the critic (or the one who undergoes this kind of experience) to gain access to a "transcendence" whose validity *for us* the contemporary interpreters has been established. If we are not in a position to accept this thesis without further evidence, then we seem to have reached an impasse.

In the end, then, the question of the "objectivity" or nonarbitrariness of the dialectical image must transpose itself from discussions of Benjamin's own understanding of it to our own. And on these terms, the fragile historicity of the dialectical image, according to which images flash up at moments of historical correspondence neither entirely knowable nor manipulable by the efforts of the critic, gains a new and unsettling relevance. It could be that the question of the arbitrariness of the dialectical image is undecidable for us according to Benjamin's own historical sensibility: itself presumably the ground for our own interpretive interest in arguing for the contemporary relevance of the dialectical image. The hermeneutical circle that ensues here—extending a historicist claim toward "relevance" in order to "save" the very historical sensibility that challenges this relevance most powerfully—approximates the devil's circle of allegorical contemplation itself and threatens a similar paralysis, in which fragments of Benjamin's own work are infinitely chopped and recombined, for the sake of a lasting, a true picture.

From this point of view, the question appears in a different light. What are the grounds on which we might be persuaded to attribute to the dialectical image the objectivity that Benjamin claimed for it? One immediate answer is the acceptance of the theology that supports the claim. I see no way to conduct a critical discussion of this possibility—one either accepts it, does not accept it, or, like most people, manages at a more or less satisfactory point in between.

Another possibility is the pragmatic option of considering what the "cash value" of the truth of the claim to objectivity would be, and this seems, at least on one level, to be what Buck-Morss has in mind. The dialectical image smashes the hegemony of capitalist dream time by confronting it with images, crystallized moments not only of stark actuality, but also of images in which "the ur-old, theological myth of worldly utopia as the origin and goal of history" springs forth from the dusty historical objects themselves. The ancient promise of happiness, denied but nevertheless contained as trace within these liberated objects, is released, explosively, as a powerful moral-political indictment of the misery of capitalist modernity. The revolutionary effect of the dialectical images, on this view, is itself what secures their objectivity. This underlies Buck-Morss's closely related claim that "what saves [the *Passagenwerk*] from arbitrariness is Benjamin's *political* concern that provided the overriding orientation for every constellation."[54] This emphasis on the political efficacy of the dialectical images is, by contemporary standards alone, particularly well placed when one considers efforts to depict Benjamin as a herald of the "hermeneutics of indeterminacy" of postmodern politics.[55]

Emphasizing the effect of the dialectical images cannot, of course, bring us to any certainty concerning their status: (arbitrary) allegorical constructions, as propaganda, can also be politically explosive, if not precisely in the sense Benjamin means. Moreover, the question of what the political effect of the dialectical images in fact is remains, read through the filter of the intervening decades and, admittedly, through the gloomy lens of Adorno's negative dialectic, also open.

Indeed, as Michael Jennings has observed, the professed need to establish the nonintentional objectivity of the images is itself difficult to reconcile with Benjamin's own intention of imbuing the images themselves with an ethical force, directed at the heart of the present, to smash the phantasmagoria of capitalism. For Jennings, Benjamin's pointed efforts "to eliminate the possibility that the relationship of the [allegorical and dialectical] images might be conceived as selective or arbitrary" fail; the result is that "the tension between a frankly subjective ethical impulse and the drive to truth is nowhere resolved in the late work."[56]

This observation, while certainly true, points to another mode for offering an answer to the problem of the dialectical image. Buck-Morss is absolutely correct in her insistence that the objectivity of the dialectical image be referred back to the question of the theology of criticism. Jennings is correct in his claim that such an attempt leads, in Benjamin's own work, to an unresolved tension. This situation is entirely appropriate. The tension refers back to the deepest and truest sources of Benjamin's frozen dialectical thinking. Images spring from contradiction. To resolve the contradiction is to determine the images; such determination, however, is the incorporation of dialectical images into a theoretical edifice that cannot help but close off whatever explosive power the images themselves possess. Dialectical images are the expressions of a dialectic of the subjective appropriation of historical-cultural objects that itself thrives upon, and is fueled by, a tension that we can characterize as "immanent transcendentalism" or "messianic Marxism." In the end, however, we are speaking here of a melancholy dialectics. The question concerning the arbitrariness of the dialectical images is the question of the relation of the images to melancholy.

Observing the iconoclastic appropriation of Jewish theology and Marxism in the theoretics of the *Passagenwerk*, Susan Buck-Morss argues that Benjamin's thought unites, in one image, the *Grübler* and the collector. This observation, while relatively undeveloped in Buck-Morss's analysis, is central. Allegory goes away empty-handed because of the form of the subject-object relations that is mandated under the sign of the *Grübler*. The *Grübler*, as Benjamin had observed in the case of Baudelaire, must always develop a violent, even a sadistic relationship to the "rescued" object. "*Any* intimacy with the things is essentially foreign to the allegorical intention. To touch them means: to rape them. To recognize them means: to see through them."[1] The object, lifted from the process of circulation, must be killed to be saved.

The collector, however, bears a different relation to the object. A way to gesture toward the kind of heroic melancholy that Benjamin achieved is to read his thoughts on the figure of the collector against the theory of melancholy allegory and to perceive how, in the dialectic between these two images, Benjamin's own final vision of materialist criticism arises. The image of the collector is recorded in *Konvolut* H, one of the shortest of the *Passagenwerk*, in the essay on Eduard Fuchs and, in what is arguably Benjamin's loveliest essay, "Unpacking My Library."

The image of the collector must emerge against that of the allegorist. Their relation to the world of things represents a relationship of precise dialectical negation. What the allegorist seizes through a redemptive will turned sadistic, the collector wants to enclose in the embrace of "ownership." Ownership is, of course, one of those concepts in which mythic and messianic elements struggle for primacy of expression. Like the image of the allegorical profusion of discrete things, the notion of ownership is meant to cast a new light upon the fate of objects. But the stark light of allegorical humiliation is gone, and instead the things, in the light given off by the image of the collector, are illuminated, anamnestically, as in childhood. The abandoned passages, department stores, and exhibition halls are crammed to overflowing—with commodities, yes, but also with magical icons, recalling the particular mode of appropriation of the child who navigates in the realm of toys, of decoder rings and painted lead soldiers, through the modern world expositions replete with "ingenious cases with built-in interior illumination, three-foot long pocket knives, officially registered umbrella handles with stopwatch and revolver."[2]

On the Kaiserstrasse, the exhibition of nineteenth-century toys is crowded; with children trudging along on their school excursions, and with the furtive, solemn, slightly dazed grown-ups, who bring to mind the image of the Christmas scene of the father, sunk deep in concentration over the model railway he has given his son, oblivious to the child who stands by and weeps.[3] In the realm of the object, memory enforces the *"Drang zum Spielen"* on the adults first. This compulsion, for Benjamin, is not merely a regression into childhood. The child who is surrounded by the giant adult world plays, and in playing reduces the world to the proper scale. The adult, playing, transforms the normal-sized world to miniature and thereby is at least momentarily released from the horror implicit within it.

Collecting takes part in this very modern tropism. "What is decisive about collecting," Benjamin notes, "is that the object is removed from all its original uses, in order for it to enter into the closest conceivable relationship with things just like it. This is the diametric contradiction of use, and thus stands under the remarkable category of completeness [*Vollständigkeit*]. What is this completeness[?] It is the grand attempt to overcome the sheer irrationality of the mere ready-to-handedness [of the object] by determining its order in a new system, the collection, made by the collector himself."[4] Relieved from usefulness, the collected objects themselves become for the collector "the scene, the stage of their fate."[5] For the true collector, the object, incorporated into the collection, is transmuted into a temporally pregnant monad, "an encyclopedia" containing within it, magically, the complete physiognomic record of the history locked inside it:[6] "The most profound enchantment for the collector is the locking of individual items within a magic circle in which they are fixed [*erstarrte*] as the final thrill, the thrill of acquisition, passes over them."[7]

In this final thrill, Benjamin observes, the object releases its freight of memory. Plato's *topos hyperouranious*, where the "immutable *Urbilder* of the things" are lodged, is a region to which the collector has a special access. "Collecting is a form of practical remembering";[8] in the act of collection, the pre- and posthistory of the collected toy, poster, magazine, fragment, begins to shimmer and pulsate with the messianic, charged, unstable energy characteristic of the moment of awakening. The unique "*Blick*" of the collector, under which the fragmented and dispersed thing is recovered, ordered, and "set right," sees "more and differently" into the world of things than the merely profane property owner.

Collectors are, Benjamin concludes, in essence physiognomists of the realm of the thing.[9] They have a special talent for the recognition of structure, pattern, and order in an otherwise allegorically fragmented world of things. This skill can only be defined as the collector's ability to see, in the moment that the newest possession enters the collection, a microscopic victory over the fate dwelling within the commodified object; a tiny anticipation of reconciliation. This makes the connection between messianic hope and revolutionary memory particularly vivid in the figure of the collector. "One has only to watch a collector handle the objects in his glass case. As he holds them in his hands, he seems to be seeing through them into their distant past as though inspired."[10]

Collecting, through a circuitous route, taps into the element within the commodity that resists being incorporated into mythic fetish, that emerges most strongly when the commodity passes out of the sphere of circulation. In this sense collecting is, implicitly, an act of political liberation. Conversely, however, "every tiny act of political signification constitutes, so to speak, an epoch in the antique store." For the project of the *Passagenwerk*, the mobilization of the dialectical image, this is enormously important: "We are constructing an alarm clock here, meant to stir the kitsch of the previous century into a convocation [*Versammlung*]."[11]

The nineteenth century as a collection-convocation, a *Sammlung-Versammlung*: this means to summon forth the powers latent in "dead nature" itself, to bring out of this juxtaposition of "like" elements a power of indictment against the conditions of their fragmentation. Already we see clearly the deep affinities between the collector and the allegorist. The activity of collecting, like allegory, is in essence an activity of the lonely one who, locked away with the things, begins to read them. Like the allegorist, who ruins the world in order to piece together from memory the Ur-old, hoped-for image of redeemed nature, the collector's interest in completeness is in essence messianic. Unlike the allegorist, however, the collector approaches the objects with love, not spleen. He embraces them, rather than seizing them. They become keys to an ancient knowledge not despite but precisely through their status as fragments. To touch them means not to violate them, but to finger them lovingly; to recognize them means not to see through them, but to allow them to fit in. The violent imposition of meaning by the allegorist is, in the collector, matched by the gentle gesture whereby the object is placed carefully in its appointed place in the glassed-in collector's case.

"One must regard the Parisian arcades as if they were possessions in the hand of the collector."[12] In collecting, the past of the object and the present of the collector lose their chronologically ordained, linear displacement and are brought together in a moment of mutual appropriation and recognition in which the messianic-anamnestic category of "completeness" exceeds and convolutes the category of ownership. There is, then, a mode of perception peculiar to the collector, one that the *Grübler* cannot master. This is the time of the sudden actuality of the fragment of the past—not just as souvenir, not as *Erlebnis*, as *mere* documentation of the discrete fragments of lived experience, but primarily as a concrete temporal constellation in which an element of that-which-has-been (*das Gewesene*) enters into the present, transforming it into a Now (*Jetzt*).

There is, to be sure, a mythic component here as well. The collector, alone with the things, "lives . . . a piece of dreamlife,"[13] like the historian who must piece together the constellation of waking from the collected/convoked dream landscape of the arcade, the "*Zeitraum*" of the nineteenth century. Collecting is mythic insofar as the objects are taken as secret storehouses of (essentially private) pleasure. But the collector is unable to effect the dialectical translation of this enchanted circle of possessions into a critical force directed against their source. The redemptive dimension of collection remains obscured by the light of enchantment that irradiates the possessed objects. The collector knows, supremely, how to rescue the objects. But for this very reason, he does not know how to *use* them—just what the brooding allegorist knows how to do *all too well*.

Collecting alone, in other words, is just as inadequate a model for the activity of the materialist critic as is allegory. Just as allegory goes away empty-handed by betraying the things for the sake of knowledge, the collector's dreamy compilation of possessions betrays critical-revolutionary knowledge for the sake of the things. Oppositions such as this one, which never occur by accident in Benjamin's thought, are the signs of an image about to emerge. This opposition is brought to crystalline focus near the close of the *Konvolut:*

> One could, perhaps, describe the most deeply hidden motive of the collector in this manner: he takes up the struggle against dispersion [*Zerstreuung*]. The scatteredness and confusion in which the things of the world find themselves touch upon him in a completely originary fashion. It was the same dramatic spectacle that so occupied the baroque era; in particular one cannot explain the worldview of the allegorist without the passionate affliction arising from this spectacle. The allegorist develops the counter-pole to the collector, one might say. He has abandoned the investigative effort to illuminate how the things relate to, fit in with one another. He tears them from their contexts and from then on leaves it to his *Tiefsinn* to illuminate the meaning of the things. The collector, on the other hand, unites that which belongs together; in this fashion he is able to instruct himself about the things through their relationship or their temporal position.[14]

As dialectical counterpoles, the collector and the allegorist thus match up perfectly with one another according to their contradictory attitude toward the thing. Yet lest we forget that dialectics mandates complexity and that opposition is another form of identity, and simply affirm the role of the collector to accomplish that redemptive encounter with the things that the melancholy allegorist cannot, Benjamin develops this opposition to its breaking point:

> Nevertheless—and this is more significant than anything that might establish a distinction between them—there hides an allegorist in every collector, and a collector in every allegorist. As far

as the collector is concerned, the collection is never finished: even if he is missing only one piece, that means that everything that he collects remains piecework [*Stückwerk*] just as the things have been for the allegorist from the very beginning. On the other side, the allegorist, for whom, indeed, the things themselves merely represent the entries in a secret dictionary that betrays their meaning, can never have enough of the things—and one can no more stand for another than can reflection predict to which meaning *Tiefsinn* will consign them. [15]

Benjamin too situates himself, carefully and with great pain, here at the crossroads, not only between subjectivity and its objects, but also between these two mutually conditioning modes of subjective appropriation of the objects. Benjamin is a collector, and not only of books. The perspective from which life itself comes to achieve the status of a collection is, according to the logic of this last dialectical passage, both the same and not the same as the allegorical intuition in which even life itself is chopped up into the killed souvenir. From the attitude of the collector, life appears not as the chronic plodding series of events but as the "moments and discontinuities" within this flow, the objects themselves that both contain and conceal the truth of a life. One need only recall "Loggien," the section in the "Berliner Kindheit um Neunzehnhundert," in which Benjamin's gaze painstakingly remembers, in precise detail, the entire visual field of the courtyard of his childhood home. No "I," no subject intervenes in this convocation of collected thing-memories, and the things, retrieved through practical memory, merge into the textual arcanum, the palimpsest through which the utopian dimension of memory, hope, glints dimly through, irradiating the entire ensemble of cherished objects with a light from a distant, nevertheless familiar planet. Not for nothing did Benjamin cherish "Loggien" above all sections of the "Berliner Kindheit," referring to it as "the most precise portrait I shall ever be able to give of myself."[16] And one could say that only through tear-blurred eyes could such a doggedly conventional collection of bourgeois implements be transmuted into incandescent ciphers of a happiness promised with every thought and withheld at every historical moment.

But we know how quickly this process of "excavating and remembering"[17] can transmute itself into allegory, and for all his effort Benjamin remains a fair theoretician, an excellent philosopher, but

unsurpassed—truly unsurpassed—as a *Grübler.* The subject that is so
intensified in the metaphysics of melancholy allegory, and so gently
dispersed in the theology of collection, can in the intersection of these
images attain a kind of diffracted magnification that Benjamin perceived all too well at work in the modern allegory of Baudelaire.

There is, as Buck-Morss observes, both collector and *Grübler* at
work in Benjamin. But this observation, far from being a mere reference to features of his theoretical development, expresses nothing
other than the heart of Benjamin's thinking. It refers, in the end, to
Benjamin's status as the quintessential modern heroic melancholic.

Between the poles of the allegorical violence and the love of the
collector there is a space, albeit a terribly small one, where criticism
can install itself. It is a space between antinomies, established by
theology. What the image of the collector possesses, and what the
allegorist so keenly lacks, is love for the object, and this love is
capable of accomplishing a terrifically important function: it overcomes melancholia and marks an end to *Grübelei.* What allegory has
that is so lacking in the spirit of the collector is the desperate search for
meaning under whose weight the false image of the world buckles, and
from which issues a messianic will, a call to make good again that
which has been broken. The things themselves constitute that null
point where the "counterpoles" of the collector and the allegorist meet:
to embrace that meeting place, to master it, and to direct the energy of
the crossing onto the heart of the present is the goal of Benjamin's
criticism.

If I nevertheless insist on referring to this criticism as a heroic
melancholy of a particular kind, it does not necessarily mean that the
allegorical side of this dialectic "wins" over the collective, any more
than Benjamin's messianic will triumphs over his physiognomic fascination. It merely indicates that the victory over melancholia that
Benjamin achieves is one that only makes sense, retrospectively, when
grasped not as the abandonment of melancholia, not as its "*Überwin-
dung,*" but as a moment in which the strength of the individual is
capable, through sacrifice, of harnessing the historical and personal
forces that define his sorrow, to render him into a productive, controlled whole. If, in the physiognomy of this project and this life we
cannot help but recognize the older theme of the heroic melancholic, it
means only that this image, which is always historically concrete

according to the motorial reaction between the contemplative subject and its a priori objects, must itself undergo the kind of sudden recovery of "actuality," of contemporary relevance, that Benjamin wrested from all historicist empathies and claimed for his own.

Benjamin recognized all too well that, in the history of the melancholy disposition, the easiest road was the one that led to "left melancholia"; to self-indulgence and passivity tricked out as social criticism. Materialist criticism instead took the longest possible path, the "planet of detours and delays," as he wrote in "Agesilaus Santander."[18] Benjamin's criticism, held in the tension between two contradictory and ultimately incompatible modes of appropriation of the fragment, derives its graphicness and its power from this tension itself. The fragment is both loved and used, both recognized and seen through; the fascination with the world of the things, with the scriptural convolution of the surfaces of the world, struggles up until the very end with the contradictions that produced it.

Subject and its objects do not reconcile; the murdered, as Horkheimer once unnecessarily thought to remind Benjamin, are truly murdered. There, Horkheimer had insisted on the need to take seriously the "completeness" of history. "Sadness," he wrote, "rather than happiness is sealed by death." But for the materialist critic, between collecting and brooding, "completeness" marks only the moment where historiography, as practical, painful, committed recollection, begins. "Recollection [*Eingedenken*] can make the incomplete (happiness) into something complete, and the complete (suffering) into something incomplete. This is theology; but in recollection we have an experience which forbids us the chance of conceiving history as essentially atheological, just as we ought not to write it immediately theological concepts."[19]

The dialectical image is neither arbitrary nor objective. Its "objectivity" is held in the same suspension as the oppressed past from which it springs. It is the expression of a kind of melancholy in which just this question itself is deferred, as is the moment of redemption, the "straight gate through which the Messiah might enter."[20] Between the hoped-for past and the remembered future, melancholy dialectics dedicates images—as candles for the dead, but also as lights whose very fragility might guide the Messiah home.

Notes

Introduction

The source for the epigraph is Gershom Scholem, "An Karl und Kitty. Mit einem Exemplar der 'Einbahnstrassen,'" reprinted in *The Correspondence of Walter Benjamin and Gershom Scholem 1932–1940*, ed. Gershom Scholem (New York: Schocken Books, 1989), 81.

1   Julia Kristeva, *Black Sun: Depression and Melancholia* (New York: Columbia University Press, 1989), 258, 12.

2   Kristeva, *Black Sun*, 258.

3   Ibid., 259.

4   Kierkegaard, quoted in Theodor W. Adorno, *Kierkegaard: Construction of the Aesthetic*, trans. Robert Hullot-Kentor (Minneapolis: University of Minnesota Press, 1989), 60.

5   Cf. Samuel Weber, Afterword, in *Just Gaming* by Jean-François Lyotard and Jean-Loup Thébaud (Minneapolis: University of Minnesota Press, 1985), 101–23.

6   Kristeva, *Black Sun*, 3.

7   Robert Burton, *The Anatomy of Melancholy* (London: E. P. Dutton & Co., 1932), 20.

8   Walter Benjamin, "Linke Melancholie. Zum Erich Kästner's neuem Gedicht-buch," in Walter Benjamin, *Gesammelte Schriften*, ed. Rolf Tiedemann and Hermann Schweppenhäuser, 7 vols. (Frankfurt am Main: Suhrkamp Verlag, 1972–), 3:279–83. (All further references to the *Gesammelte Schriften* will be abbreviated as GS followed by volume and page number.)

9   See Bernd Witte, *Walter Benjamin—Der Intellektuelle als Kritiker. Untersuchungen zu Seinem Frühwerk* (Stuttgart: Metzler Studienausgabe, 1976), 141.

10 Walter Benjamin, "The Author as Producer," in *Reflections: Essays, Aphorisms, Autobiographical Writings*, ed. Peter Demetz (New York: Harcourt Brace Jovanovich, 1978), 226.

11 See Witte, *Walter Benjamin*, for an excellent discussion of literary review-as-

praxis, especially section 4, "Der Kritiker als Rezensent. Zu Theorie und Praxis einer funktionaler Kritik."

12　See Erich Kästner, *Gesammelte Schriften* (Köln: Verlag Kiepenheuer & Witsch, 1959), 5:181, 263, 507; cf. also R. W. Last, *Erich Kästner* (London: Oswald Wolff, 1974), 94. Particularly interesting in this regard is a comparison of Kästner and Benjamin on the notion of childhood as a reserve of memory, which can be (through pedagogic writing) tapped and mobilized as a political-critical force for present concerns: "Childhood," writes Kästner, "is the quiet, pure light that shines consolingly out of the past into the present and the future. Truly to hold childhood in memory means to know again, suddenly and without long contemplation, what is genuine and what false, what is good and what bad. . . . Childhood is like a lighthouse" (Last, 94). And later: "There are two kinds of time. One can be measured by the ruler, the compass and the sextant. Just like roads and plots of land are measured. But our memory, the other means of reckoning time, has nothing to do with the meter and the month, the decade and the hectare. What we have forgotten, that is old. But the unforgettable is yesterday. The yardstick is not the clock, but the value" (Last, 121). There is, to be sure, a sentimentalism at work here in this that is for the most part absent in Benjamin's understanding of childhood; what Kästner wants to preserve as a nourishing light, Benjamin wishes to exploit as an arsenal.

13　The debate continues; *Fabian* has in fact become regarded as an emblematic literary work for the cynical exhaustion of the Weimar left and its unwillingness to "act" against the rise of fascism. Cf. Dirk Walter, *Zeitkritik und Idyllensehnsucht: Erich Kästners Frühwerk als Beispiel linksbürgerlicher Literatur in der Weimarer Republik* (Heidelberg: Carl Winter Verlag, 1977).

14　Benjamin, "Gebrauchslyrik? Aber nicht so!" GS 3:183–84.

15　For a view of some of the principal contributions to this debate, see Michael Stark ed., *Deutsche Intellektuelle 1910–1933* (Heidelberg: Verlag Lambert Schneider, 1984), especially the last section, "Ohnmacht des Geistes oder Linke Melancholie," with texts from Tucholsky, Mehring, Lion Feuchtwanger, Kracauer, and Döblin.

16　Benjamin, GS 3:279, 280, 280–81. Citing himself (as "a perceptive critic"), Benjamin would quote much of this passage verbatim in "The Author as Producer" two years later (*Reflections*, 232).

17　Benjamin, GS 3:281.

18　Ibid., 283.

19　Ibid.

20　Cf. Tiedemann's observation that "Linke Melancholie" provides "one of the earliest documents of Brecht's influence on Benjamin" (Benjamin, GS 3:644).

21　Erwin Panofsky and Fritz Saxl, "Dürers 'Melancolia I': Eine quellen- und typengeschichtliche Untersuchung," *Studien der Warburg Institut 2* (Leipzig, 1922).

22　Aby Warburg, *Heidnisch-antike Weissagung in Wort und Bild zu Luthers Zeiten* (Heidelberg: Carl Winter Universitätsbuchhandlung, 1920). Reprinted in *Aby M. Warburg. Ausgewählte Schriften und Würdigungen*, ed. Dieter Wuttke (Baden-Baden: Verlag Valentin Koerner, 1980).

23 Gershom Scholem, "Walter Benjamin and His Angel," in *On Walter Benjamin: Critical Essays and Recollections*, ed. Gary Smith (Cambridge: MIT Press, 1988), 58–59.

24 Since the appearance of Scholem's essay, other attempts to unriddle the "secret names" Benjamin describes in "Agesilaus Santander" have resulted in very different interpretations of the meaning of the text. Werner Fuld discovered that the two "secret names" that Benjamin claimed to bear were not a fictive or occult reference to the anagrammatic "Angelus Satanas," but rather the quite real "Benedix Schönflies," the latter the maiden name of Benjamin's mother (Fuld, *Walter Benjamin: Zwischen den Stühlen. Eine Biographie* [München: Fischer Verlag, 1974], 23ff.). Jürgen Ebach has suggested that this discovery actually makes the text more, rather than less obscure (Ebach, "Agesilaus Santander und Benedix Schönflies. Die verwandelten Namen Walter Benjamins," in *Antike und Moderne. Zu Walter Benjamins "Passagen,"* ed. Norbert Bolz and Richard Faber [Würzburg: Königshausen & Neuburg, 1986], 148ff.). The question would thus be the relation between the two sets of secret names, Benedix Schönflies and Angelus Satanas; moreover, why Benjamin chose "Agesilaus Santander"—a Spartan emperor and Spanish town—remains obscure. Ebach attempts to riddle out the significance of this obscurity, pointing to the image of the lamed warrior to be found in the legends of Agesilos and the biblical Jacob, and Benjamin's own lamed ankle, injured on Ibiza, on the motif of blessing in Jacob's story and Benjamin's own "Benedix."

25 "Benjamin was born under the sign of Saturn, as he expressly testifies only here in all the writings of his known to me. Thus the angel, to whom astrological charracterology was no less familiar than to the author of *The Origin of the German Trauerspiel* and to his melancholy nature, could make him pay for the disturbance of his heavenly and hymnal performance" (Scholem, "Walter Benjamin and His Angel," 71).

26 This juxtaposition is deeply developed in Witte's *Walter Benjamin*, 58–64, 125–32.

27 Theodor W. Adorno, "Introduction to Benjamin's *Schriften*," in Smith, *On Walter Benjamin*, 4.

28 Scholem, "Walter Benjamin and His Angel," 54, 85.

29 Adorno, "Introduction to Benjamin's *Schriften*," 9.

30 "History is not the ground of human happiness. The periods of happiness are blank pages in it, for they are the periods of concord, of the missing contradiction" (G. W. F. Hegel, *Vorlesungen über die Philosophie der Geschichte*, Jubiläeumsausgabe, 56).

31 Adorno, "Introduction to Benjamin's *Schriften*," 15.

32 See Hellmut Flashar, *Melancholie und Melancholiker in den medizinischen Theorien der Antike* (Berlin: de Gruyter & Co., 1966).

33 The work of the Warburg Institute is the paradigm example in this regard, discussed in chapter 3. Cf. also Bridget Gellert Lyons, *Voices of Melancholy: Studies in Literary Treatments of Melancholia in Renaissance England* (New York: Barnes and Noble, 1971).

34   See Klara Obermüller, *Melancholie in der deutschen Baroklyrik* (Bonn: Bouvier Verlag, 1974); Helen Watanabe O'Kelly, *Melancholie und die melancholische Landschaft. Ein Beitrag zur Geistesgeschichte des 17ten Jahrhunderts* (Bern: Fincke Verlag, 1978); Lawrence Babb, *The Elizabethan Malady: A Study of Melancholia in English Literature from 1580 to 1642* (Lansing: Michigan State University Press, 1951).

35   Gabrielle Ricke, *Schwarze Phantasie. Melancholie im 18. Jahrhundert* (Hildesheim: Gerstenberg Verlag, 1981); Bernhard Buschendorf, *Goethes Mythische Denkform. Zur Ikonographie der 'Wahlverwandtschaften'* (Frankfurt: Suhrkamp Verlag, 1986).

36   Elanor Sickels, *The Gloomy Egoist: Moods and Themes of Melancholy from Gray to Keats* (New York: Columbia University Press, 1932).

37   Franz Loquai, *Künstler und Melancholie in der Romantik* (Frankfurt: Verlag Peter Lang, 1984); Henning Mehnert, *Melancholie und Inspiration. Begriffs- und wissenschaftsgeschichtliche Untersuchungen zur poetischen "Psychologie" Baudelaires, Flauberts und Mallarmes* (Heidelberg: Carl Winter Verlag, 1978).

38   See Flashar, *Melancholie und Melancholiker*, 8ff.

39   Thus the earliest Hippocratic tables could be composed in this way:

Blood	Yellow Bile	Black Bile	Phlegm
sanguine	choleric	melancholic	phlegmatic
warm/wet	warm/dry	cold/dry	cold/wet
Spring	Summer	Autumn	Winter
Air	Fire	Earth	Water
Youth	Adulthood	Late Adulthood	Old Age
Heart	Liver	Spleen	Brain
Joy	Pride	Sadness	Fear

See Flashar; Raymond Klibanski, Erwin Panofsky, and Fritz Saxl, *Saturn and Melancholy: Studies in the History of Natural Philosophy, History, and Art* (London: Nelson, 1964), 10.

40   Stanley Jackson, *Melancholia and Depression from Hippocratic Times to Modern Times* (New Haven: Yale University Press, 1986), 30, 31.

41   It was under the Greek physicians of the Roman Empire that melancholia truly emerged as a fully recognized pathology with a detailed symptomatology and diagnostic protocol; Galen and Rufus of Ephesus are the most significant contributors. Rufus was particularly influential in providing an elaborate symptomatology of melancholia, ranging from the most severe symptoms—dementia, delusions, coma, or paralysis—to mild ones such as distended veins and abdomen, coldness of extremities, lethargy, even constipation or flatulence. Thus the origin of Benjamin's critique of Kästner's poems, which "do not improve the atmosphere" (cf. Jackson, *Melancholia and Depression*, 37–39; Flashar, *Melancholie und Melancholiker*, 12).

42   Cf. Jackson, *Melancholia and Depression*, 44ff.; Flashar, *Melancholie und Melancholiker*, 32.

43   Michel Foucault, *Madness and Civilization: A History of Insanity in the Age of Reason* (New York: Vintage Books, 1973), 122.

44   Sigmund Freud, "Mourning and Melancholia," in *The Standard Edition of the Complete Psychological Works of Sigmund Freud* (London: Hogarth & Co., 1968), 14:246, 248, 246.

45   Kristeva, *Black Sun*, 10, 13, 189.

46   Ibid., 100.

47   Ibid., 100, 102.

48   *Problemata Physica xxxi*, quoted in Klibanski, Panofsky, and Saxl, *Saturn and Melancholy*, 18. There is widespread skepticism that Aristotle is the author of this passage. Cf. Klibanski, Panofsky, and Saxl, 16; Flashar, *Melancholie und Melancholiker*, 32.

49   Klibanski, Panofsky, and Saxl, *Saturn and Melancholy*, 23, 24.

50   "Those who have a little of this temperament are ordinary, but those who have much of it are unlike the majority of people. For if their melancholy habitus is quite undiluted they too are melancholy; but if it is somewhat tempered they are outstanding. If they are not careful they tend toward melancholy sickness" (Klibanski, Panofsky, and Saxl, *Saturn and Melancholy*, 26).

51   Ibid., 128ff.

52   Cf. Obermüller, *Melancholie in der deutschen Baroklyrik*, 16, 15.

53   For example, William of Auvergne regarded melancholia as a pathological state that nevertheless contained a spiritually uplifting moment, insofar as it "withdrew men from physical pleasures and worldly turmoil, prepared the mind for the direct influx of divine grace, and educated in cases of exceptional holiness to mystic and prophetic visions" (quoted in Klibanski, Panofsky, and Saxl, *Saturn and Melancholy*, 70). In this case melancholia was a sign of the soul's yearning for recovery of originary divine purity. For Hugues de Fouilli, melancholia thus emerges as a feeling of profound grief, produced by a preponderance of bile from the spleen, but nevertheless *signifying* "longing to be united with the Lord" (quoted in Klibanski, Panofsky, and Saxl, *Saturn and Melancholy*, 108).

54   Walter Benjamin, *The Origin of German Tragic Drama*, trans. John Osbourne (London: Verso, 1977), 148–49. Henceforth referred to as "O."

55   Cf. Babb, *The Elizabethan Malady*, 184. Babb traces the genealogy of melancholy as fashion from the Florentine Neoplatonists (e.g., Ficino et al.) to Elizabethan England, where it promptly established a "vogue" of melancholy, fueled by "the general acceptance of the idea that [melancholy] was an attribute of superior minds, of genius" (184). This vogue is most visible in the sudden appearance of melancholy characters on the Elizabethan stage, of which Hamlet is the most complex and best known. One could speculate that the sudden appearance of tormented, black-clad melancholy artists in Elizabethan England finds its rough parallel in the wave of *stürmische* characters—and suicides—following the publication of *Werther*.

56   Cf. Flashar, *Melancholie und Melancholiker*, 21.

57   Cf. Loquai, *Künstler und Melancholie in der Romantik*, chap. 3.

58   Cf. O'Kelley, *Melancholie und die melancholische Landschaft*, 71ff.

59   As Bridget Gellert Lyons has shown, the image of the Renaissance melancholic malcontent as an overstylized, hyperbolic rebel became a popular and familiar

tragic and comic figure on the Elizabethan stage. Hamlet's feigned/unfeigned jeremiads, for example, are on Lyons's reading a quasi-comical reference to this standard dramatic figure (cf. Lyons, *Voices of Melancholy*, 17–18).

60　Wolf Lepenies, *Melancholie und Gesellschaft* (Frankfurt: Suhrkamp Verlag, 1969), 17. Cf. also Robert Merton, *Social Theory and Social Structure*, 2d ed. (New York: The Free Press, 1968), 209ff. The jump from Merton's theory of the varieties of social anomie to a theory of melancholia is, to be sure, a big one. Merton discusses several adaptive behavioral strategies in response to the experience of social anomie. Among these, rebellion implies the conscious rejection of the purposive-intentional content of socially sanctioned behavior, and its replacement with wholly private sets of means and ends. Merton contrasts this sort of rebellion with retreatism, in which the "supreme value of the success-goal has not yet been renounced" although the possibility of its attainment has vanished, and the ability for instrumental action is thus repressed. Lepenies's adaption notwithstanding, it is clearly this latter form of retreatism, rather than rebellion, that comes closest to Merton's own conception of anomic social exclusion. Merton classifies as "retreatists" those who are marginalized from society but do not possess, like the anomic rebel, any access to a coherent plan of instrumental action whatsoever. He lists these "true aliens" as "psychotics, outcasts, vagrants, vagabonds, tramps, chronic drunkards, and drug addicts," but certainly not as disaffected intellectuals (cf. Merton, *Social Theory*, 207).

61　Lepenies, *Melancholie und Gesellschaft*, 17, 11, 13.

62　Ibid., 54–55ff.

63　"And thus the native hue of resolution / Is sicklied o'er with the pale cast of thought, / And enterprises of great pitch and moment / With this regard their currents turn awry, / And lose the name of action."—(*Hamlet*, 3.1.83–87).

64　Lepenies, *Melancholie und Gesellschaft*, 7.

1　Trauer and Criticism

1　Gershom Scholem, *Walter Benjamin: The History of a Friendship* (London: Faber & Faber, 1982), 25.

2　Walter Benjamin, *Briefe*, comp. Gershom Scholem and Theodor W. Adorno (Frankfurt: Suhrkamp Verlag, 1978), 126, 125–26.

3　Benjamin, *Briefe*, 127, quoted in Anson Rabinbach, "Between Enlightenment and Apocalypse: Benjamin, Bloch, and Modern German-Jewish Messianism," *New German Critique* 34 (Winter 1985): 106.

4　Cf. Benjamin, "Das Leben der Studenten," GS 2:75–87.

5　Benjamin, *Briefe*, 93.

6　Concerning the decisionistic foundation of Zionism and its relation to the experience of anti-Semitism, Scholem has written that "the Jewish post-assimilatory renaissance meant a revolt against the life-styles of the parents' home or of the circle of families like it. This was a conscious breakaway, a volitional act, a decision. . . . At the time, I did not have an abstract-conceptual awareness of assimilationism. My awareness was an emotional one." Scholem continues:

The revolt, or the break . . . was against self-deceit. A person living in a liberal-Jewish, German assimilationist environment had the feeling that those people were devoting their entire lives to self-delusion. We did not come to Zionism in search of politics. . . . Some of us, to be sure, went on to become real political Zionists, but the Zionist choice was a moral one, an emotional one, an honesty-seeking experience.

("With Gershom Scholem: An Interview," in *On Jews and Judaism in Crisis*, ed. Werner J. Dannhauser [New York: Schocken Books, 1976], 2.) The irony in this sentiment is that, for the secular Jewish messianists, the turn not only to politics, but also to a politics that specifically sought to address and overcome the pathology of assimilationism by appeal to a reinvigorated Jewish identity is, nevertheless, as *praxis* conceived as the negation of the *in*decisiveness of the older generation, and thus arises from the same discourse of passivity and activity, power and powerlessness. In other words, a discourse of politics is from the beginning alienated from the political and is obliged to articulate itself in moral-aesthetic or theological terms, terms that tended often to worsen the gap between theory and practice. On this phenomenon, see Hans-Hellmuth Knütter, *Die Juden und die deutsche Linke in der weimaren Republik* (Düsseldorf: Droste Verlag, 1971), 59ff.

7   Cf. Benjamin's letter to Carla Seligsohn from 4 August 1913 (in Benjamin, *Briefe*, 89).

8   Primary representatives of such a project were figures such as Kurt Hiller, Heinrich Mann, and Rene Schickele.

9   Theodor W. Adorno, "Benjamin the Letter Writer," in Smith, *On Walter Benjamin*, 333–35. Adorno indicates another factor at work in Benjamin's participation in the youth movement: "Between [Benjamin's] own proclivities and the circle he joined there was a gulf that he seems to have attempted to bridge by indulging his need to dominate. . . . Flashes of imperiousness dart through the often nebulous early letters like lightning bolts in search of tinder" (334). Indeed one of the odder dimensions of Benjamin's involvement in the youth movement— a dimension that persists throughout—is the simultaneous appeal for the formation of a spiritual community (*Bund*) of companions on the one hand, and on the other, the equally emphatic call for the achievement of an absolute form of spiritual solitude.

10   Witte, *Walter Benjamin*, 19, 20–22.

11   Benjamin, "Das Dornröschen," GS 2:10.

12   Benjamin, "Erfahrung," GS 2:54.

13   Benjamin, "Gedanken über Gerhart Hauptmanns Festspiel," GS 2:59–60.

14   Benjamin, 2:75.

15   Ibid.

16   Peculiarities abound in "Das Leben der Studenten": not only is the emphatically messianic conception of the role of criticism in historical time hardly touched on in the rest of the essay, but also the essay itself is an expanded version of Benjamin's inaugural address to the Berlin *Freie Studentenschaft* and must have been one of the strangest inaugural manifestos ever given. The profound dis-

couragement in the possibilities for youth, the sense of the growing inability of the youth movement to distance itself critically from the university and from the older generation, and the mystical antipractical opening point to the distance that already separated Benjamin from his colleagues in the youth movement, but also from Kurt Hiller, whose own activism contrasted sharply with Benjamin's insistence on the abstract purity of critique. Nevertheless, "Das Leben der Studenten" was first published in Hiller's journal *Das Ziel* in 1916. As the editors of the *Gesammelte Schriften* point out, Hiller had a consistently low opinion of Benjamin and regretted publishing the essay. As Hiller later wrote to Adorno, Benjamin broke contact with Hiller almost immediately upon the publication of "Das Leben der Studenten": "[Benjamin] simply dismissed (humanistic) Activism as flat and false; for him, an analytic contemplation was the answer, which aimed not at changing the world but at conceiving (*begreifen*) it" (GS 2:916). Hiller dismisses Benjamin's later work in toto as " 'trendy,' but deathly boring, completely superficial, sticks meant to trip up the humanistic realization of the briskly marching spirit—typically counterrevolutionary" (GS 2:916–17).

17   Benjamin, "Das Leben der Studenten," GS 2:75.

18   Benjamin, *Briefe*, 131–32.

19   Cf. Michael Jennings, *Dialectical Images: Walter Benjamin's Theory of Literary Criticism* (Ithaca, N.Y.: Cornell University Press, 1987).

20   Benjamin claimed that the essay represented "a certain systematic intention, which however makes the fragmentary character of thought very clear" (*Briefe*, 129).

21   Perhaps even more than the two short essays on the *Trauerspiel*, it is the language essay that Benjamin had in mind when he claimed, at the opening of the *Ursprung* study, that it was "conceived" (*entworfen*) in 1916. Cf. GS 1:203; cf. also Benjamin's letter to Belmore (*Briefe*, 454; GS 2:935), which makes frequent reference to the language essay's "*Verwandtschaft mit der Vorrede des Trauerspielbuchs.*"

22   On the significance of Benjamin's early reading of Humboldt and the influence of his professor, Ernst Lewy, see Scholem, *History of a Friendship*, 21–22, 104–10. An expert discussion of the sources of Benjamin's early language mysticism is presented in Winfried Menninghaus, *Walter Benjamins Theorie der Sprachmagie* (Frankfurt: Suhrkamp Verlag, 1980), 9–50.

23   Menninghaus, *Walter Benjamins Theorie der Sprachmagie*, 16.

24   "On Language as Such and on the Language of Man," in Walter Benjamin, *Reflections*, 314, translation altered; "There is no event or thing in animate or inanimate nature that does not in some way partake of language, for it is in the nature of all to communicate [*vermitteln*] their spiritual content" (314); 316, translation altered; 317.

25   Benjamin, "On Language as Such and on the Language of Man," 325; 323, translation altered.

26   Cf. Menninghaus, *Walter Benjamins*, 17. Much of the language essay is dedicated to speculations on the power of the Adamic name to perfectly "re-present" the creative word of God, and thereby to capture the essence of the named thing;

these speculations show a particular interest in the occult doctrine of the secret name, which, insofar as it captures a person's essential being, gains great power and must not be divulged. Speculations such as these, never far from the esoteric concerns of the Kabbalah, also underlie the notion of secret names and astral or occult forces that appear in "Agesilaus Santander." In the language essay, for example, Benjamin observes that "by giving names, parents dedicate their children to God; the names they give do not correspond—in a metaphysical, not etymological sense—to any knowledge, for they name newborn children. In a strict sense, no name ought (in its etymological meaning) to correspond to any person, for the proper name is the word of God in human sounds. By it each man is guaranteed his creation by God, and in this sense he is himself creative, as is expressed by mythological wisdom in the idea (which doubtless not infrequently comes true) that a man's name is his fate" ("On Language as Such and on the Language of Man," 324).

27   Benjamin, "On Language as Such and on the Language of Man," 318, translation altered.

28   Friedrich Schlegel, quoted in Eva Fiesel, *Die Sprachphilosophie der deutschen Romantik* (Tübingen: Verlag J. C. B. Mohr, 1927), 49. (Benjamin reviewed Fiesel's solid but somewhat plodding monograph in 1928; he admitted that its large scholarly apparatus qualified it as "competent," but observed that, insofar as it was unmoved by the spiritual energy of the romantics themselves and thus timidly shrank to the safe refuge of scholarship, it remained a "typical *Frauenarbeit*"—forgetting, apparently, that the romantics themselves did not share his misogynistic objections to womens' admission into the sphere of the *Geistigen*. Cf. GS 3:96–97.)

29   Cf. Menninghaus, *Walter Benjamins Theorie der Sprachmagie*, 22–32.

30   Benjamin, "On Language as Such and on the Language of Man," 326–27, translation altered; 328.

31   Ibid., 329; 330, translation altered; 329, translation altered; 329–30, translation altered.

32   Susan Buck-Morss, *The Dialectics of Seeing: Walter Benjamin and the Arcades Project* (Cambridge: MIT Press, 1989), 229–52.

33   Michael Jennings has argued that Scholem's assertion that a reading of Jewish mysticism underlies the structure of the language essay is undermined by Benjamin's own silence on the matter, as well as the fact that Scholem's own "serious" work on the Kabbalah began only after 1916, the year that the language essay was composed (Jennings, *Dialectical Images*, 95). Jennings will argue instead that, in addition to the romantics, Molitor, and von Baader, it is Hölderlin who provides the relevant source for Benjamin's mysticism; in fact, Jennings claims, the language essay is a reworking of the essay "Zwei Gedichte von F. Hölderlin" from 1914. What Scholem in fact claims (in *History of a Friendship*, 34) is that the language essay arose as a response to "a rather long letter to Benjamin about the relationship between mathematics and language." Indeed, Scholem observes that even Benjamin's interest in von Baader and Molitor (the Germanist who was largely responsible for introducing the Kabbalah into a Western philosophical

discourse) began only in the first few months of 1917; Scholem recalls that it was only then that the two held "our first conversations on the Kabbalah; at that time I was still far from a study of its sources, but I already felt an obscure attraction to its world" (*History of a Friendship*, 38). It is nevertheless likely that Scholem was the relevant source for much of Benjamin's use of Jewish mysticism in the language essay; although the first "serious" conversations on the Kabbalah may have occurred subsequent to the composition of the essay, and it is certainly the case that Benjamin and Scholem had held numerous and extensive conversations on themes of Judaism and philosophy well before such time. Cf. Scholem, *History of a Friendship*, 24–25, 31–32.

34   Cf. Gershom Scholem, *Kabbalah* (New York: Dorset Press, 1974), 124.

35   Menninghaus, *Walter Benjamins Theorie der Sprachmagie*, 43.

36   Cf. Irving Wohlfarth, "On Some Jewish Motifs in Benjamin," in *The Problems of Modernity: Adorno and Benjamin*, ed. Andrew Benjamin (London: Routledge, 1989), 191–92.

37   Cf. Menninghaus, *Walter Benjamins Theorie der Sprachmagie*, 21.

38   See ibid., 39; Witte, *Walter Benjamin*, 11.

39   In this I am in essential agreement with Menninghaus's assertion that the language essay does not seek to *discover* anything new about the nature of linguistic phenomena: "Es geht vielmehr von einer—genauer: von seiner—vorausgesetzten Spracherfahrung aus und versucht, diese Spracherfahrung nicht sowohl zu überprüfen als allererst zu konzeptualisieren, in ein theoretisches Modell einzubringen. Allein unter dieser Perspektive ist auch zu verstehen, warum Benjamin, wenn er die Arbitrarität des Zeichens thematisiert, nicht einen gegebenen Sprachcorpus untersucht, sondern das I. Buch Mose aufschlägt" ["It has far more to do with a—or more precisely, his—postulated experience of language; an attempt, not so much to verify this experience as to conceptualize it and incorporate it within a theoretical model. This is the only perspective from which we can understand why Benjamin's thematization of the arbitrariness of the sign turns to the book of Genesis, instead of a given linguistic object"] (*Walter Benjamins Theorie der Sprachmagie*, 39; my translation).

40   See n. 33.

41   "Das Urteil der Bezeichnung," "Lösungsversuch des Russelschen Paradox," frgs. 1, 2 GS 6:10–11: "Der Name ist etwas (ein Element) am Gegenstand der Intention selbst, was sich aus ihm herauslöst; daher ist der Name nicht zufällig" ["The Judgment of Description," "Attempted Solution of Russell's Paradox," fragments 1, 2 GS 6:10–11: "The name is something (an element) objectively real to intention itself; that is, what is released from within it. Thus the name is not arbitrary"; my translation].

42   As Irving Wohlfarth puts it, nature so endowed with the language of lamentation "would . . . resemble the Jewish mother who, when her son calls, does not stop complaining that he never calls her" ("On Some Jewish Motifs in Benjamin," 169).

43   Michael Jennings has argued convincingly that it is precisely a transcendence of subjectivity in poetic creativity that Benjamin had earlier found in Hölderlin. The

1914 essay "Zwei Gedichte von F. Hölderlin" had depicted the poet as "sur-render[ing] subjectivity in the interest of the All" (Jennings, *Dialectical Images*, 126–28). Jennings observes that, contrary to Benjamin's reading, Hölderlin himself continued to vacillate between the transcendence and the concentration of selfhood in the act of poetic creation.

44   See Witte, *Walter Benjamin*, 10.

2   *Trauerspiel* and Melancholy Subjectivity

1   Witte, *Walter Benjamin*, 123–28.

2   Walter Benjamin, "A Berlin Chronicle," in *Reflections*, 15.

3   See Scholem, *History of a Friendship*, 113.

4   See Scholem, *History of a Friendship*, 95: "One of his close acquaintances told me that for her and her female friends he had not even existed as a man, that it had never even occurred to them that he had this dimension at all. 'Walter was, so to speak, incorporeal.' Was the reason for this some lack of his vitality, as it seemed to many, or was it a convolution of his vitality . . . with his altogether metaphysical orientation that gained him the reputation of being a withdrawn person?"; cf. also Adorno, "Benjamin the Letter Writer," in Smith, *On Walter Benjamin*, 329: "Not that he was ascetic, or even gave such an impression by his appearance; but there was something almost incorporeal about him."

5   Adorno, "Benjamin the Letter Writer," 330.

6   Theodor Adorno, "A Portrait of Walter Benjamin," in *Prisms* (Cambridge: MIT Press, 1981), 231, 235.

7   Theodor W. Adorno, *Negative Dialektik* (Frankfurt: Suhrkamp Verlag, 1975), 277.

8   Benjamin, GS 4:113.

9   Charles Rosen has perceptively observed that the climax of the drama of fate, above all in Shakespeare, incorporates the stage itself into the heart of the fateful moment: "This reference to the stage at the climax of tragedy is not a poet's game, an irrelevant frivolity. Richard with his looking glass, like Hamlet with the skull of Yorick, or Lear judging the footstool, is a figure of allegory, frozen for a moment into an emblematic stiffness" (Rosen, "The Ruins of Walter Benjamin," in Smith, *On Walter Benjamin*, 148).

10   Benjamin, "Über das Programm der kommenden Philosophie," GS 2:157–71; "On the Program of the Coming Philosophy," trans. Mark Ritter, *The Philosophical Forum* 15:41–51, 44, 44–45.

11   Cf. the discussion of this point in Jennings, *Dialectical Images*, 89.

12   Benjamin, "On the Program of the Coming Philosophy," 46.

13   For a thorough discussion on the relation to Hegel in the Kant-critique of the program essay, cf. Rolf Tiedemann, *Studien zur Philosophie Walter Benjamins* (Frankfurt: Suhrkamp Verlag, 1973), 32–34.

14   Benjamin, "On the Program of the Coming Philosophy," 46.

15   "Method is a digression. Representation as digression—such is the methodological nature of the treatise" (Benjamin, O, 28).

16   Benjamin, GS 1.1208.

17   Benjamin, O, 28.

18   Ibid., 28–29, translation altered.

19   Ibid., 29.

20   Ibid., 32, 27. The relation between the Goethean *Urphänomen* and Benjamin's "allegorical" construction in the *Trauerspiel* book and in the doctrine of dialectical images will recur; see also Witte, *Walter Benjamin*, 127. For contrasting views concerning the importance of the *Urphänomen* for the formation of Benjamin's critical theory, cf. Michael Jennings, 133–35. Jennings emphasizes Benjamin's attack, in the closing pages of his dissertation, on the creeping mythology inherent in Goethe's attempt to attribute to the *Urphänomen* a nonlinguistic, natural existence. Cf. also Susan Buck-Morss, *The Dialectics of Seeing*, 71–74. Buck-Morss insists far more than Jennings upon the paradigmatic nature of the *Urphänomen* for Benjamin's critical theology of history: the insistence that the totality of the historical event could be encapsulated in compressed and therefore explosive form in the unique, individual fragment was, for Buck-Morss, the conscious and deliberate conveyance of Goethean morphology into historiography; Buck-Morss notes that Simmel's reading of Goethe was a vital transition from a philosophy of nature to the insight that the material physiognomy of historical processes can be read like a text.

21   Benjamin, O, 33, 34.

22   Ibid., 34.

23   Cf. Susan Buck-Morss, *The Origin of Negative Dialectics: Theodor W. Adorno, Walter Benjamin, and the Frankfurt Institute* (New York: The Free Press, 1977), 92.

24   Benjamin, O, 34, 34–35.

25   Ibid., 34.

26   This point forms the central claim of the twin essays, "On the Mimetic Faculty" and "Doctrine of the Similar," that Benjamin composed in 1933. Benjamin's clear intention with the essays had been the reformulation of the theology of language from 1916 (cf. letter to Scholem, *Briefe*, 575).

27   Scholem, *History of a Friendship*, 61.

28   Benjamin, O, 45.

29   Ibid., 46.

30   Cf. Benjamin, "Trauerspiel und Tragödie," GS 2:133–37.

31   Benjamin, O, 62.

32   Benjamin, GS 2:204.

33   Benjamin, O, 62.

34   Ibid., 64.

35   For a reconstruction of Gryphius's political thought, see Harald Steinhagen, *Wirklichkeit und Handeln im baroken Drama. Historisch-ästhetische Studien zum Trauerspiel des Andreas Gryphius* (Tübingen: Max Niemayer Verlag, 1977), and Wilhelm Vosskamp, *Untersuchungen zur Zeit- und Geschichtsauffassungen im 17ten Jahrhundert bei Gryphius und Lohenstein* (Bonn: Bouvier Verlag, 1967).

36   Benjamin's attraction to the protofascist Schmitt is one of the odder bibliograph-

ical adventures of the *Ursprung des deutschen Trauerspiels*. Benjamin appears to have accepted Schmitt's theory of sovereignty without reservation. It could be that the radical "nihilism" that Benjamin espoused in the late teens and early 1920s subsisted at such a level of spiritual abstraction that, true to form, the unmistakably fascist content of Schmitt's theorizing either did not arouse his attention or simply did not interest him; at any rate, as late as 1930—long after Schmitt had laid his own political cards on the table—Benjamin could still send Schmitt a copy of the *Trauerspiel* study, along with a letter in which Benjamin expressed his recognition of "how greatly the book owes to you its representation of the doctrine of sovereignty in the seventeenth century"; the letter continues by referring to Schmitt's later work, *Die Diktatur*, which Benjamin describes as "a confirmation of my research methods in the theoretics of art" (GS 1:887). Schmitt never responded. Years later, Schmitt did discuss the *Ursprung des deutschen Trauerspiels* briefly in his work, *Hamlet oder Hekuba: Der Einbruch der Zeit in das Spiel* (Düsseldorf: Eugen Diedrichs Verlag, 1956). There, Schmitt weakly praised Benjamin's work but admitted that he was left "puzzled" by Benjamin's treatment of Hamlet, since, as Schmitt argued, the play fundamentally bypasses the Christian categories that Benjamin found there and instead explores pagan or barbaric forms of tragic sensibility—Benjamin's point, as we shall see, was that *Hamlet*, by transcending the formal parameters placed upon it by the *Trauerspiel*, does not thereby become a tragedy, but rather the perfection (not the extreme) of the *Trauerspiel*, and in this sense liberated from the generic designation itself. For a further discussion of Benjamin's relation to Schmitt, see Michael Rumpf, "Radikale Theologie. Benjamins Beziehung zu Carl Schmitt," in *Walter Benjamin—Zeitgenosse der Moderne* ed. Peter Gebhardt, Martin Grzimek, Dietrich Harth, Michael Rumpf, Ulrich Schödlbauer, and Bernd Witte (Kronberg: Scriptor Verlag, 1976), 37–50, and David Pan, "Political Aesthetics: Carl Schmitt on Hamlet," *Telos* 72 (1987): 153–59.

37   Benjamin O, 65.

38   Liselotte Wiesenthal has argued for a deep theoretical connection between Schmitt's conception of the extreme (*Grenzbegriff*) and Benjamin's development of the extreme in the *Erkenntniskritische Vorrede*, thus claiming that Benjamin's interest in Schmitt extended well beyond a reading of baroque (or contemporary) political theory. Cf. Wiesenthal, *Zur Wissenschaftstheorie Walter Benjamins* (Frankfurt: Athenäum Verlag, 1973), 17.

39   Benjamin, O, 66, 72.

40   Ibid., 72.

41   Ibid., 71.

42   "The hero, who scorns to justify himself before the gods, reaches an agreement with them, in a, so to speak, contractual process of atonement which, in its dual significance, is designed not only to bring about the restoration but above all the undermining of an ancient body of laws in the linguistic constitution of the renewed community" (Benjamin O, 115).

43   Thus the stage of the *Trauerspiel* "is not strictly fixable, not an actual place, but it too is dialectically split. Bound to the court, it yet remains a travelling theater;

metaphorically its boards represent the earth as the setting created for the enactment of history" (Ibid., 119).

44   Ibid., 129.

45   Ibid., 131, 132, 133–34.

46   Cf. Benjamin, GS 1:134–35.

47   Benjamin, O, 66.

48   Ibid., 119.

49   Cf. Benjamin, "Goethes Wahlverwandtschaften," GS 1:141–49, 149–51.

50   Benjamin, O, 93, 139.

51   Cf. Max Weber, *The Protestant Ethic and the Spirit of Capitalism* (New York: Charles Scribner's Sons, 1958), 83–88.

52   Benjamin, O, 139.

53   On the connection between melancholia as *Tiefsinn* and Benjamin's frequent use of the word *tief* (deep), see Ferruccio Masini, "Allegorie, Melancholie, Avante-Garde: Zum *Ursprung des deutschen Trauerspiels*," *Text und Kritik* 31/32 (July 1979): 97.

54   Benjamin, GS 1:318. Translation altered.

55   Witte, *Walter Benjamin*, 133.

56   Ibid., 133.

57   Benjamin, O, 140.

58   Ibid., 45–47.

59   Benjamin, GS 5:592 (N 9a, 3).

60   Cf. Susan Buck-Morss, *The Dialectics of Seeing*, 206–15.

61   See Ernst Gombrich, *Aby Warburg: An Intellectual Biography* (London: The Warburg Institute, 1970), 195.

62   Aby Warburg, "Heidnisch-antike Weissagung in Wort und Bild zu Luthers Zeiten," 202, 202ff.:

> In logic, which creates the cognitive space between human and object through conceptually distinctive descriptions, and magic, which by the (ideal or practical) superstitious connection between human and object destroys this same space, we observe in the prophesying thought of astrology a still unified, primitive tool, that the astrologer can use both to measure and to cast spells. The epoch in which logic and magic, like trope and metaphor (as Jean Paul once wrote) 'blossom grafted upon a single stem' is, in reality, timeless, and in the representation of this polarity by the cultural sciences, heretofore untapped support can be found for a deepened positive criticism of a historiography whose doctrine of development is completely conditioned by the concept of time.

63   See Gombrich, *Aby Warburg*, 212.

64   See Warburg, "Heidnisch-antike Weissagung in Wort und Bild zu Luthers Zeiten," 255–62:

> "Thus Dürer has rendered the saturnine demon harmless through the thoughtful activity, true to character, of the creature under the influence of cosmic currents [*durch denkende Eigentätigkeit der angestrahlten Kreatur*];

the planet-child, through its own contemplative activity, to save itself from the curse of the demonic star, from the threat of 'the most ignoble complex.' It is the compass of genius, and not a mere gravedigger's shovel, that melancholia holds in her hands [in Dürer's engraving *Melancolia I*]. Magically summoned forth, Jupiter comes to help Saturn through his beneficial, taming effect. The salvation of humanity through this counter-image of Jupiter is, in the print, so to speak already accomplished, the act of demonic duel, as Lichtenberger beheld it, is over, and the magic number-square hangs on the wall like an ex-voto in thanks to the good, victorious stellar genius. (261)

65 Warburg was diagnosed with acute melancholic dementia and was placed under the care of Ludwig Binswanger, himself a noted theorist of melancholia (see Gombrich, *Aby Warburg*, 215). Binswanger later attempted to link the melancholy syndrome to a pathologically altered interior time consciousness via a reading of Husserlian phenomenology. On this reading, melancholia was marked by the subject's inability to maintain the distinction between protension and retention, thus hopelessly regarding the future as a field of closed-off possibilities and seeing the past as a mass of volatile, tormenting memories. Cf. Ludwig Binswanger, *Melancholie und Manie. Phänomenologische Studien* (Pfullingen, 1960).

66 Panofsky and Saxl, "Dürers 'Melancolia I.'

67 See Lepenies, *Melancholie und Gesellschaft*, 217–18.

68 See Paul Oskar Kristeller, *The Philosophy of Marsilio Ficino* (New York: Columbia University Press, 1943), 208–9.

69 Ficino, *De Vita Triplici*, quoted in ibid., 211. This Christianized version of Neoplatonic anamnesis and the emotional dimension entailed by it is, as Panofsky and Saxl observe, a very familiar feature of Renaissance speculation, as in Erasmus or in Ficino's contemporary Guainerio, who associates this sadness with the melancholy temperament, but not, apparently, with the Aristotelian conception of melancholy genius or with Arabian astrology, as Ficino did. For Guainerio, episodes of ecstatic insight disclose particles of forgotten, occult knowledge to the soul, and the melancholy temperament is one in which this sort of *mémoire involontaire* becomes particularly sensitive. Cf. Klibanski, Panofsky, and Saxl, *Saturn and Melancholy*, 96–97.

70 Ficino, *De Vita Triplici*, quoted in Klibanski, Panofsky, and Saxl, *Saturn and Melancholy*, 259, 270–71.

71 For an excellent discussion of the relation between Warburg's interpretation of Dürer and that of his disciples, in particular of Panofsky, see Sylvia Ferretti, *Cassirer, Panofsky, and Warburg* (New Haven: Yale University Press, 1989), 197–236.

72 Warburg's work, like that of Giehlow, is essential in determining the ground convictions of Benjamin's theory of Renaissance and baroque melancholia; Benjamin only became familiar with Saxl and Panofsky's subsequent study (1923) in 1924, once the first draft of the *Ursprung des deutschen Trauerspiels* was finished; the great amount of this work that became included in the finished version of the *Trauerspiel* study indicates the significance that Benjamin attached to it. At the

end of 1924, Benjamin wrote Scholem: "Now after the draft is finished, a capital book has come into my hands, one which I would name as the last word in an incomparably fascinating research. . . . Panofski [*sic*]-Saxl: Dürers Melacolia I, Berlin Lpz 1923 (Studien der Bibliothek Warburg). Don't miss it" (Walter Benjamin, *Briefe*, ed. Gershom Scholem and Theodor W. Adorno, 2 vols. [Frankfurt: Suhrkamp Verlag, 1978], 366. Hereafter referred to as B.]

George Steiner claimed, in the introduction to the English translation of the *Ursprung des deutschen Trauerspiels* that "it is Aby Warburg's group . . . which would have afforded Benjamin a genuine intellectual, psychological home, not the Horkheimer-Adorno Institute for Research in the Social Sciences with which his relations were to prove so ambivalent and, during his lifetime, sterile. Panofsky could have rescued Benjamin from isolation; an invitation to London might have averted his early death" (in Benjamin, O, 19). This thesis is entirely plausible. Nevertheless, Benjamin's admiration for the Warburg Institute in general, and Saxl and Panofsky in particular, was not mutual. It seems unlikely that anyone could have rescued Benjamin from his isolation, which had far less to do with admittedly difficult, often impossible material and intellectual circumstances, and far more to do with an essential personal disposition; moreover, the older conviction that the Frankfurt School proved a stifling, even an oppressive or manipulative force in Benjamin's life has gradually been abandoned. Benjamin's productivity—staggering, when one thinks about it—would have surely been different had things worked out differently; in the end, it is an open question whether the Warburg Institute would have been more or less beneficial for it than the Institute for Social Research.

In any event, the Warburg Institute certainly showed little respect for the *Ursprung des deutschen Trauerspiels*, and I suspect the reason for this had a great deal to do with Benjamin's willful and unabashed—and entirely characteristic— imposition of his own theology of historical happening upon the objects of research. For the far more precise and "scholarly" minds of the Warburg Institute, this epistemological *chutzpah* was intolerable. Years after the *Trauerspiel* study was complete, Benjamin still hoped for a review from the Warburg circle, believing (as he wrote to Kracauer in 1928) that the centrality of the Warburg Institute for his own mode of research was becoming increasingly clear to him, and he reports that to his great pleasure "the report came, indirectly, that Saxl is intensively interested in my work" (GS 1:910). Several months earlier, Benjamin wrote to Scholem that Hoffmannsthal had sent the special printing of the melancholy chapter to Panofsky, who, according to Benjamin, responded by returning a "cool, resentment-laden letter" (Benjamin, B, 457; GS 1:911). The letter has, unfortunately, not survived. There was no Warburg review of the *Trauerspiel* book, nor were there any further contacts between the institute and Benjamin.

73   Benjamin, O, 140, 147–48.
74   Ibid., 149, 150.
75   Ibid., 151.
76   Ibid., 153.
77   Ibid., 154, 140.

78   Ibid., 155, 156.

79   Ibid., 156; 157, translation altered.

3   *Melancholia and Allegory*

1   Witte, *Walter Benjamin*, 125, 127.

2   "Neither in knowledge nor in reflection can anything whole be put together, since
     in the former the internal is missing and in the latter the external; and so we must
     necessarily think of science as art if we expect to derive any kind of wholeness
     from it. Nor should we look for this in the general, the excessive, but, since art is
     always wholly represented in every individual work of art, so science ought to
     reveal itself completely in every individual object treated" (Johann Wilhelm von
     Goethe, *Materialen zur Geschichte der Farbenlehre*, quoted in O, 27.

3   Benjamin, B, 366, quoted in Witte, *Walter Benjamin*, 125.

4   As he completed the draft of the *Trauerspiel* book, Benjamin wrote Scholem that a
     few "constitutive crimes" concerning his ignorance of primary sources notwith-
     standing, he believed that the accumulation of quotations—even if mainly from
     secondary sources—allowed "'allegory' . . . in all its totality to spring out
     momentarily, so to speak" (B, 366, quoted in Witte, *Walter Benjamin*, 127).

5   Witte, *Walter Benjamin*, 130, 129.

6   See Hans Robert Jauss, *Toward and Aesthetic of Reception: Theory and History of
     Literature* (Minneapolis: University of Minnesota Press, 1982), 2:172.

7   Cf. Tillich's claim that religious symbols, insofar as they participate in the same
     reality that they represent, point beyond themselves. Their paradoxical nature is
     thus contained in the cognitive dimension of the symbol, an inadequacy that is
     only resolved in the extension of the normative claim that the symbol also makes:
     any religious symbol that claims an exhaustive or complete expression of unity
     slides into an idolatrous image (Paul Tillich, *Dynamics of Faith* [New York:
     Harper and Row, 1974], chap. 3).

8   As Goethe wrote, "Allegory changes a phenomena into a concept, a concept into
     an image, but in such a way that the concept is still limited and completely kept
     and held in the image that expressed it. . . . The symbol changes the phenomenon
     into the Idea, the Idea into the image, in such a way that the Idea remains always
     infinitely active and unapproachable in the image, and will remain inexpressible
     even though expressed in all languages" (Goethe, quoted in Hazard Adams,
     Philosophy of the Literary Symbolic [Tampa: Florida State University Press,
     1983], 54).

9   Jennings, *Dialectical Images*, 167.

10   Benjamin, O, 163.

11   Winfried Menninghaus, "Walter Benjamin's Theory of Myth," in *On Walter
     Benjamin: Critical Essays and Recollections*, ed. Gary Smith (Cambridge: MIT
     Press, 1989), 313.

12   Benjamin, O, 165.

13   Benjamin, GS 1:135.

14   Benjamin, GS 6:60.

15   Benjamin, O, 160.

16   Ibid., 166.

17   Ibid.

18   Hans Heinz Holz, "Prismatisches Denken," in *Über Walter Benjamin* ed. Theodor W. Adorno (Frankfurt: Suhrkamp Verlag, 1968).

19   Cf. Theodor W. Adorno, "Die Idee der Naturgeschichte," *Gesammelte Schriften* (Frankfurt: Suhrkamp Verlag, 1973), 1:351.

20   Benjamin, O, 166.

21   This observation has been made frequently; it appears particularly strongly in Terry Eagleton, *Walter Benjamin or Towards a Revolutionary Criticism* (London: New Left Books, 1981): "History then, as always for Benjamin, progresses by its bad side. If there is a route beyond reification, it is through and not around it; if even apparently dead objects, in the sepulchral splendour of the *Trauerspiel*, secure tyrannical power over the human, it remains true that the tenacious self-absorption of melancholy, brooding upon such husks, embraces them in order to redeem them" (20).

22   Karl Giehlow, *Die Hieroglyphenkunde des Humanismus in der Allegorie der Renaissance, besonders der Ehrenpforte Kaisers Maximilian I. Ein Versuch* (Leipzig, Vienna: Jahrbuch der kunsthistorischen Sammlungen des allerhöchstern Kaisershauses, 1915).

23   Benjamin, O, 168, 170, 171.

24   An excellent analysis of the allegorical dimension of natural history is provided in Susan Buck-Morss's work, both her earlier *Origin of Negative Dialectics*, chap. 3, and *The Dialectics of Seeing*, 159–77.

25   Benjamin, O, 173.

26   Ibid., 175, 176.

27   Ibid., 140.

28   Ibid., 183–84.

29   Georges Perec, *Life: A User's Manual* (Boston: David R. Godine, 1987), xv.

30   Ibid., xvii.

31   Benjamin, O, 224, 217–18.

32   Qualified support for the assertion that the (baroque) image of the corpse is not just "a" but "the" origin of the *Trauerspiel* can be found in Liselotte Wiesenthal, *Zur Wissenschaftstheorie Walter Benjamins*, particularly in the context of Wiesenthal's development of the concept of the "extreme" as the heart of Benjamin's epistemology: "Das Leichenemblem ist so Extremphänomen, aber nicht gewonnen im unmittelbaren Zugriff auf die Natur, sondern auf der 'höhern' Stufe der 'Konfiguration' der Extremphänomen als 'Idee.' Das Leichenemblem wird damit zur Idee des Trauerspiels" ["The corpse emblem is therefore an extreme phenomenon. It is achieved not in the unmediated grasp of nature, but rather on the higher level of a 'configuration' of the phenomenon as 'idea.' Thus the corpse emblem emerges as the idea of the *Trauerspiel*"] (126; my translation). The point raises once again the argument that the "origin," like the "extreme phenomenon" or the "dialectical image," can be grasped as Benjamin's attempt to transpose the Goethean *Urphänomen* from nature to history; cf. *Passagenwerk*, n. N 9a, 4, and

interpretations in Jennings, *Dialectical Images*, 136–37, and Buck-Morss, *The Dialectics of Seeing*, 71–73.

33 Benjamin, O, 224, 224–25.

34 Ibid., 230.

35 Ibid., 231; translation altered.

36 Ibid., 232; translation altered.

37 Once again, the centrality of the "extreme formulation" is developed at length in Wiesenthal, *Zur Wissenschaftstheorie Walter Benjamins*, esp. 56–73.

38 Benjamin, O, 232, 232–33; translation altered.

39 Ibid., 233; translation altered.

40 Cf. Gershom Scholem, *The Messianic Idea in Judaism and Other Essays on Jewish Spirituality* (New York: Schocken Books, 1971), 45ff.

41 Cohen, quoted in Gershom Scholem, *Major Trends in Jewish Mysticism* (New York: Schocken Books, 1954), 36.

42 Benjamin, O, 234.

43 Witte observes that "nothingness" must lie at the end of the allegorical intention in order for it to transmute itself into God's presence and points out that absolutely arbitrary subjectivity must be revealed as the essence of the allegorical mode, for "eben dadurch repräsentiert sie aber die Hoffnung auf eine Rettung von Welt und Kunst im theologischem Bereich" ["precisely in this manner, however, it represents hope for the rescue of world and art in the theological dimension"] (Witte, *Walter Benjamin*, 128; my translation). Wolin too underscores the role of subjective contemplation in the self-deconstruction of baroque allegory: "The sphere of knowledge which corresponds to the guilt-laden context of creaturely existence voluntarily sets its own baseness in relief in order thereby to indicate the theological sphere in which the light of salvation resides in fact. The highest function that objects and personages in the realm of the profane can perform is to serve as allegorical references to the superior realm of redeemed life" (Wolin, *Walter Benjamin: An Aesthetic of Redemption*, 73–74). Both Witte and Wolin speculate on the problematized relationship between the "theological," albeit faithless resolution of the allegorical intention for the baroque and Benjamin's own equally theologically inspired allegorical critique; in both cases, however, the observation of an affinity, both in terms of the intellectual physiognomy of allegory and between baroque allegory and expressionism, are noted without being explained, as they would have to be in light of Benjamin's own historical conceptions developed in the *Vorrede*. Cf. Witte, *Walter Benjamin*, 132–34, and Wolin, *Walter Benjamin*, 75.

44 Susan Buck-Morss, *The Dialectics of Seeing*, 174.

45 Ibid., 175.

46 Cf. Buck-Morss's discussion of Adorno's Kierkegaard study in *The Origin of Negative Dialectics*, 114–21, 116.

47 Adorno, *Kierkegaard*, 53.

48 Ibid., 54, 59.

49 Ibid., 62–64.

50 Ibid., 64.

51   Ibid., 60–61.

52   Ibid., 64, cf. 124.

53   Ibid., 123, 125.

54   Ibid., 126.

55   Adorno, "Introduction to Benjamin's *Schriften*," in *On Walter Benjamin*, ed. Gary Smith, 8–9, 11–12.

56   Cf. Theodor W. Adorno, "Die Aktualität der Philosophie," in *Gesammelte Schriften*, vol. 1 of *Philosophische Frühschriften* (Frankfurt: Suhrkamp Verlag, 1973), 335.

57   Benjamin, O, 235. Bernd Witte has observed that the origin and particular meaning of the invoked phrase "*ponderación misteriosa*" remain unexplained: Benjamin himself does not name the source, which is his own citation of Borinski's quote of the obscure Spanish baroque dramatist Lorenzo Gracian Barcellona. For Witte, this constitutes another example of Benjamin's own allegorical method, in which the fragment, imbedded in academia, is wrested out and heterogeneously quoted for its pyrotechnic effect (Cf. Witte, *Walter Benjamin*, 132, 220.

4   Melancholia and Modernity

1   Cf. Benjamin, 7:735–43. Cf. also Michael Jennings, *Dialectical Images*, 19–20, 215–19 for a reproduction of essential portions of the plans for the Baudelaire book not contained in the *Gesammelte Schriften*.

2   Ibid., 20.

3   Cf. Susan Buck-Morss, *The Dialectics of Seeing*, 206.

4   Cf. Michel Espagne and Michael Werner, "Vom Passagen-Project zum 'Baudelaire': Neue Handschriften zum Spätwerk Walter Benjamins," *Deutsche Vierteljahrhefte für Literturwissenschaft und Geistesgeschichte* 4 (1984): 593–657.

5   Jennings, *Dialectical Images*, 218. Additional relevant material for the structure of the first section of the planned Baudelaire book is reproduced in Benjamin, GS 7:737; these do not agree, however, with the structure mentioned above. Benjamin's plans consist of a number of different themes or headings, each carefully designated by a complex system of variously colored icons; the work is divided into: 1: Idee und Bild; 2: Antike und Modern; 3: Das Neue und Immergleiche. (GS 7:739.) Various themes are then arranged carefully under these. Under the first, the themes repeat, inexactly, the content of the earlier division of "Baudelaire as Allegorist": "Sensitive Anlage; aesthetische Passion; Melancholie, Allegorie; Rezeption; Gautier Note; Verfehmung des Organischen."

6   Cf. Benjamin, GS 1:1065.

7   Eugène Marsan, "Les cannes de M Paul Bourget et le bon choix de Philinte," Paris, 1923, quoted in Benjamin, GS 5:321–22.

8   Walter Benjamin, "On Some Motifs in Baudelaire," *Illuminations*, ed. intro. by Hannah Arendt (New York: Schocken Books, 1969), 155, 156.

9   Cf. Walter Benjamin, "Zentralpark" (GS 1:657–90); "Central Park," trans. Lloyd Spencer with Mark Harrington, *New German Critique* 34 (Winter 1985): 32–58.

10   Cf. Benjamin, GS 1:1150.

11   Benjamin, "Central Park," 44.

12   Susan Buck-Morss has also recorded this feature; cf. *The Dialectics of Seeing*, 177.

13   Benjamin, GS 5:460.

14   Benjamin, GS 1:1150.

15   Cf. Benjamin, GS 5:339, 340 (J 20, 3; J 20a, 1) for examples of this attitude.

16   Ibid, 366 (J 33, 4).

17   Ibid.

18   In this regard, see Benjamin's by now much-discussed attempt to reformulate Marxist doctrine such that the ideological superstructure emerges as the "expression" of its economic base. "The superstructure is the expression of the base. The economic conditions under which society exists come to expression in the superstructure, precisely in the way that an overfilled stomach can, for the sleeper, find expression in the content of dream rather than its reflection" (GS 5:495 [K 2, 5]).

19   Benjamin, "Central Park," 33. See also GS 5:592 (N 9a, 5). The repetition of this critique of "apologia" as a secret agent of historicism in the "N" *Konvolut* indicates its central—if undeveloped—methodological significance.

20   Benjamin, GS 5:592 (N 9a, 3).

21   Cf. Benjamin, "Central Park, 37, 37–38.

22   Cf. Benjamin, GS 5:431 (J 63, 4).

23   Benjamin, "Central Park," 38; cf. GS 5:348 (J 24, 5): "Are the flowers soulless? does this enter into the title "Flowers of Evil"? In other words: are flowers a symbol of the whore? Or, perhaps, with this title the flowers are directed towards their true place."

24   Benjamin, "Central Park," 36.

25   Cf. Benjamin, GS 5:343 (J 21a, 4): "Baudelaire injects into the lyric the figure of a sexual perversion that seeks its objects in the streets. The most characteristic feature, however, is that he does so with the line 'quaking like an extravagant' in one of his most perfect love poems, 'A une passante.'"

26   Benjamin, GS 5:307.

27   Benjamin, "Central Park," 36.

28   Benjamin, GS 1:667.

29   Cf. Benjamin, GS 5:438 (J 66a, 9); "Central Park," 36: "Impotence is the fundament of the *Passionsweg* trodden by masculine sexuality."

30   Cf. Benjamin, GS 5:438 (J 66a, 9).

31   Benjamin, "Central Park," 38.

32   Benjamin, GS 5:426 (J 61, 3).

33   Benjamin, GS 1:1150–51.

34   Benjamin, "Central Park," 41 (cf. GS 5:413).

35   Ibid., 41.

36   Benjamin, GS 1:1151.

37   Benjamin, GS 5:465.

38   Ibid.

39   Benjamin, "Central Park," 46; cf. GS 5:408.

40 Benjamin, GS 5:466.

41 Benjamin, "Central Park," 55.

42 Cf. Friedrich Nietzsche, *The Use and Abuse of History*, trans. Adrian Collins (New York: Bobbs-Merill, 1957).

43 Cf. Benjamin, GS 5:431 (J 63, 4).

44 Nietzsche, *Use and Abuse of History*, 7–8.

45 Cf. *The 18th Brumaire of Louis Bonaparte*, reprinted in *A Marx-Engels Reader*, ed. Robert C. Tucker (Princeton, N.J.: Princeton University Press, 1978), 596–97.

46 Cf. Kierkegaard, *Either/Or* (Princeton: Princeton University Press, 1944), reprinted in *A Kierkegaard Anthology*, ed. Robert Bretall (Princeton: Princeton University Press, 1973), 26.

47 "The 'abyssal' sensibility is to be defined as 'meaning.' It is always allegorical" (Benjamin, GS 5:347).

48 Ibid., 348.

49 For an excellent discussion on the relation between Nietzsche's conception of resentment and the doctrine of hypertrophied memory in Benjamin's reading of Baudelaire, see Irving Wohlfarth, "Resentment Begins at Home: Nietzsche, Benjamin, and the University," in Smith, *On Walter Benjamin*.

50 A longer and in many senses congruent discussion of this point is to be found in Buck-Morss, *The Dialectics of Seeing*, 177–201. While Buck-Morss undervalues the central role of melancholy *spleen* in Benjamin's appropriation of Baudelaire, her discussion is excellent in documenting Benjamin's introduction of Marx's reading of commodity fetishism to explain the "rage" underlying Baudelaire's allegorical imagination.

51 Benjamin, GS 1:1151.

52 Benjamin, "Central Park," 34, 42; cf. GS 5:424 (J 60, 5).

53 Benjamin, GS 1:1151; cf. also GS 5:422 (J 59, 10).

54 Benjamin, GS 5:466 (J 80, 2, J 80a, 1).

55 Benjamin, "Central Park," 42.

56 The best reading of Adorno's essay is Buck-Morss, *The Origin of Negative Dialectics*, 52–62.

57 Cf. Benjamin, "Central Park," 46; cf. also GS 5:408 (J 53, 3).

58 Benjamin, GS 5:438–39 (J 67, 2).

59 Ibid., 474 (J 84a, 2, 4).

60 Ibid., 437 (J 66a, 4).

61 Benjamin, "Central Park," 35, 51, 33.

62 Ibid.

63 Charles Baudelaire, "Short Poems in Prose," in *My Heart Laid Bare and Other Writings* (New York: Haskell House, 1950), 128.

64 Baudelaire, "Le Soleil," in *Les Fleurs du mal* (Paris: Gallimard, 1972), 115.

65 Benjamin, GS 1:573.

66 Charles Baudelaire, *Intimate Journals*, trans. Christopher Isherwood (San Francisco: City Lights Press, 1983), 27.

67 Benjamin, "Central Park," 46.

68 Baudelaire, "La Destruction," *Les Fleurs du mal*, 146.

69   Benjamin, GS, 5:1147. It is interesting to note that the deliberate confusion of
     gender in "La Destruction" (the Demon is male, its form female) is matched
     precisely in Benjamin's commentary upon it, in which the male "genie" of
     allegory acts as the representative of "mistress" allegory herself.

70   Benjamin, "Central Park," 46; cf. GS 5:330 (J 15a, 3) and 435 (J 65a, 4):
     "'L'appareil sanglant de la Destruction' is the court of allegory."

71   To make things more complex still: Benjamin was surely familiar with Panofsky
     and Saxl's investigation of the process whereby the successive appropriations and
     losses of allegorical representations of melancholia from classical and Hellenistic
     Greece, through Rome, Arabia, and thence Christian Europe had produced such
     an allegorically overloaded Father Saturn/Chronos, wielding a razor-sharp sickle
     as allegory both of his dominion over time (i.e., the "Grim Reaper") as well as of
     his patricide and castration. The transformation of this Saturn-Chronos, wielding
     his sickle, to Dame Melancholy, who limply holds a compass but allows the sharp
     blades of construction and destruction to lie at her feet, is the richest—arguably,
     the quintessential—moment in the Warburg School's long preoccupation with
     melancholia. Cf. Klibanski, Panofsky, and Saxl, *Saturn and Melancholia*, esp.
     284–376.

72   Benjamin, "Central Park," 42; see also GS 5:416 (J 56a, 6).

73   Benjamin, "Central Park," 39; see also GS 5:401 (J 50, 2). The "destruction" of
     Baudelaire's allegory that "attaches itself to the rubble" is in this sense related as a
     polar opposite to that of the "destructive personality" discussed in the following
     chapter.

74   Benjamin, "Central Park," 42; cf. also GS 5:455 (J 74a, 5).

75   Benjamin at any rate attributes it to Proust; cf. GS 1:1141.

76   Baudelaire, *Les Fleurs du mal*, 112.

77   Baudelaire, *Intimate Journals*, 97.

78   Benjamin, GS 1:1141.

79   Ibid., 1151.

80   Benjamin, "Central Park," 43; see GS 5:429: "The conception of the eternal
     recurrence transforms the historical event itself into a mass-produced article."

81   Benjamin, "Central Park," 43.

82   Cf. Benjamin, GS 5:425 (J 60, 7), 424 (J 60, 6).

83   Benjamin, "Central Park," 55. "Key figure" (*Schlüsselfigur*) in this context should
     not be understood merely as "central" or "most significant" figure, but rather as
     origin, according to the terminology of the *Vorrede* of the *Trauerspiel* book. In a
     conceptually constructed constellation of fragments, one crystallized image con-
     stitutes the key, whose application to the puzzle makes the solution to the puzzle
     spring forth, and thereby lose its character as a puzzle. The notion of the originary
     (later dialectical) image as a *Schlüsselfigur* may well have arisen during Benja-
     min's discussions with Adorno at Königstein in the late 1920s; in his 1931 "Ac-
     tuality of Philosophy," Adorno too will refer to *Schlüsselkategorien*: "The purpose
     of interpretive philosophy is to construct keys which allow reality to spring open"
     (cf. Adorno, "Die Aktualität der Philosophie," in *Gesammelte Schriften* 1:340).

84   Henning Mehnert, *Melancholie und Inspiration*, 82–88.

85   Benjamin, "On Some Motifs in Baudelaire," in *Illuminations*, 181.

86   Ibid., 182.

87   Benjamin, "Central Park," 44.

88   Baudelaire, "La Chambre double," in *Le Spleen de Paris: Petits poèmes en prose* (Paris: Livre de Poche, 1972), 33–36.

89   Benjamin, "Central Park," 44; cf. also GS 5:414 (J 55a, 6).

90   Benjamin, "Central Park," 49.

91   There is an obvious affinity in this kind of metaphor to Heidegger's reading of George; cf. Martin Heidegger, "On the Nature of Language," in *On the Way to Language* (New York: Harper and Row, 1971), 118.

92   Benjamin, "Central Park," 49.

93   Benjamin, "On Some Motifs in Baudelaire," 183, 184.

94   Benjamin, GS 7:764. This section of notes, considering the "axes" of coordinate fields guiding Benjamin's composition of the essay on Baudelaire, takes on a tremendous significance in Susan Buck-Morss's recent attempt to argue that Benjamin's theory of the dialectical image—indeed his thinking in general—can be captured by reference to the schematism of coordinate fields. This argument is analyzed in the concluding chapter.

5   On the Road to the Object: Surrealism as Postmelancholy Criticism

1   Louis Aragon, *Le Paysan de Paris* (Paris: Gallimard, 1953), 60.

2   Ibid., 61.

3   Ibid., 61–62.

4   Ibid., 63.

5   Benjamin, GS 2.3:1018.

6   Benjamin, GS 2.2:620.

7   Ibid.

8   Cf. Susan Buck-Morss, *The Dialectics of Seeing*, 160–62.

9   Benjamin, GS 2.3:1021, 1022, 1024.

10   Walter Benjamin, "Surrealism: The Last Snapshot of the European Intelligentsia," in *Reflections*, 178–79.

11   Ibid., 179.

12   Ibid.

13   André Breton, "Manifesto of Surrealism," in André Breton, *Manifestoes of Surrealism*, trans. Richard Seaver and Helen R. Lane (Ann Arbor: University of Michigan Press, 1969), 26, 21–22, 32.

14   Ibid., 36–37 (Breton's emphasis). Breton is quoting from Baudelaire, but he does not name the specific text.

15   Benjamin, "Surrealism," 180, 183.

16   Cf. Susan Buck-Morss, *The Dialectics of Seeing:* "If Aragon sees the modern world as mythic, he does not order this vision into a mythological system that would explain (and hence legitimate) the given. Rather, Aragon is recording a fact that the theory of instrumental rationality represses: Modern reality in this still-primitive stage of industrialism *is* mythic, and to bring this to consciousness

in no way eliminates the possibility of a critique, for which, indeed, it is the prerequisite" (260). The problem for Benjamin would be the ability of the surrealists to "bring to consciousness" the explosive critique of ideology latent within the dream image of modernity.

17 Ibid., 260–61.

18 Benjamin, "Surrealism," 182, 181–82.

19 Cf. Benjamin's letter to Hoffmannsthal, which describes the surrealism essay as the "*Gegenstück*" to the essay on Proust, as well as the "prolegomena" to the *Passagen-Arbeit* (GS 2.3:1020; *Briefe*, 496).

20 Walter Benjamin, "The Image of Proust," in *Illuminations*, 204, 202.

21 Ibid., 313, 203, 204 (translation altered), 204.

22 Ibid., 211.

23 Ibid., 205, translation altered.

24 Ibid., 209.

25 For a treatment of the relation between Proust's and Kierkegaard's allegories and their relation to Benjamin, see Robert Hullot-Kentor, Introduction to *Kierkegaard* by Theodor W. Adorno, xix.

26 Benjamin, "The Image of Proust," 210.

27 Ibid., 212.

28 "There has never been anyone else with Proust's ability to show us things; Proust's pointing finger is unequalled. But there is another gesture in amicable together- ness, in conversation: physical contact. To no one is this gesture more alien than to Proust" (Ibid., 212.) To no one except, perhaps, Benjamin himself. The comment calls to mind Adorno's recollection of Benjamin: the isolated thinker driven to effect a point of connection between private reflection and social movements even at the expense of the dialectical integrity of the thought itself. For Adorno Benjamin was unsurpassed as an example of isolated thought. "The preponderance of spirit radically alienated him from his physical and even his psychological existence . . . friends hardly dared put a hand on his shoulder" (Theodor Adorno, "Introduction to Benjamin's *Schriften*," in *On Walter Benjamin*, ed. Gary Smith, 15–16.

29 Cf. Benjamin, "The Image of Proust," 214.

30 Benjamin, "Surrealism," 185.

31 Ibid., 186.

32 Ibid., 187.

33 Cf. Scholem, *Walter Benjamin: The History of a Friendship*, 180. Glück is a figure in Benjamin's intellectual biography about whom very little is known; Scholem recalls that Glück was a bank executive whom Benjamin had befriended during Benjamin's most acute spiritual crisis in 1931; Scholem recalls that Glück, Benjamin's "closest relationship" at the time, was a Viennese whom Benjamin had met through Brecht. Without literary ambition himself, Glück nevertheless seems to have made a strong enough impression upon Benjamin that the latter wrote to Scholem that Glück had served as the model "(*cum grano salis*)" for "The Destructive Character." There is no explanation for what this grain of salt may be.

34 Walter Benjamin, "The Destructive Character," in *Reflections*, 301, 302–3.

35   Benjamin, "Surrealism," 191.

36   Benjamin, GS 5.1:574, cf. 574 (N 1a, 8): "Method of this work: literary montage. I have nothing to say. Only to show. I shall not make off with anything valuable, or appropriate any lofty formulations. But the rubbish, the refuse: this I want not to inventory but to do justice to it in the only way possible: to use it."

37   Walter Benjamin, "N [Theoretics of Knowledge; Theory of Progress]," trans. Leigh Hafrey and Richard Sieburth, *The Philosophical Forum* 15, nos. 1–2 (1983–84): 3.

38   Benjamin, GS 5:579 (N 3a, 3).

39   Breton, "Second Manifesto of Surrealism," in *Manifestoes of Surrealism*, 123–24.

40   Breton, "First Manifesto of Surrealism," in ibid., 38.

41   Breton, "The Surrealist Situation of the Object," in ibid., 268.

42   Peter Bürger, *Theory of the Avant-Garde* (Minneapolis: University of Minnesota Press, 1984), 66.

43   Benjamin, "Surrealism," 184, 180.

44   Breton, "Second Manifesto of Surrealism," in *Manifestoes of Surrealism*, 176–78, 179, 182.

45   Breton, "Surrealism in Its Living Works," in *Manifestoes of Surrealism*, 297–99.

46   Ibid., 301, 303.

47   Theodor W. Adorno, "Looking Back on Surrealism," in *Notes to Literature* (New York: Columbia University Press, 1991), 87.

48   Ibid., 88.

49   Ibid., 89.

50   Susan Sontag, "Under the Sign of Saturn," in *Under the Sign of Saturn* (New York: Farrar, Straus, and Giroux, 1980), 124.

51   Bürger, *Theory of the Avant-Garde*, 66.

52   André Breton, quoted in Michel Carrougues, *André Breton and the Basic Concepts of Surrealism* (University: University of Alabama Press, 1974), 84.

53   Bürger too argues that the surrealist be viewed as a contemporary melancholic. Despite the historical specificity of the phenomenologies of baroque and avant-garde melancholy, claims Bürger, the two modes of aesthetic production ought both to be regarded as "melancholy" insofar as they are both allegorical. "What Benjamin calls melancholy here is a fixation on the singular, which must remain unsatisfactory, because no general concepts of the shaping of reality correspond to it. Devotion to the singular is hopeless because it is connected with the consciousness that reality as something to be shaped eludes one. It seems plausible to see in Benjamin's concept of melancholy the description of an attitude of the avant-gardiste who, unlike the aestheticist before him, can no longer transfigure his social functionlessness" (*Theory of the Avant-Garde*, 71).

6   *The Trash of History*

1   Buck-Morss, *The Dialectics of Seeing*, 67.

2   Tiedemann, "Dialectics at a Standstill: Approaches to the *Passagenwerk*," in *On Walter Benjamin*, ed. Gary Smith, 284.

3   Benjamin, GS 5:595–96 (N 11, 4), 1262.

4   Cf. Ibid., 1041–43; 1035.

5   Buck-Morss, *The Dialectics of Seeing*, 209–12, 211.

6   Ibid., 54, 211.

7   Benjamin, GS 5:578 (N 3, 1), 592 (N 9, 7).

8   Cf. Buck-Morss, *The Dialectics of Seeing*, 215: "The whole elaborate structure of the *Passagenwerk* must be seen within the temporal axis that connects the nineteenth century to Benjamin's 'present,' the dimension which, by transforming emblematic representation into philosophy of history and historical image into political education, provides dialectical images with their explosive charge."

9   Benjamin, O, 153.

10   Benjamin, GS 5:591–92 (N 9, 7).

11   Ibid., 577 (N 3, 1).

12   Cf. Theodor W. Adorno, *Against Epistemology: A Metacritique*, trans. Willis Domingo (Cambridge: MIT Press, 1983).

13   Benjamin, GS 5:578 (N 3, 1).

14   Ibid.

15   Ibid.

16   Not incidentally, this statement—that the image of the present or the past "shining their light" on each other is merely a nostalgic veil for an act of appropriation—also clearly illuminates the distance between Benjamin's conception of memory and that of *die neue Sachlichkeit*; in the introduction, it will be recalled, Erich Kästner had described childhood memory as "the quiet, pure light that shines consolingly out of the past and into the present and the future"; the dialectical image is Benjamin's firmest rejection of this sort of consolation.

17   "A decisive rejection of the concept of 'timeless truth' is called for. And yet truth is not—as Marxism supposes—merely a temporal function of cognition, but rather is bound to a temporal nucleus, present at the heart of both the knower and the known. This is true in the sense that the eternal is far more of a dress's faint rustle than an idea" (Benjamin, GS 5:578 [N 3, 2]).

18   Ibid., 588 (N 7a, 3).

19   Ibid., 592 (N 9, 7).

20   "For a fragment of the past to be struck by the contemporary, no continuity must exist between them" (Benjamin, GS 5:587 [N 7, 7]).

21   Ibid., 580 (N 4, 1).

22   Ibid., 577 (N 2a, 4).

23   "N [Theoretics of Knowledge, Theory of Progress]," *The Philosophical Forum* 15, nos. 1–2 (1983–84): 22.

24   Benjamin, GS 5:575 (N 2, 6), 595 (N 10a, 3).

25   Ibid., 570–71 (N 1, 4).

26   Ibid., 595 (N 10a, 2), 594 (N 10a, 2).

27   Ibid., 594 (N 10, 3), 587 (N 7, 6).

28   Ibid., 578 (N 3, 1).

29   Ibid., 574 (N 2, 1), 575 (N 2, 6).

30 Cf. esp. Buck-Morss, *The Origin of Negative Dialectics*, chaps. 9–11; cf. also Wolin, *Walter Benjamin: An Aesthetic of Redemption*, chap. 6.

31 Theodor W. Adorno, letter to Walter Benjamin, 2 August 1935, in *Aesthetics and Politics* ed. Fredric Jameson (London: NLB, 1977), 115.

32 For Adorno, the problem consisted of Benjamin's insistence on presenting the dialectical image as the sudden, *immanent* product of the dreaming collective of the nineteenth century itself. The problem with this evocation of immediate transferral of dream images into dialectical image, for Adorno, is that it undialectically fails to reflect that the dream image is in fact no dream; that the "Hell" of concrete social relations under capitalism, once (surrealistically) transfigured as dream time, in order to grasp the nature of the dialectical image as a moment of waking, is not illuminated *as* Hell by the image itself. "It seems extremely significant to me that this version of the dialectical image, which can be called an immanent one, not only threatens the original force of the concept, which was theological in nature, introducing a simplification which attacks not so much its subjective nuance as its basic truth; it also fails to preserve that social movement within the contradiction, for the sake of which you sacrifice theology" (Jameson, *Aesthetics and Politics*, 111). This, for Adorno, was the inevitable result of Benjamin's ultimately pointless embrace of crude concepts such as the collective consciousness or collective dream. For Adorno, the adoption of these terms served, ultimately, to excuse Benjamin from the task of theoretically working out the relation between critical subjectivity and the dialectical image itself: Benjamin flees from this problem by "disenchanting" it; but "disenchantment of the dialectical image leads directly to pure mythical thinking" (113).

33 Cf. Jameson, *Aesthetics and Politics*, 111–14: "A restoration of theology, or better yet, a radicalization of the dialectic into the glowing center of theology, would at the same time have to mean the utmost intensification of the social-dialectical, indeed economic, motifs" (114).

34 Walter Benjamin, letter to Greta Karplus, 16 August 1935, quoted in Buck-Morss, *The Dialectics of Seeing*, 218.

35 Jameson, *Aesthetics and Politics*, 127.

36 Ibid., 127, 128, 129.

37 Ibid., 129–30. "God knows, there is only one truth, and if your intelligence lays hold of this one truth in categories which on the basis of your idea of materialism may seem apocryphal to you, you will capture more of this one truth than if you use intellectual tools whose movements your hand resists at every turn" (131).

38 Benjamin, GS 5:1033.

39 This analogy is by Michael Steinberg, in "History and Negative Aesthetics in Adorno and Benjamin; or, 'The Third Man,'" unpublished MS.

40 Gary Smith cites a letter from Adorno to Kracauer in which Adorno complains that while the *Vorrede* did indeed put forward the invaluable doctrine of fragmentary thinking, of the postidealist strategy of the construction of constellations, it still suffers from "blatant, historically oblivious, and in the end, veritably mythological Platonism, which not by accident must take frequent recourse to phenomenology" (Theodor W. Adorno, letter to Kracauer, Cronberg, 12 May 1930,

Unpublished letter in Deutsches Literaturarchiv, Marbach am Neckar. Quoted in Gary Smith, "Thinking Through Benjamin," in *Benjamin: Philosophy, History, Aesthetics*, ed. Gary Smith [Chicago: The University of Chicago Press, 1989], xxvii).

41   Theodor W. Adorno, "Die Aktualität der Philosophie," in *Gesammelte Schriften*, 1:335.

42   Jameson, *Aesthetics and Politics*, 127, 131.

43   Benjamin, GS 5:570 (N 1, 3), (N 1, 1).

44   On this question, see Tiedemann, "Dialectics at a Standstill: Approaches to the *Passagenwerk*," in Smith, *On Walter Benjamin.*

45   Buck-Morss, *The Dialectics of Seeing*, 170.

46   Ibid., 222.

47   Cf. Ibid., 222–27. The reference is to the strategy of interpretation of Benjamin usually associated with such figures as Rainer Nägele, Rodolphe Gasché, John Wellbury, and Werner Hamacher. For a representative selection, see Rainer Nägele, ed., *Benjamin's Ground: New Readings of Walter Benjamin* (Detroit: Wayne State University Press, 1988).

48   Buck-Morss, *The Dialectics of Seeing*, 228.

49   Ibid., 230.

50   Scholem, *Major Trends in Jewish Mysticism*, 26, quoted in Ibid., 236–37.

51   Buck-Morss, *The Dialectics of Seeing*, 237, 241.

52   Ibid., 239–40.

53   Cf. Michael Löwy, *Rédemption et utopie: Le Judaisme libertaire en Europe Centrale* (Paris: Presses Universitaires de France, 1988), 47–48.

54   Buck-Morss, *The Dialectics of Seeing*, 242, 54.

55   Cf. Gregory Hartmann, *Criticism in the Wilderness: The Study of Literature Today* (New Haven, Conn.: Yale University Press, 1980). A concise criticism of this strategy of appropriation can be found in Jennings, *Dialectical Images*, 10.

56   Jennings, *Dialectical Images*, 51.

Afterword

1   Benjamin, GS 5:423 (J 59a, 4).

2   Ibid., 269 (H 1, 1).

3   Benjamin, GS 4:514.

4   Benjamin, GS 5:271 (H 1a, 2).

5   Benjamin, "Unpacking My Library," in *Illuminations*, 60.

6   Cf. Benjamin, GS 5:271 (H 1a, 2).

7   Benjamin, "Unpacking My Library," 60.

8   Benjamin, GS 5:271 (H 1a, 2).

9   Ibid., 274 (H2, 7; H2a, 1); cf. also "Unpacking My Library," 60.

10   Benjamin, "Unpacking My Library," 60–61.

11   Benjamin, GS 5:271 (H 1a, 2).

12   Ibid., 272 (H 1a, 5).

13   Ibid., 271 (H 1a, 5).

14   Ibid., 279 (H 4a, 1).

15   Ibid., 280 (H 4a, 1).

16   Cf. Benjamin's letter to Scholem, 31 July 1933, reprinted in Scholem, *The Correspondence of Walter Benjamin and Gershom Scholem 1932–1940*, 68.

17   Cf. Benjamin, "Ausgraben und Erinnern," GS 4:400–401. This fragment is virtually replicated in a central passage of the *Berlin Chronicle:*

> Language shows clearly that memory is not an instrument for exploring the past but its medium. It is the medium of past experience, as the ground is the medium in which dead cities lie interred. He who seeks to approach his own buried past must conduct himself like a man digging. . . . For the matter itself is only a deposit, a stratum, which yields only to the most meticulous examination what constitutes the real treasure hidden within the earth: the images, severed from all earlier associations, that stand—like precious fragments or torsos in the gallery of the collector—in the prosaic rooms of our later understanding. ("A Berlin Chronicle," in *Reflections*, 25–26)

18   Cf. Gershom Scholem, "Walter Benjamin and His Angel," in *On Walter Benjamin*, ed. Gary Smith, 57.

19   Cf. Benjamin, GS 5:588–89 (N 8, 1).

20   Benjamin, "Theses on the Philosophy of History," in *Illuminations*, 264.

Index